PENGUIN BOOKS

C.I.A.
The Myth and the Madness

Patrick J. McGarvey was born in Philadelphia in 1935. He took his B.A. at the University of Omaha and later studied Mandarin Chinese at Yale's Institute of Far Eastern Studies. A veteran of fourteen years in the United States intelligence community, he has served in Korea, Japan, Taiwan, Vietnam, and Washington. While at the Pentagon he received an "Outstanding Performance Award" for his work at the Paris peace talks and during the Tet offensive. McGarvey is married and lives near Washington with his wife and his four children.

P9-CAL-903

PATRICK J. McGARVEY

C.I.A.

The Myth and the Madness

Penguin Books Inc
Baltimore • Maryland

Penguin Books Inc
7110 Ambassador Road
Baltimore, Maryland 21207, U.S.A.

First published by Saturday Review Press, New York, 1972
Published in Penguin Books 1973
Reprinted 1974

Printed in the United States of America

To my wife, Cass, and our children,
Kathy, Pat, Meghan, and Maureen

The highest duty of the writer is to remain true to himself and to let the chips fall where they may. In serving his vision of the truth the artist best serves his nation.

JOHN F. KENNEDY
October, 1963

Contents

C.I.A.

The Myth and the Madness

I

The Malaise of Intelligence

◪◪◪

At no time in American governmental life has there been an institution similar to our national intelligence community headed by the Central Intelligence Agency. Now nearly twenty-five years old, the CIA's history remains largely unverifiable. Its factual record is shrouded in official secrecy, yet those of its deeds that are known have been glorified by even its harshest critics.

Powers almost occult have been attributed to the CIA, and the result has been the emergence of perhaps the greatest myth of the twentieth century.

And, as I was told in the CIA officer-training program, the leaders of the intelligence community prefer it that way. They purposely have done nothing to dispel any of the myths that have arisen over the years, because in their words, "they are oftentimes of great advantage to us."

One of my reasons for writing this book is to shed some light on the most damaging, persistent myth afoot today about the CIA—that it is an efficient, well-run machine capable of almost any act of trickery or intrigue. An honest portrayal of what intelligence is all about must conclude that the CIA is an insufferable bureaucratic morass with little or no central direction, sorely needing drastic change. It is not the purpose of this book, however, to foster or promote the naive notion that we do not need a CIA.

This book is not an attempt to expose the CIA. It is simply a pulling together of my personal experiences in intelligence. They are not unusual events for intelligence work. They include ordinary, tragic, and humorous incidents. From some of them a few whopping conclusions can be drawn; others contain no profundities, simply a human message.

At the outset it is perhaps worthwhile to describe the feelings I've had about writing this book. I first rejected the notion, convinced that the project would somehow emasculate the American government. Calmer thinking prevailed after the passage of time, and I decided to write of intelligence, realizing that my view from the trenches—or as I like to call it, the lower intestines—was so narrow that I in no way could damage this nation's security. I was not privy to the inner circle of government, but I was affected by some of the goings-on at those levels. I made no policy decisions, but I had a few doubts about the ones I was carrying out. I am not wracked with pangs of conscience, nor do I now lose sleep over intelligence. I personally think there's a helluva lot wrong in intelligence, and I think a lot can be done to correct the problems.

The first writing came off as crisp, flaky, and unappealing as a saltine to a thirsty man. I spoke in pontifical, academic language laced heavily with governmental clichés. The most difficult thing I experienced was injecting myself into the intelligence community. This state of mind, I realized, was brought about by the constant indoctrination at CIA on security. The place is as armor-plated as Fort Knox, and they have armed guards constantly prowling the dark corridors at night. Even with all that, however, they insist that every piece of paper in the place be locked in a safe at night. If the guards find a scrap of paper in your desk drawer or in the wastebasket once, you are severely reprimanded. If they find it twice, you're fired. The indoctrination is so thorough that CIA has every secretary and file clerk in the place thinking that a wrong word by them to anyone outside the agency would trigger World War III. I've been away from intelligence three years and I still get those wormy feelings in my intestines if I think too long about the security angle of writing about it.

While I was writing this book, I was in touch with a good many guys still working in intelligence. Many of them came forth and volunteered information about their own personal experiences. They wanted me to convey their feelings about the organization, and they got a special thrill out of telling their tales out of school. At one point in the writing eight of us gathered at the Key Bridge Marriott in Washington for an all-night party that ended up in spontaneous storytelling. One anecdote triggered another from everybody there. The delight with which they delivered their stories is an indication of how badly things have gone wrong at CIA.

An appreciation of intelligence and its effectiveness is not gained solely by a study of the organizational structure of the intelligence community. This reveals little of the conflicts and contradictions that plague intelligence, for they all stem essentially from the human beings that people the complex machinery and make it run or slow it down or cause it to react. This book will focus on these human aspects of intelligence—intangibles such as attitudes, moods, the politics of a particular point of view, and the feuds, horse trades, and acts of omission that somehow always escape the formal record.

A well-known Washington-based newspaperman once told me, "There's nothing wrong with CIA. I don't think of it as a sinister outfit. I think of it as a dark lump of something sitting in a dark corner of a damp basement. Imagine that someone tossed a heavy canvas over this lump and let it sit there for twenty-five years. The results, in terms of the nefarious, wormy, sinister little things that would grow under that canvas, are what CIA is today. They've been covered with the canvas of secrecy for twenty-five years now, and brother, a helluva lot of slimy things have grown up under there. Individually these little growths are relatively harmless, but they do give off a collective odor. My solution would be to remove the canvas and allow the sun to shine on the lump for awhile. Those dark little creepies and crawlies would wither and die under those conditions, and the lump would shrink back to its original size and shape."

Many knowledgeable observers have concluded in recent years that something is amiss in United States intelligence. They have seized on the headline stories of intelligence failures, such as the *Pueblo* and *EC-121* incidents, and have probed to uncover what went wrong. This approach misses the more persistent and widespread fundamental problems and tries to capture and describe only those elements that directly affect the particular event under study.

Stepping back from my own fourteen years' experience, I can only describe the fundamental problems of intelligence in a vague way. An indefinite feeling of debility or lack of health persists. This malaise involves over 150,000 persons today employed in intelligence. It is as fleeting as those first waves of nausea, yet it is as undeniably present. It can be seen in the lackadaisical manner in which a Marine Corps colonel at the Defense Intelligence Agency wryly shrugs off the downing of a United States Navy reconnaissance plane off the coast of North Korea as "typical of most Navy operations." It is evident in the cavalier manner in which CIA and State Department officials treat their counterparts at the Defense Intelligence Agency, thinking of them as little more than narrow-minded military men who have no perception of the "fine interworkings" of intelligence. The fact that many men at CIA stereotype their counterparts at the State Department as limp-wristed, hand-wringing, nervous Nellies and that DIA military staffers view both CIA and State men as fuzzy-headed liberals points up a parochialism that is bound to influence the product which they deal with regularly.

Old hands and young ones alike throughout the intelligence community endure common frustrations. Their social lives are constricted by their involvement in intelligence. Many drink just a little too much, and some, if they have the good sense, seek the help of psychiatrists; CIA has an "approved" list. The phenomenon of the "burned-out" intelligence officer, or the spy who has come in from the cold, is a real one. It is accepted blandly as part of the game. It is "understood" at CIA. The agency takes care of these guys whether their collapse came about from a series of hard tours overseas or from too long on the firing line of current intelligence and the endless paper wars of Washington. Jobs and high-sounding titles are created for them to await their retirement.

The euphemisms convey only a vague impression, and they mask the harsh reality of the phenomenon of men beaten to a moral pulp by their profession. The operational chief of the base in Central America from which the Bay of Pigs invasion was launched was relegated to the CIA training facility afterwards. I ran into him during my training there. He couldn't make it through the day without a half-pint. By early evening he could be found standing at the bar in the CIA club silently staring into his glass. He wouldn't join bar conversations. He'd simply stand till he fell. The bartender was thoroughly familiar with his nightly ritual and used to come from behind the bar at about ten-thirty and guide Ray to the door, where he'd call a jeep to take him back to his quarters. His wife had divorced him, and he spent all of his time on the CIA training facility, either drinking or instructing us on amphibious landings. Whenever the question of the Bay of Pigs came up during a lecture, and it invariably did, he refused to answer it. Most of the time he'd be fighting back tears; some of the time he got so worked up at the mere mention of the Bay of Pigs that he'd have to dismiss the class.

Witnessing the decline of men who have spent a lifetime in intelligence, the young become cynical rather early. They learn that the system exists for the system's sake and that no upstart will ever change it from within. Many have tried to change it, but at great personal expense. One man, Tom, who was an expert on the Soviet air forces, started a donnybrook several years ago over the strength of the MIG defenses in Eastern Europe; he ended up being transferred to a staff job with little hope of promotion. The United States Air Force had put forth a budget request to increase the size and quality of United States tactical air squadrons in Europe on the premise that the East European air forces were keeping older MIG-15 and MIG-17 fighters in their active inventory. They listed them as members of the air defense forces and considered them as line units. Tom's analysis of their use, based on solid information also available to Pentagon analysts, indicated that they were being used solely for the training of new pilots. The Air Force countered this argument with the assertion that they could be quickly activated to join the regular line air defense units. Tom's boss as this point acceded to the Air Force logic and told Tom to pull in his horns. Tom refused and, after assembling all of his evidence, sat down over a weekend to write a paper detailing his position on the subject. He indicated that aerial photographs and communications intercepted from East European and Soviet radio demonstrated that the older MIGs had been considerably remodeled for training purposes. All armament had been removed, and a tandem seat had been installed so that an instructor pilot could fly with the students. He pointed out that other evidence indicated that the Soviets no longer manufactured the parts to reconfigure the MIGs for combat status. Once remodeled for training, the MIGs in Tom's opinion could not be transformed back into combat fighters. They therefore posed no threat to NATO forces, and they should not be considered ample justification for the requested increase in United States tactical air units in Western Europe.

On Monday Tom presented his paper to his boss and requested permission to forward it to the Bureau of the Budget analysts working on the Air Force request. His boss was angered but couldn't refuse directly. Instead he asked Tom to assemble all the evidence he had on the subject. When this was done he instructed Tom to arrange a meeting with the Air Force intelligence staff to coordinate his findings. The meeting resulted in a deadlock. The Air Force disagreed with Tom's findings because their files didn't have the reports that indicated the spare parts were no longer being manufactured. They insisted on writing up a special intelligence collection requirement and alerting the field collectors to the problem so they could ferret out the information. Tom realized this was a delaying tactic which would take several months for collection—by which time the budget would have been approved.

He informed his boss of the results of the meeting and asked that CIA send a special uncoordinated report to the Budget Bureau alerting them to the possibility of new evidence changing the situation. His boss refused. Tom, on his own, called the Budget Bureau analyst and told him of the situation. The Budget Bureau then requested the CIA and the Air Force to meet at the bureau on the subject. Tom won the battle, and the Air Force request was denied. Two weeks after the meeting, he was transferred to a staff job processing paperwork requesting support from the photographic shop.

Many CIA analysts compromise some of their principles for the higher principle of serving as guardian of the real truth in government. Yet even this higher principle is subject to hard questioning, for within their purview they are often able to contrast the high-sounding rhetoric of the administration with the hard-nosed top secret cables winging back and forth from field stations to Washington spelling out the "real meaning" of the President's latest policy statement. I witnessed the flurry of cable traffic describing the details of the tough negotiations with the South Korean government in 1965 concerning their entry into the Vietnam War. Their price was high, over $3 billion. They wanted our government to pay their troops' salaries, provide pensions for the families of men killed, supply the troops with food, clothing, and ammunition, allow their troops access to the American base exchange system, and also come across with a long list of other forms of military and economic aid. I read the dispatches from Bangkok and saw the price we were paying for the entry of Thai troops into the Vietnam War—$50 million a year—and for the use of Thai real estate to build American air bases—$750 million. All of this, of course, was secret, but the action of the Thais and Koreans was ballyhooed publicly as a "generous move on their part to defend freedom and democracy." The program itself was entitled "Show the Many Flags" by glib State Department staffers who pumped out press releases celebrating the "spontaneous" support the American cause was gathering.

It is a pervasive sickness. It reduced men to little more than vegetables. The middle levels of the intelligence community are filled with men who simply go through the motions of their work. At the Defense Intelligence Agency a middle-aged civilian professional named Sam, who has been in intelligence since World War II, had risen to the post of Senior Civilian in the Far Eastern Office. He and I clashed over a Joint Chiefs of Staff paper I was working on in 1966, when the military wanted to expand the bombing campaign in Laos. At issue was the effectiveness of the bombing that had preceded the new campaign. The evidence at best was soft, consisting largely of unsubstantiated pilot reports of the number of trucks destroyed and damaged and the numbers of bridges knocked out. Sam and I conferred at length on the substantive arguments over the evidence, but he finally dropped all pretenses and said, "Pat, there is one thing you haven't learned yet. The cold fact is that the J-3 has already decided that we are going to step up our bombing in Laos. He now is going through the fire drill of substantiating the exercise. We can in no way influence his decision." I asked what the operations staff would do if our report, a necessary ingredient in the formal decision-making process, were to con- clude that the effectiveness of the previous bombing efforts was in serious doubt and that an expansion of the effort would also have dubious impact on the stated goal of cutting off the flow of supplies into South Vietnam. Sam thought a minute and with a wry smile replied, "They'd take your report, call a meeting with you and perhaps six staffers from the service intelligence and operations staffs, and spin you around in circles. It would probably last from about 11:00 A.M. to past midnight. You could fight all you want, but the results would be the same. They'd water down the original paper to the point where your objections would merely be footnotes to the opinions of the others assembled." Sam closed with a sage comment, "Save yourself the misery of sitting in one of those damned conference rooms for twelve hours, and give 'em what they want." I didn't, but the paper came out just as Sam had predicted.

The walls of Sam's office were and still are adorned with certificates citing him for "Outstanding Performance," "Sus- tained Superior Performance," and unexcelled dedication to his duties. Each one of these, by the way, gives Sam four years added seniority in the event that a reduction in civilian person- nel strength is ordered.

It requires an unrealistic sense of loyalty to a vague high principle for a professional intelligence officer to rationalize all of his actions taken in the line of duty. In Vietnam, when the CIA decided to gear up a "counterterror" program to eliminate Vietcong cadre in the hamlets, it hurriedly threw together an informant system in the hamlets and villages. American CIA men who supervised the operation were unable to go down to the villages to check out the information being supplied by the tipsters that the South Vietnamese police had recruited because the presence of a white man in the village would disrupt the routine there. Also, most of us were unable to speak Viet- namese, and our traveling to the villages wouldn't net any information. Once sufficient information had been gathered on the living patterns of the village residents, the theory had it that "ringers" would start showing up. One man, for example, might spend every Tuesday night away from his village. He might also receive visitors at his home at irregular hours. Tidbits began to build up on an individual, and, in time, he was "fingered" by the CIA field officer and the Vietnamese police as a "suspected Vietcong agent." Some were thought more dangerous than others, so the decision was made to kill them.

In one province, after eight "suspected Vietcong agents" had been killed by the local police over a two-month period, it was learned that one policeman had used his position to settle a family feud that had been brewing for three generations. He had his relatives write the informant reports and "identify" the members of the other family as Vietcong agents. In another case a police team member relieved his entire family of its lifetime of debts by fingering the family's creditors and seeing to it that they were killed. In still another case we discovered that a police official regularly turned in reports from a network of eighteen nonexistent informants—whose monthly salaries he drew from the local CIA field officer. These incidents were fairly widespread. Several of us, who figured we had a tiger by the tail, tried to get our boss in Saigon to reconsider the worth of the entire program and, perhaps, cancel it. The answer we got was: "It's funded in the budget, and we're not going back to Washington and tell them it isn't working. Moreover, the concept has been bought at the White House, so it has to work."

Our frustrations doubled when we tried to take action against the various police officials, using the Vietnamese legal system. The boss in Saigon said, "We can't do this. The South Vietnamese are our allies. It wouldn't look good in the press." At this point several guys paid their own way back to the States, happy not to be returning to the stateside world of intelligence.

There, intelligence requires that a man divest himself of his daily chores before he hits the parking lot each afternoon and seeks comfort at home in his rose garden, his horse breeding, his tennis skill, or his martini. His life has the typical frustrations that plague all organization men—with one important difference. These men are not dealing with ad accounts or marketing programs. They are involved with paperwork and action programs that concern human lives, national policy and, in the broadest sense, the fate of the free world.

Their wives learn quickly not to pry too deeply. A wife knows that her husband is dealing with the nation's secrets, but she also perceives that his work is somehow making a different man of him. Some rebel, and as the statistics show, the divorce rate is high in the intelligence profession. Others adapt, but they have to put up with the old man spilling his guts out—if only partially. When they question their husbands in an honest desire to find out what's troubling them, they usually are warded off with some inanity about classified material. At the same time, some Washington wives are privy to every single thing their husbands are involved with and actually render more national decisions than the security officers throughout the community would like to concede.

And raising children isn't easy. You can't rely on Dr. Spock. When we were in Saigon my son was in first grade. The first morning a school bus came to pick him up. It was like a typical suburban scene—with one exception. A Vietnamese policeman and an American GI with a submachine gun came to the gate around our walled villa to escort him onto the bus. The bus itself had the windows covered with cyclone fencing so a Vietcong couldn't toss a grenade into it. When he came home from school that day he was wired for sound. "Hey Dad! Man, what a cool school! They got sandbags on each corner of the roof with machine guns up there. Soldiers with machine guns walk up and down the hallway all day. Man, its neat! They got barbed wire all over the place, and when we go into our room we all have to lift our desk tops real slow to see if there's a bomb in there."

These are just a few of the superficial symptoms of the malaise. It starts with the men, but it has a decided influence on what they do, how they do it, and how each organization operates. It is part of a larger, more ominous trend, whose earmarks are a grotesque diffusion of responsibility, an accelerating dehumanization of the entire profession of intelligence, an enormous propensity for error, and the ever-growing phenomenon of a suffocating bureaucracy. Put simply, there is a crisis brewing within the United States intelligence community, one that conceivably could result in disaster. Men in the community are today shrinking from the hard decisions and only partially fulfilling their responsibilities.

When the deliberations concerning the invasion of Cambodia were underway in the White House, the intelligence community was deeply involved. It met its responsibilities chapter and verse, but, as one official described it, "CIA interpreted their marching orders too literally. They did not include a full-blown estimate of the internal Cambodian political, social, and economic consequences of the military maneuver or treat as fairly as they could the likely course of military action on the part of the Vietcong over the long haul. They sensed the old man was serious about the Cambodian venture and didn't want to make waves."

Another disquieting—but ignored—element is the fact that many able men are simply leaving. One man in his late thirties, who worked in the CIA director's office and was dubbed a "comer" in the organization, resigned because, in his words, "the bureaucracy finally got to me. I realized that changes were vitally needed, but the director refused to listen to anyone proposing changes. He only wants yes-men around him." The cases of men leaving in disgust are frequent. One analyst with a Ph.D. in history left a promising $16,000-a-year job to teach in a community college in Kentucky for $8,500 a year because he felt he "could contribute more to the nation there than he could at CIA." Another quit after eighteen years, took his savings from the bank, and bought himself a lobster boat which he now plies daily through the Atlantic off the coast of Maine. "Maybe out there away from the bureaucracy and the insanity I can regain my own perspective on life," he remarked at his farewell luncheon in a posh Washington restaurant. His quip did not fall on deaf ears, because for weeks afterward many of us at the party lamented the fact that we didn't have the guts to take a step like "ole Frank" did. And this seems to be the nub of the problem. Too many men at the working level simply no longer care about their work. To some it's a kind of a joke; to others it's "better than diggin' ditches." Most will stay on because it's too difficult to start over somewhere else. A common expression among intelligence staffers looking for work elsewhere is, "Who the hell needs tailgunners after the war?" Once you've spent the youthful portion of your career in intelligence it's difficult to translate that experience into a marketable commodity. Many stay because they realize this harsh fact and they are caught up in the suburban swirl of mortgage, two cars, kids near college age, and daughters to marry off.

The crisis involves CIA most directly but also affects nine other federal departments and agencies. The prospects, frankly, seem grim. One can almost predict an increasing number of intelligence failures on the scale of the *Pueblo* incident—and perhaps another war because of the present dry rot that infects our national intelligence structure.

There is little room for complacency on this crucial aspect of our national life. There have been more failures and, less excusably, more mediocrity than the United States should be willing to accept. The most generalized and persuasive argument for radical change is simply that the present system has not worked.

The past ten years are punctuated with a succession of intelligence failures that in no way counterbalance the bromide about "unsung successes." Simultaneously during the past decade there have been a number of attempts at reform that, not coincidentally, match the number of failures. These post-mortems are designed to identify and rectify problem areas. They have all resulted in glib, well-written final reports exonerating many, blaming none, recommending minor alterations, and in all cases, missing entirely the basic problems of a lack of central direction and control.

Time, the great healer, blunts the effects of these problem-oriented studies. The bureaucracy, stung for a bit, recoils—only to emerge after the passage of several months stronger and more determined not to "get caught" like that again. At the Pentagon, after the post-mortem on the shootdown of the United States Navy reconnaissance plane off the coast of North Korea in April, 1969, there was a lively interest for several months in risk assessments. Generals and admirals made certain that the procedures set up by the Joint Chiefs of Staff were followed. They checked the paperwork personally. Six months later the paper was being checked by the majors and captains in the Pentagon. Within a year the paperwork was spot-checked by a major, and the entire community slid back to its old way of making a "quick and dirty" rundown of the JCS criteria when sending in reconnaissance mission proposals. Why? Because that way it's easier to get the enormous amount of paperwork finished before the mission is to run.

At the Defense Intelligence Agency, after severe reprimands in the post-mortem for "misplacing" the message that could have prevented the *Pueblo* seizure, the responsible colonel installed an elaborate microfilming setup in the message center. He ordered that all incoming message traffic be filmed and stored for easy retrieval for any future post-mortems. He wanted to be able to prove what time it came in and what time it was sent to the responsible party in the Pentagon. With the message flow numbering in the thousands daily, the filming backlog now delays by three or four hours the cable traffic from the message center to the desk analysts responsible for reporting current developments to the defense establishment.

Radical change is needed. It is not simply a matter of the feelings or reputations of the men who now run the intelligence community. It is a matter of the nation's best interest being served. It will require hard decisions—decisions that will set the bureaucracy spinning, that will crush empires, fire men, reorganize the basic missions, and redefine the role of intelligence in United States national life. Any other approach is simply self-delusion. The age of evolutionary change went out the window with the dawning of the nuclear age. As the time required for destroying entire nations has diminished, the time for rectifying our national machinery of foreign policy has been compressed. Those who argue otherwise are luxuriating mentally in a former era.

A review of the better-known intelligence failures of the past ten years bears stark witness not only to the rapidity with which national crises arise, but also to the spreading nature of intelligence problems. The U-2 incident in May, 1960, torpedoed chances of a summit meeting in a twinkling. The hastily gathered and inaccurate intelligence during the Gulf of Tonkin crisis in 1964 was the basis for a costly, ineffective, four-year widening of that conflict. Yet, before the bombing decision was made, a CIA staffer who attended the White House sessions told me, "We knew it was bum dope that we were getting from the Seventh Fleet, but we were told to give only the facts with no elaboration on the nature of the evidence." The reason, in his words: "Everyone knew how volatile LBJ was. He didn't like to deal in uncertainties." The USS *Liberty,* an American intelligence ship, probed too closely to the Arab-Israeli war in June, 1967, because a warning message had been "misrouted." This prompted an attack which destroyed the ship and killed thirty-four American men—an incident which could have sucked the United States into that war had the Joint Chiefs of Staff's impulsive advice, which I witnessed, been followed. They proposed a quick, retaliatory air strike on the Israeli naval base which launched the attack. The next year the North Koreans seized a similar ship, the *Pueblo,* and interred its crew. Again we were on the brink of war because of intelligence, the supposed secret arm of government. The JSC again recommended an air strike. The *Pueblo* incident was followed by the shoot-down of a United States reconnaissance plane off the coast of North Korea a little over a year later. And again the JCS wanted to mount an air strike. The atmosphere was different because Nixon was in office then. The smart money at the Pentagon was saying that Nixon wouldn't allow the North Koreans to get away with this. After all, they reasoned, he was the guy who campaigned about the *Pueblo,* calling the North Koreans a fourth-rate military power. There were three or four days immediately after the shootdown when the decision had not been made. The majority of the military officers in our organization were strutting around claiming that Nixon would show those bastards. I couldn't resist the temptation to start calling bluffs by offering ten-to-one odds that he wouldn't do anything more than issue a "stern warning" statement. I had seventy takers and earned the nickname of "Patty the Greek." I have to admit that as the bets rolled in, and I realized that I stood to lose upwards of seven hundred bucks, I was nervous. Fortunately, I collected seventy bucks when it was all over. The administration issued one of those "we view this with alarm" statements.

The Bay of Pigs was the first proxy war CIA chose to fight. It was followed by others. A CIA-backed air force of ex-Cuban freedom fighters suddenly appeared in the Congo. Tibetan guerilla forces suddenly sprang into being along the Communist Chinese border. As Southeast Asia heated up, we fielded and led a mercenary army in Laos.

During the past decade American intelligence activities have also stained and strained the fabric of our domestic life. The Diem coup and CIA's involvement with Michigan State University as a cover for Vietnam operations set the stage for the credibility gap as far as the Vietnam venture is concerned. The disclosure of CIA's involvement with the National Student Association embittered many of the young in this country. CIA's involvement with the Green Berets in political assassinations in Vietnam even threatened the fiber of the American system of justice. The efforts of Army intelligence to ferret out information on potential domestic trouble spots and politicians led to the creation of a centralized computer file on the political activities of American college students and other citizens in clear violation of the charter of the intelligence community. And, today, as this kind of thing continues, it is even more disconcerting that many responsible officials know it and fail to remedy the situation.

Part of this inaction, I am convinced, is due to the character of the American psyche. Intelligence seems to be a virility symbol for many Americans—one that immediately equates the profession with such allegedly masculine ventures as murder, coup-plotting, intrigue, and a dash of illicit love making. Their minds somehow entangle the violence of pro football, the screen antics of James Bond, and lingering World War II memories of parachuting behind enemy lines with an exaggerated sense of "duty, honor, country." Some men in responsible positions within government would consider it decidedly "unmanly" to question the American intelligence establishment.

The saddest aspect of this attitude is that it is based on myth. The contrast between the commercial version and the actual profession of intelligence is stark—like comparing the life of a Carmelite nun to that of a jet-set swinger. A career in intelligence is dull. Bureaucracy, conformity, and paper mill are more meaningful power phrases to an intelligent professional than *coup d'état*, clandestine operations, or even spy. The lion's share of intelligence work is of a nine-to-five, deskbound nature. It is not even a brisk trade. Long hours of idleness characterize the daily work routine for more men in intelligence than one can easily imagine. The bull sessions in the office are broken up with jaunts to the cafeteria for coffee and bird-watching in mid-morning. Two-hour lunch breaks to various Washington restaurants are common. The Far Eastern analysts and operators frequent the Peking and Yenching Chinese restaurants. European analysts are seen at Tre Scalini, the Two Caesars, or the Chez François. The Syriana and other Middle Eastern and African restaurants draw their share of intelligence officers. Most afternoons are broken with another trip to the cafeteria for more coffee and forty-five minutes of gossip about the fellows who stayed behind. In the autumn and early winter months the Washington Redskins are subject to closer analysis than the Soviet strategic missile threat. Men in the scientific shop at CIA programmed one of their computers to replay the entire game each Monday to assist in their analyses. Quiet mutinies abound and go unnoticed. One man at the Defense Intelligence Agency prides himself on his ability to get a project extended. His championship was earned by getting twenty-four consecutive one-month extensions on a six-month research project. And lamentably, he is looked up to by his peers as a very clever fellow who knew how to beat the system.

The reason for all United States intelligence efforts is the finished product—the report that informs the President of developments abroad vital to American interests. And today there are considerably more people engaged in the complex intelligence community processing, analyzing, and reporting on the flow of paper than there are collecting it. In addition, the remarkable advances in technology which have afforded the United States the use of such devices as satellite-borne cameras, electronic impulse sensors, and infrared and microwave receivers have injected the necessity for having a wide variety of technical specialists operating in terrain once occupied by the lone-wolf spy. One element, the National Photographic Interpretation Center, employs about 3,000 people processing and reporting on satellite and aerial photography. The National Security Agency, in Washington alone, has close to 13,000 people working on communications and electronic intelligence. The service research organizations such as the Air Force's Institute of Technology at Wright Patterson Air Force Base in Ohio employs thousands developing electronic surveillance gear and studying Communist military and technological hardware. Industrial contractors also supply a good deal of the engineering talent needed.

Another and more readily discernible reason for the state of affairs within the intelligence community is its low and fragmented visibility. Submerged, dispersed, and under the control of several federal departments, the community has never been looked at as a whole in the past decade. This is not to say that responsible men have not tried to peek behind the cloak of secrecy which enshrouds the intelligence establishment. They have. But they have only done it in pieces. An Appropriations Committee will review Defense Intelligence as it scrutinizes the budget for the military services. A presidential commission will study military intelligence only as it applies to the pecking order in the Pentagon. A lonely scholar will try to penetrate the entire problem but is unable to get too deeply into the secret corridors and inhale the working-level atmosphere of intelligence. Former high officials of government will write of their experiences with intelligence. Special congressional committees will investigate the individual incidents such as the *Pueblo* seizure and touch on parts of the intelligence community's problems. And even though these efforts have not afforded a full view of intelligence problems, all have separately come to the same conclusions—that the intelligence community is in chaos and drastic presidential action is needed.

The most visible portion of the American intelligence establishment is the Defense Department's intelligence arm, the Defense Intelligence Agency. The most outspoken and perhaps most knowledgeable man on this subject on Capitol Hill is Congressman Jamie Whitten, of the House Appropriations Committee, who for years has watched the growth of the intelligence community. His thoughts on the subject are well known and feared throughout the community, but regrettably, have received little public attention.

At a hearing before his committee reviewing the 1969 budget of the DIA, Whitten informed Admiral Vernon Lowrance, the deputy director of DIA, that he had conducted a special staff investigation of DIA because he had been hearing many reports of inefficiency. He presented the report to Admiral Lowrance, remarking, "The report describes the current condition of our defense intelligence assets. After reading the report one could only conclude that the management of your intelligence assets is in a state of complete disarray, Admiral. Based upon the information in the report, one could justly say that our intelligence operations appear to be chaotic. I will cite a few examples before we go into the details.

"1. The report states that a number of intelligence activities are not included in the consolidated intelligence program procedure.

"2. The report indicates that the consolidated intelligence program is not an adequate device for managing intelligence programs.

"3. Intelligence reports are filed on film clips without an evaluation as to their importance.

"4. There is a lack of performance standards for intelligence positions.

"5. There is inefficient organization in assignment of work.

"6. Subordinates do not know their supervisors, and supervisors, in some instances, did not know who they were supposed to supervise.

"7. There appeared to be a lack of overall control of employees.

"8. Many intelligence costs are not included in the consolidated intelligence program.

"9. As a result of various deficiencies, the office responsible for Southeast Asian activities had 517 linear feet of file drawer space filled with data unprocessed by the analysts.

"Before going into the details, Admiral, would it not appear from the types of deficiencies disclosed in the report that some change is needed in the scope of your management activities of the defense intelligence community?"

Later on during the same hearing, Whitten, running short of patience with the admiral, interrupted him to deliver a rather stinging soliloquy. "I have been on this committee a good many years. I have listened to all sorts of intelligence reports. The witnesses continually refer to the 'intelligence community.' I can appreciate the fact that in the absence of intelligence we would be in a very bad way. I have about decided, however, that something about the size of a Sears, Roebuck catalogue full of intelligence can also leave you in a bad way. You can have so many reports and so much information and such a large community of intelligence that it seems as though before we got the book read the Tet offensive happened. I say that because these are the things on my mind. We have intelligence groups all over the place. It is a matter of record that expenditures in the name of intelligence are hidden in various and sundry areas of appropriation. I have heard it goes in excess of four to five billion dollars a year. This committee went into the *Pueblo* incident, went into the Cuban problem when it dawned on us that the Russians had those missiles based there. We dealt with the USS *Liberty* when it was fired upon. We have gone into the matter of the Tet offensive and the Vietnam situation. In all of these areas there are many people who feel that our intelligence just broke down. Rightly or wrongly, that is the feeling of many, many people."

Melvin Laird, long a skeptic of the Pentagon's bureaucracy while serving as a congressman, turned his staff to internal problems at the Department of Defense soon after assuming command there. His 1970 Defense budget singled out intelligence as a major management problem. "Intelligence," Laird said, "is both critical and costly. Yet we have found intelligence activities diffused with management overlapping or nonexistent. Deficiencies have provoked criticism that became known even outside the intelligence community. These criticisms can be summarized in five principal points:

"1. Our intelligence product was being evaluated poorly.

"2. Various intelligence-gathering activities overlapped and there was no mechanism to eliminate the overlap.

"3. There was no coordinated long-range program for resource management and programming.

"4. Significant gaps in intelligence gathering went unnoticed.

"5. The intelligence community failed to maintain frank and unrestricted channels of internal communication."

Laird assured Congress that he was making changes that would cure these basic ills within the Defense Department, but over a year later the President's Blue Ribbon Panel, which studied the Pentagon, noted that the situation was worse than ever. The panel chairman, Gilbert Fitzhugh, remarked at a July, 1970, press conference: "I believe that the Pentagon suffers from too much intelligence. They can't use what they get because there is so much collected. It would almost be better that they didn't have it because its difficult to find out what's important."

He went on to characterize operations within the entire Pentagon; his comment sets the tune for intelligence work there and applies with equal validity to the rest of the community. "Everybody is so busy at the Pentagon putting out brushfires that the five-to-fifteen-year view of things lies unattended. Frankly, we think it's an impossible organization to administer in its present form, just an amorphous lump. The basic difficulty we found was the diffusion of responsibility. There is nobody below the level of Secretary and Deputy Secretary that has the purview of the whole operation of the department. The same people have an interest in everything, so that they are all bogged down with too much detail work, too many responsibilities, too many man-killing jobs—and nobody really has the responsibility for anything."

A special subcommittee of the House Armed Services Committee was convened to investigate the USS *Pueblo* and *EC–121* incidents. They delved deeply into the problems of intelligence, which are so closely intertwined with the elaborate United States military command structure that it is impossible to separate them. At each level of military command there exists an intelligence component serving the local needs of the military commander and Washington at the same time.

The report concluded with the unanimous view "that there exists serious deficiencies in the organizational and administrative military command structure of both the Department of the Navy and the Department of Defense. If nothing else, the inquiry reveals the existence of a vast and complex military struc ture capable of acquiring almost infinite amounts of information but with a demonstrated inability in these two instances to relay this information in a timely and comprehensible manner to those charged with the responsibility for making decisions."

The subcommittee report went on to note that because of "the vastness of the military structure with its complex division into multiple layers of command and the failure of the responsible authorities at the seat of government to either delegate responsibility, or in the alternative, provide clear and unequivocal guidelines for emergency situations, our military command structure is now simply unable to meet the emergency criterion outlined and suggested by the President himself. The absent or sluggish response by military commanders in the *Pueblo* and *EC–121* incidents demonstrates the need for a complete review of our military and civilian command structure and its capability to cope with emergency situations."

The subcommittee closed the report with a recommendation that "the President establish a special study group of experienced and distinguished civilian and military personnel to approach this problem on an emergency basis and make such recommendations for changes in the National Security Act and the military structure itself that will provide our nation and its military forces with a genuine capability to respond directly to an emergency of a national security nature."

Some might conclude from the testimony above that intelligence is not really the issue under study and that it is simply another case of military mismanagement. That is true to a degree. But it must be kept in mind that intelligence is a vital part of all military operations and organizations. Since the director of the CIA is responsible for ensuring the efficient use of intelligence by the entire United States government, the gut issue is intelligence. This point, lamentably, has been missed by these various studies and investigations. Intelligence is thought of as a mere adjunct to an event such as the *Pueblo* and the *EC–121*, when in reality it is the major purpose. Intelligence seems to be creating almost as many dangerous situations as it brings to the attention of the President. Aren't supposedly secret operations to gain crisis-preventing information actually prompting the dramatic confrontations they were designed to detect in advance? Congressmen, with a few notable exceptions, ascribe a degree of sanctity to the CIA and treat the director and all other intelligence officials with a hushed reverence that borders on the ridiculous. They fail to think of intelligence simply as another bureaucracy, and treat it, instead, as a super-patriotic group of dedicated men above the human foibles and organizational frailities common to the rest of government. They have contented themselves to conduct what Senator J. W. Fulbright described to me as "what amounts to a ritualistic convening of special subcommittees which gather to hear only what the intelligence community wants them to hear." This approach is based on the confidence most congressmen have that the CIA is under proper control in the conduct of foreign operations. To a large extent that is true, but there are changes in the nature of intelligence problems that have yet to be perceived on Capitol Hill.

An important difference exists between the intelligence crises of the early sixties—which saw such exploits as the Bay of Pigs, the Diem coup, and the Congo Air Force caper—and the late sixties, which are noteworthy for the USS *Liberty,* the *Pueblo,* and the *EC–121* incidents. The former were operations primarily mounted by the clandestine service of CIA with an immediate political goal in mind. The latter were sophisticated collection missions mounted and directed by the analytical side of the intelligence community with more esoteric technical goals in mind. It is beyond dispute that the Bay of Pigs was a watershed for CIA in terms of its influence on policy making. It brought the problem of the role of operational intelligence in policy making into sharp focus and spurred not only a public furor but White House action. Prior to the Bay of Pigs fiasco, no matter how much administrative or political control there might have been, Allen Dulles ran the CIA largely as he saw fit. After that, however, the politically oriented operations of the CIA abroad were mounted only at the direct order of the President. John Kennedy reconstituted a control mechanism that he had let pass out of existence, and his administration spent a great deal of effort rearranging control over clandestine operations from the White House; nevertheless, the Congo operations, and particularly the Diem coup, made official Washington gun-shy of further exploits, because of the backlash at home. Word went out from Washington to CIA stations abroad that henceforth the policy on political action programs was to be "hands off." In Saigon, where I served, several long-time agents whose specialty and experiences had been in political action—they kept up close personal relationships with men like South Vietnam's General Khanh, Thieu, and Ky—were quietly sent back to stateside tours of duty after more than a decade's service in Vietnam. Similar operatives in other areas were pulled back to headquarters.

In the late sixties the analytical side of the intelligence community was largely responsible for the intelligence crises which this nation faced. No longer is the matter of control of agency operations as pertinent as is the much more subtle and involved question of the intelligence community's competence to deal wisely with the array of technical collection devices at its disposal. This new intelligence milieu is considerably more complicated and impersonal than in the former era, when decisions to mount political operations were made by individual men who were accountable for their actions. Now the decisions are made by a corporate phalanx of seemingly innumerable technically oriented committees with no single entity or person accountable for the entire impact of the program.

It is easier to say the entire system is at fault. The half-decisions and acts of omission surrounding tragedies like the *Pueblo* are not really conspiratorial in nature, like the Diem coup.They represent a combination of bureaucratic inertia, the military's penchant for "positive thinking," the failure of the entire intelligence community to organize itself to meet the

needs of technical collection, propensity on the analytical side
of the profession to collect more and more information regardless of its worth, and the failure to have a realistic program for
assessing collection.

The scope of the problems of national intelligence today are
broad indeed. They strike at the heart of the system and concern seemingly mundane matters such as organization of the
community, the duplication of effort within the profession, and
the overall work environment. A career at CIA, for example,
is vastly different from a career at DIA, the National Security
Agency, or the State Department. Pay, promotion, and personnel policies vary widely from agency to agency and even within
agencies. In contrast to the Hollywood image of rugged in-
dividualism, today's intelligence scene is dominated by the
committee, the mainstay for intelligence decision making—
belittling initiative, rewarding compromise, and contributing to
the emergence of corporate yes-men.

On May 12, 1966, United States aircraft flying over North
Vietnam on a bombing mission inadvertently strayed off course
and crossed into Chinese Communist air space. The Chinese,
of course, reacted by scrambling MIGs and downing one
United States aircraft. The incident was reported within minutes by field collection stations. The evidence on hand—radar
tracking data—indicated that the United States aircraft had
penetrated Chinese air space. The United States pilot reports,
however, which came in within an hour of the incident, insisted
that the pilots had not strayed across the border. The Chinese,
they claimed, had entered North Vietnamese air space to intercept them—an allegation with rather significant import, as it
could have represented a widening of the Vietnam War to
include the Communist Chinese. It boiled down to a case of
which evidence the intelligence community would accept in
reporting the event to the policy makers of government. CIA
analysts, long accustomed to the accuracy and validity of radar
reports, opted to write their analysis for President Johnson on
that basis, discounting, in other words, the validity of the pilot

reports. The Defense Intelligence Agency, however, opted to place more value on the pilot reports and so reported the situation to Pentagon officials.

In the coordination of the daily report for the President, DIA, which has a say in the final wording of the report, insisted on giving greater credence to the pilot reports. This resulted in a compromise report to the President which altogether avoided taking a position on exactly where the event had occurred. It read something like this: "Preliminary evidence indicates that US and Chicom aircraft today engaged in combat in the vicinity of the China–North Vietnam border. One US aircraft was downed by enemy fighters. At this time it is uncertain if the combat occurred over Chinese or North Vietnamese territory."

The committee, then, had decided to avoid the gut issue and await further evidence. It only informed the President of the bare facts of the incident without qualifying the evidence. Before the additional evidence came in, the United States Air Force Chief of Staff, having read the initial DIA assessment, which is not coordinated with CIA, publicly discussed the issue with newsmen and categorically denied that United States aircraft had penetrated Chinese air space. The elaborate radar and navigation gear on United States aircraft would not allow pilots to make such a gross error, he insisted. The next day the Chinese Communists published photographs of both the pilot they had captured and the wreckage of his aircraft. The President was finally fully informed of the actual sequence of events when this additional evidence appeared. No one at CIA, however, seemed to recall the swiftness of some of LBJ's decisions—such as in the Gulf of Tonkin caper—or the fact that LBJ drew heavily on the Joint Chiefs of Staff for advice concerning Vietnam.

These problems, and the uncertainty and indecisiveness they breed, converge at a point where the integrity of intelligence is most important—at the policy-making level of government. An intelligence estimate or current report, despite its slick packaging, has nothing to sell it but consistent credibility. Rumors of internal bickering, such as the long-standing enmity between Richard Helms, the director of CIA, and the man who almost got his job in 1966, Ray Cline, now the director of the State Department's intelligence bureau, inevitably percolate to the top of government. Personality clashes between two strong men —like Helms and his former deputy director at CIA, retired Admiral Rufus Taylor, who retired in disgust—do not go unnoticed; they tend to lessen the credibility of intelligence reports and almost insure that they will not receive the attention they should.

And today this is happening. Henry Kissinger, Nixon's national security adviser, has sidestepped many of the established intelligence processes, according to well-placed sources who have witnessed the decline of CIA in the past two years. On the delicate issue of Vietnam, for example, Kissinger has not asked for a single National Intelligence Estimate, yet he has asked the community to supply him and his staff with the facts and with an assessment of the evidence. He is, in effect, writing his own estimates. Specialists in Middle Eastern affairs disclose that Kissinger has stopped asking for broad estimates of that situation. Here, too, he wants only the facts and an assessment of the evidence. A friend revealed that Kissinger sent back a CIA study assessing the likelihood and effects of a British entry into the Common Market with "Piece of Crap" scrawled across the cover. Obviously, Kissinger recognizes that essential facts are vital to the recommendations he puts before the President, but it is apparent that the intelligence product with which he has been dealing has not earned his respect. H. H. Ransom, a scholarly student of the intelligence establishment, has written on this point. "Fundamental problems of perception and receptivity remain," he said. "Many officials in the last analysis continue to serve as their own intelligence experts. Intelligence by committee still tends to suppress what at times may be vitally significant dissent. Duplication, institutional rivalry, and jurisdictional jealousy continue to deposit sand in the gears, and the irresistible force of the National Intelligence Estimate collides on frequent occasions with such immovable objects as budgetary ceilings, partisan selfishness, or the omnipresent obstacle of unwillingness to believe unpleasant or unexpected information."

The memoirs and press conference quips of former government officials are replete with remarks about the quality of intelligence in the sixties. Roger Hilsman, Assistant Secretary of State for Far Eastern Affairs under Kennedy and Johnson, asserted: "The blunt truth is that the President knows very little that you and I don't know. And, even that little extra is going to leak out sooner or later." At the very start of the information-gathering process, according to Hilsman, there are inevitable limits. The subjectivity of intelligence agents can easily lead them to ask different questions, and thus get different answers from what is before them, whether the subject is a Vietcong prisoner or a pile of captured documents. Hilsman argues that the intelligence pipeline is further bent because even good data gathered in the field must pass through many channels before arriving at their destination. If the information was not digested, of course, it would be unmanageable. So at each step it is scrutinized, reinterpreted, perhaps expanded, more often cut down. An error at one stage can be magnified in the result. Having matured as an officer in the Office of Strategic Services during World War II, Hilsman was under no illusions about the nature of the intelligence game when he left his academic post to serve the Kennedy administration. He knew from personal experience of the distortions that abound in intelligence reporting, and his skepticism served him in good stead.

John Kennedy learned skepticism about intelligence estimates the hard way—from the Bay of Pigs. He reflected once, "I don't think the intelligence reports are all that hot. Some days I get more out of *The New York Times.*" During his conduct of the Vietnam War, Lyndon Johnson often relied heavily on the counsel of his senior military and civilian advisers. Yet in 1966 he confessed: "I can't think of a thing I know that the press doesn't know right now. Oh yes, some details, a few little secrets, but there isn't one important activity we are in that I haven't seen in the papers or on TV in some way." It is a seemingly sad commentary on intelligence, which spends four to five billion dollars a year amassing information for the President, that their product is only on a par with the American press. On the one hand it bears testimony to the limits of intelligence-gathering potential, and on the other hand it suggests that a great deal of money and effort is being wasted. More importantly, executive disaffection with, or lack of faith in, the intelligence product results inevitably in poorly informed presidential decision making.

The broader implications of the internal rumblings, the disarray and the disenchantment within the intelligence community, are not lost on the American public or the world at large. Instinctively, college students of today link CIA with the worst of the nation's weakening institutions. The seemingly endless string of failures in the past decade has resulted in the CIA's becoming a foreign policy liability, and its status at home remains under a serious cloud of suspicion. Arnold Toynbee was prompted to write soon after the Cambodian invasion in May, 1970: "To most Europeans I guess America now looks like the most dangerous country in the world, since America is unquestionably the most powerful country. The transformation of America's image in the last thirty years is very frightening to Europeans. They feel that at any moment America may intervene in their own internal affairs with the same appalling consequences that have followed from American intervention in Southeast Asia. For the world as a whole the CIA has now become the bogey that Communism has been for America. Whenever there is trouble, violence, suffering, tragedy, the rest of us are now quick to suspect that CIA had a hand in it. Our phobia about the CIA is no doubt as fantastically excessive as America's phobia about world Communism. But, in this case too, there is just enough convincing evidence to make the phobia genuine. In fact, the roles of America and Russia have been reversed in the world's eyes. Today, America has become the world's nightmare." This sense of ill-being concerning American intelligence activities is an exaggerated and even misplaced sentiment. That Toynbee wrongly chose to stress political intervention on the part of CIA as the culprit does not invalidate, however, his conclusion that America has become the world's nightmare largely because of its intelligence activities. It simply adds further credence to the idea that intelligence is suffering from a malaise. The vagueness of intelligence problems eludes even the trained eye.

The many myths that surround CIA and intelligence in general must be torn away and replaced with a clearer picture of just what it is that American intelligence does and how it does it. A clear knowledge of the complexity of the community as it is now organized is a prerequisite to understanding the bureaucratic culture that prevails. Even then, however, there are no simple answers to the problems. Regrettably, a full examination of United States intelligence seems to raise more questions than it answers. It suggests, among the more important items, that considerable thought should be given to the conventional wisdom of allowing a professional intelligence officer to run the entire intelligence apparatus when the weight of evidence, over the past five years in particular, points clearly to the conclusion that the intelligence community is becoming less and less able to fulfill its basic mission of supporting the President.

"Conviction that CIA is a necessity to national security is not in itself sufficient," wrote Lyman Kirkpatrick, the former executive director of CIA. "There must also be assurances that the agency is under proper control and operating competently. Like any other part of the United States government, the CIA is the servant of the American people. Their control of it through Congress and the President can be decisive. It can be the type of organization that the people of America want and need. It can be either strong and efficient and adequately controlled, or it can be weak and ineffective. If it is the former then I have confidence in the future. If the United States intelligence effort is the best in the world, then our policy makers should be the best informed. This information, in turn, should enable them to guide the nation and hopefully lead the world on the path of peace. If CIA is weak and ineffective, then the Communists will have won a major victory in the cold war, and the security of this nation will be in grave jeopardy."

Regrettably the present state of affairs within the United States intelligence establishment indicates that the problems so outnumber the solid achievements that the system has grown cumbersome and approaches the "weak and ineffective" state of which Kirkpatrick warned. As it now stands, the intelligence establishment is of doubtful future value.

Any critical examination of the intelligence establishment requires a working understanding of just how the intelligence pie is divided.

I do not pose as an expert on the organization of United States intelligence. As a matter of fact this book is being written because I still do not comprehend fully after fourteen years' experience the complex structure of intelligence. The establishment is so large, so cumbersome, and so diffuse today that it almost defies rational understanding by one person. In the officer-training program I attended at CIA, our instructors spent four solid weeks, eight hours a day, explaining the elaborate organization. We were dazzled with an endless array of color-slide briefings carefully explaining the fine lines of authority. That was in 1963, and the intelligence community has continued to expand, never contracting.

My admitted ignorance does not preclude, however, an appreciation of the broad outlines of what is going on in intelligence. When the story of the United States Army's spying on American political figures broke in December, 1970, for example, I was able to put the operation into its proper context and conclude that the entire affair was grossly distorted in the press.

The basic facts were correct. United States Army agents were infiltrating student groups and tailing domestic political candidates. These acts were patently violating the charter of military intelligence, and should have been stopped, but they in no way posed the threat to civil liberties that the press implied. My own brutal, first-hand experience with military intelligence has shown that the United States Army is incapable of pulling off something as sophisticated as pressuring elected officials with blackmail tactics. Senator Ervin, who disclosed the issue, would have us believe that the Army Chief of Staff for Intelligence is daily fingering through dossiers on American political figures and passing selected tidbits along to his superiors at the Pentagon for their use in dealing with Congress. The image was a conspiratorial one heavily laden with suggestions of a military takeover. Probably the Army Chief of Staff for Intelligence did not even know that units under his command were collecting such information. Moreover, the kinds of intelligence in the files were what is known in the trade as garbage—useless tidbits of minutiae about when and where a candidate spoke and what he said. A better, more complete dossier could have been compiled by anyone who clipped newspapers and news magazines. As a matter of fact, the Army could have saved considerable expense by writing to the candiates' offices requesting to be put on their mailing lists. This would have provided them with a much more complete profile of the candidate.

This incident is not discussed to build an excuse for the Army, but rather to dispel one more myth of an all-powerful United States intelligence corps capable of ferreting out scandalous information and deviously wielding it in the power arena of Washington. The Army had no business collecting such information, and, in my opinion, heads should have rolled in the intelligence community for the tawdry affair. The man to whom Congress should have directed its ire is Richard Helms, the director of CIA, whose charter makes him responsible for all United States intelligence activities.

The structure of national intelligence that funnels information to the President is called the "intelligence community"— a mélange of ten federal departments and agencies employing about 150,000 people.

At the top of the pyramid sits the President. Directly beneath him is his Foreign Intelligence Advisory Board, a group of men from outside government who supposedly review and assess the CIA and other executive departments or agencies in the foreign intelligence fields.

Below them sits the National Security Council (NSC), playing an important overseer role in intelligence matters. They are privy to CIA and other agency programs and activities and, theoretically, insure that these blend with broad foreign policy objectives.

Under the NSC and directly responsible to it is the United States Intelligence Board (USIB), which is chaired by the Director of Central Intelligence, Richard Helms. You will note that his title is not the Director of Central Intelligence Agency. Known in town as "The DCI" (Director of Central Intelligence), Helms's responsibilities are far broader than merely running the CIA.

A CIA booklet sent to curious inquirers describes Helms's duties this way: "The DCI is responsible for coordinating the foreign intelligence activities of the United States. He is Chairman of USIB which advises and assists him in this coordinating role. The Deputy Director of CIA is a member of the Board representing CIA. The other Board members are heads of the Intelligence organizations of the State Department's Bureau of Intelligence and Research, the Pentagon's Defense Intelligence Agency, and the National Security Agency, plus representatives of the Atomic Energy Commission and the FBI." The four service intelligence chiefs, it should be added, sit in as observers on these meetings and are not without a great deal of influence.

"Acting in consultation with USIB the DCI makes recommendations to the NSC concerning the Intelligence structure of the government as a whole, to insure that each element is functioning properly in the national intelligence effort"—a point relevant to the previously mentioned issue concerning United States Army snooping.

The six USIB members and the four service observers, then,

operate as a corporate body with equal status under the chairmanship of the DCI. Each of these agencies has slightly different intelligence functions to perform. The responsibilities of the CIA are to advise the NSC of what intelligence is doing, to seek NSC approval for proposed intelligence programs that could prove embarrassing to the United States, to report the findings of intelligence collection and analysis to the policy-making arm of government, and to make recommendations to the NSC for the coordination of such intelligence activities.

The Defense Intelligence Agency (DIA) was established on August 1, 1961, by Secretary Robert S. McNamara. It controls Department of Defense intelligence resources and reviews the intelligence activities of the military departments.

The National Security Agency (NSA), the code-breaking arm of the intelligence structure, was established by presidential directive in 1952 as a separately organized agency within the Defense Department. NSA has two primary functions: a security mission of monitoring secure United States communications and an intelligence information mission, which involves manning listening posts the world over for monitoring the communications of other nations and processing this usable intelligence for other components of the community.

The State Department's intelligence activities are carried on in the Bureau of Intelligence and Research (INR). They produce intelligence studies and spot reports essential to foreign policy determination and execution for the Secretary of State.

The Atomic Energy Commission is a consumer and producer of intelligence in the critical field of nuclear energy. It is represented on the USIB by an intelligence division expert. It provides technical guidance to CIA and other members in collecting nuclear intelligence, processes information on nuclear energy, and develops estimates on the atomic-weapons capability of foreign powers.

The FBI is a major member of the national intelligence community, yet its direct role in the production of positive foreign intelligence is limited. Its counterintelligence operations often turn up information of value to positive intelligence.

While it is necessary to adhere to the formal organizational chart of intelligence to understand how the job is done, a slavish recitation of functions and authority misses a key element in today's intelligence problem—the human factor. Compartmented, isolated from reality, and swamped with paper, today's intelligence officer is truly a faceless individual. Remote from decision making and identifiable responsibility, each intelligence officer represents one facet in a collective effort that at best can be described as an amorphous lump. To get behind the semantic swirl of management jargon accompanying all organizational charts and understand what really goes on in intelligence, it is necessary to return to the basics.

Our national intelligence effort is a cyclic process involving four elements—collection, processing, reporting, and control. By reviewing each function, a clearer picture of United States intelligence should emerge in a way that will make the individual's role in the corporate hierarchy better understood.

II

The Octopus

The collection efforts of United States intelligence are directed against three targets—technical details, human thinking, and authoritative documents. The field today is dominated by technology.

The spy-in-the-sky satellites are the best-known technical devices employed, but they represent only a mere fraction of esoteric "black box" intelligence devices in use today. Overall, their "take" is small when compared to the less notorious technical collection systems. This is not meant to belittle the system, however; in one ninety-minute circling of the globe the satellites—dubbed SAMOS (Satellite Antimissile Observation System)—collect more information than an army of fifty thousand foot spies collects in a year.

The twenty-two-foot-high, five-foot-round satellite, looking much like a Cuban cigar, is packed with devices that pick up the murmurings of radars, the crackling of radios, the point-to-point secure communications of the world's nations, and the work of Chinese and Soviet scientists at their separate nuclear-weapons and space-research stations. Equipped with a variety of cameras these unusual spies can detect a chalk line on the ground from a hundred miles up.

Launched from Vandenberg Air Force Base in southern California on the average of once a month, SAMOS satellites can be triggered to unload their electronic take in a split-second spurt of energy that can be intercepted at ground stations, replayed, and amount to several hours of electronic intelligence. Their photo-intelligence take is ejected after about a week in orbit and intercepted in midair over the Pacific, where the Air Force enjoys a 70 percent success rate in catching them.

At present, there are two breeds of the SAMOS satellite in use. The first, using a Thor-Agena rocket, makes broad sweeps of the Soviet Union, China, and other target countries from an altitude of more than one hundred miles. The second, launched aboard a Titan III-B booster, carries higher-resolution cameras and is normally employed as a follow-up to the first, flying at lower altitudes. In 1970 a total of nine United States reconnaissance satellites were launched. Six of these were of the Titan III-B variety and were launched between June and late October, when there was intense United States interest in what was happening along the Suez Canal and at Russian ICBM bases, where a slowdown in construction was spotted and eventually announced by the Pentagon.

United States spy satellite activity has declined in the past several years. In 1968, sixteen satellites were launched; in 1969, twelve; and only nine were lofted in 1970. Using average times in orbit, the United States had one spy satellite over the Soviet Union on 180 days of 1970.

The Soviet Union, on the other hand, launches three times as many spy satellites as the United States. During 1970, twenty-nine recon satellites—each remaining in orbit for an average of eight to thirteen days—photographed United States installations on an average of 290 days. Most Americans don't think about being spied upon. The farmers in North Dakota would be surprised to know that the Russians are watching their crops grow with as much interest as they are. The stockyards of Omaha are scrutinized to see how the American beef industry is doing. The oil fields of Oklahoma and Texas are watched. The suburban sprawl of the East Coast is kept under surveillance so that Soviet demographers can have an accurate fix on the American population. Many a present-day Tom Sawyer has been photographed on the Mississippi as the Soviet Union keeps tabs on the river's commerce. Lastly, those cocky New York honeys who sunbathe nude on penthouse roofs are no doubt the subject of very close examination by Soviet photo-intelligence experts.

When the Son Tay prisoner-of-war-camp raid into North Vietnam flopped, it was revealed that the United States Air Force had practiced for the raid at Elgin Air Force Base in Florida. They went to such elaborate precautions that they dismantled the mockup of the prison camp every morning before dawn so that the Soviets wouldn't see it in their reconnaissance.

In the collection phase there are few difficulties with the satellite program. The only factor that does cause some problems is the weather. Missions come back with the most important targets obscured by layers clouds. When United States intelligence was trying to determine the exact number of SA-2 (surface-to-air) missiles that the North Vietnamese had in operation during the height of the bombing campaign in 1966, mission after mission would return with one-frame shots of the entire country of North Vietnam only to reveal great swatches of monsoon clouds over as much as two-thirds of the country.

The men involved in the collection program for the satellites are technicians concerned more with the operation of the system than with the intelligence it collects. Air Force teams, abetted by a few CIA staffers with technical skills, spend all of their time with launch preparation, firing, and successful tracking and retrieval of the satellite. I spent some time at Hickam Air Force Base in Hawaii, where the photo capsule is recovered by Air Force teams flying C-130 turboprop jets rigged with special trapezelike snares. The teams who snared them did not know what the capsule contained. They didn't care either. Their primary concern was getting the job done and bringing the capsule back to Hickam, where it was then taken by CIA men to the National Photographic Interpretation Center at the Washington Navy Yard.

An equally lucrative and more widespread source of technical intelligence is signals intelligence, or communications intelligence, known as COMINT. In essence, this means all forms of intelligence that can be gleaned by listening in to the radio communications of a foreign nation from afar. The most obvious targets are clear text, radio language communications—the kind required at airports, among army units maneuvering in the field, ship-to-shore naval traffic, and air-to-ground civilian airline radio communications. COMINT does not monitor a nation's domestic commercial radio stations; however, its targets include most other forms of radio communications, despite the fact that they are encoded or broadcast in other unintelligible forms such as single side band, teletype, automatic or manual Morse code, or telegraphic code. All forms of a target country's radio communications—be it merchant shipping, industrial development, foreign trade, or internal transportation—are monitored in varying degrees, depending on the country's potential threat to the United States. Obviously, the Soviet Union and Communist China are high priority targets for all forms of communication.

Controlled by the National Security Agency, America's radio intercept network is extensive. There are slightly over fifty stations active at any given time of the day. They are located in at least fourteen foreign countries. They range in size from small mobile field units of a company of men, as used in Vietnam, to a sprawling complex of men and machines numbering in the thousands, such as the Air Force Security Headquarters in West Germany. Worldwide, there are approximately thirty thousand servicemen manning these listening posts. A minimum of four thousand radio intercept consoles are in operation at all times. With each set listening in on from one to five targets, the diversity of intelligence collected is broad indeed.

These overseas sites are manned and administered by the three services primarily because of the isolated nature of the duty. I spent eight of my fourteen years in intelligence in the COMINT business, and most of that time was frittered away on lonely outposts. The most bizarre was a little island, three miles square, sitting on the 38th parallel in the Yellow Sea off the cost of Korea. Sixty of us lived in potbelly-heated tents and worked in sandbagged mountaintop bunkers, our ears covered with headsets and our tape recorders alert to any Chinest Communist activity over North Korea or China. A battalion of Korean marines shared the island with us. Things were pretty dull there, with the major social event of the month being the arrival of a South Korean Navy LST on the beach. It brought our food and other supplies. It also brought eight government-inspected whores from Inchon. The Korean marines had a merit system whereby each was given five ass chits a month. If he was a bad boy they took one of his chits away. It worked! Anyway, the Korean marines would all line up in front of the eight-door garage, in which the whores traded, and use their tickets. The LST was on the beach for about four to five days. By the third day the Korean marines had all spent their chits, so the sixty American GIs would line up at ten bucks a crack to relieve their inner tensions.

Other depressing sites are northern Japan, the tip of the Aleutian Islands, and the Khyber Pass. The bulk of the men at such stations are young enlisted men on their first hitch, trained especially for this work.

All sites maintain a round-the-clock operation, with men sitting at radio recorder consoles monitoring a particular frequency for voice traffic, others watching Morse or teletype frequencies, and still others searching a spectrum of the broadcast bands for any unexpected emissions. On the whole, the work is routine, with the daily trivia of a military airfield's training activity or the amblings of a particular Soviet army battalion through a field exercise closely watched from dawn to dusk.

During the summer I spent on Pyaeng Yang Do, the sixty of us were forced to double up after a typhoon wiped out half our tents. For two months the guy who just got off the midnight shift would come down from the mountaintop and jump into the bunk of the guy who relieved him. With linen change once a week, the process earned the name "hot-sacking it," a delightful practice in which we shared one another's farts, wet dreams, and perspiration. During this same period the supply sergeant instituted the three-squares-a-day program of toilet paper consumption, since no LST had arrived for two months. When the regular issue toilet paper ran out, we switched to using six-ply paper that we stole from the operations bunkers atop the mountain. It was fine, except for the damage rendered by the five layers of carbon paper.

Light moments break the boredom occasionally. We'd amuse ourselves by annoying the officers in our outfit. There were only three of them, yet they had the audacity to construct a separate outdoor john for themselves and cordon it off as officer country. To add to the insult, they equipped theirs with a potbelly stove. The compound in which we lived was nestled in the crotch of two hills, with officer country being three tents and an outhouse on the right slope and enlisted rats living in tents on the left slope. The entire facility was surrounded with concertina wire, and we had to pull four-hour guard tours around the clock. During the winter, when it would get to twenty below with a fierce wind blowing in from Manchuria, we sort of resented the fact that we had to scrape the ice and snow off the three-holer seats before using them in the morning, while the officers' bodies were never exposed to more than a ten-degree change in temperature. The guy on guard during the night took to rolling up snowballs and dropping them down the flue atop the officers' john, quenching the flame and presenting them with the same dilemma each nippy morning.

Predawn radio checks by Chinese Communist troops that we were monitoring would reveal many personal insights for the operators. On more than one morning that obvious crackling whiskey voice and slower-than-normal speech would indicate a hangover. Belching, yawns, and hiccups punctuated the first hour's work. Small talk between Chinese troops revealed that their gripes were similar to ours—too much guard duty, lousy food that day, KP or no three-day passes for the troops. An intimacy among operators invariably grows at these isolated sites. After months of listening to a particular Communist soldier on the radio, an invisible kinship normally developed, as well as a rather complete feel for the type of guy it was that we were listening to. One Chinese radio operator had a numbers operation going over the airwaves for months. Another would nightly describe a particular girl he had allegedly screwed instead of broadcasting the dictated one-to-ten number count for the prescribed five minutes of radio signal strength check each hour. This intimacy came in handy when suddenly the particular radio network decided to change all their call signs for security. Most voices were known to the operators, and recovery of the new call sign system was rapid.

Every detail of activity intercepted at all these sites is recorded, analyzed, and forwarded to NSA for additional study. In cases where encoded traffic is unbreakable, useful intelligence can still be gained from an analysis of the time, length, and recipients of the coded messages. For unusual developments, a message system known as CRITIC is employed by intercept sites. These are used when a sudden development of vital interest to the United States government occurs, such as the Gulf of Tonkin affair, when North Vietnamese torpedo boats intercepted a United States destroyer, or the Soviet invasion of Czechoslovakia. A short message giving the basic facts gleaned from COMINT is sent to NSA under a priority that automatically disseminates the message from its point of origin to the White House and all other interested Washington agencies within five minutes.

My first exposure to the CRITIC system occurred on Pyaeng Yang Do. We had an old reject from World War II, a guy named Davey Pendleton, about forty-five years old and unable to hold more than two stripes at any time because of his continuing love affair with the sauce. Old Davey would fill his canteen with gin or vodka each day before setting out for his solitary post in a packing crate that held radio direction finding and radar equipment. He'd rationalize it as medicinal to ward off the chills. One afternoon the Chinese Communists decided to shift a squadron of MIGs from an airfield just east of Peking to another up in Manchuria. Davey picked them up on his radar, and the guys in the other bunker picked them up on voice radio networks. Davey cranked up his direction-finding gear. His readings of their position showed that they were heading out over the Yellow Sea toward South Korea on a route that would take them directly over our island. Poor Davey panicked and called the naive young second lieutenant allegedly in charge of us. The lieutenant also panicked and dispatched a CRITIC to our headquarters in Japan and all the way back to the White House. Within minutes the fire gong went off at three air bases in South Korea and Japan, and two squadrons of American jets were scrambled to intercept the MIGs. Navy units battened their hatches and sounded general quarters, and army units lolling along the DMZ were goosed into action by red alert klaxons. The military command hierarchy throughout the Far East was tensed, ready, and quivering. As time went on and the MIGs didn't materialize, a cable from our Japan headquarters asked us to recheck our bearings on the squadron. By this time the major and the captain were on the mountaintop peering into the equipment themselves. They saw nothing other than the normal rotation of a MIG squadron from Peking to Manchuria.

They sent a follow-up message to the CRITIC telling the United States military chain of command it was a false alarm.

The major then told the captain that he'd like to see Pendleton in his tent. Davey had gulped down the remainder of his canteen and was in no shape to see anybody. The captain insisted that we pry him out of hiding in the outdoor john and present him to the major. We did, and Davey wobbled into the CO's tent and reported. The major was shocked at the sight of him and asked, "Pendleton, have you been drinking?" Davey elfishly replied, "Sir, I've been known to quaff a wee libation before nightfall to ward off the chillblains." Davey lost both his stripes.

The COMINT land stations are backed up by flying, sea-borne, and mobile land radio intercept units around the world. These were necessitated in the 1950s by the massive shift among Communist military units to VHF radio. Complete coverage of their activity demanded that United States units get closer to the transmitters, as terrain features like mountains would impede ground intercept of VHF broadcasts.

After serving my tour on the island I volunteered for flying duty out of Kimpo Air Base near Seoul. It was considered good duty. We bunked in a little compound of quonset huts on the edge of the airstrip and were such a hush-hush organization that we were relieved of guard duty and KP. We wore no insignia of rank, and the pilots had such a fondness for us that they'd smuggle us into the officer's club. The work routine was pleasant and mostly uneventful. We had one minor hitch uncommon to most military organizations, however. The pilots in our unit were not cleared for the top secret stuff we were dealing with, so they had to get aboard the airplane ahead of us and lock themselves in the pilot's compartment. We then would climb aboard with our radio receivers and tape recorders and set the equipment up in racks in the belly of the C-47 before takeoff. During the flight they were not allowed back in the fuselage of the plane where we worked. Moreover, we had our own separate radio that kept us in contact with our operation on the ground. They'd call us and ask us to shoot a direction-finding bearing on a target they were watching, and we'd pass along air traffic that we could pick up ahead of the ground station. On the few occasions that the North Koreans or Chinese Communists would send a MIG up to sniff around us they gave us the authority to vector the pilot out of the area. The pilots had been briefed to expect this.

We didn't take too much advantage of the pilots under these circumstances, but on many occasions we would vector the pilot out of the Yellow Sea and onto a course that took us to Japan. Normally we'd forget to tell the pilot to assume his old course until we were far enough away so that his fuel demanded that we continue on to Japan. This stunt was best pulled on a Friday flight because we'd end up spending the weekend in Tokyo. There was always a scramble of guys to get on the Friday flight. We'd appear dressed for a routine work day in fatigues, but we all carried a ditty bag with civilian clothes on the off-chance that we'd end up in Japan.

After the Korean tour I volunteered to join a flying unit based outside of Tokyo flying RB-50 recon missions from Japan to the Philippines, listening to Chinese Communist air defenses. At Clark Air Base outside of Manila we had a deal cooked up with the maintenance chief—he would lose whatever spare parts we needed to keep the plane flying. On the way down our crew chief would disable the heating system or the radio, and once on the ground at Clark we would have to wait for a week or ten days for them to fly in the parts from Japan. In the town of Angeles Pompanga outside of Clark they had these lovely thousand-year eggs that stank. Once we brought a couple of them back with us and inserted them into the heating ducts in the pilot's compartment. Airborne and flying at ten thousand feet, we needed heat. When the pilot turned the forward heat on, the plane took a noticeable dip and flew an erratic course for the next couple of minutes. He decided to land on Taiwan, where we spent another week awaiting the arrival of spare parts.

Daily in Europe and the Far East, several dozen United States airborne listening posts fly an average of six hours along the borders of Communist countries. Although the exact number of recon missions flown by the military is difficult to trace, the House Armed Services Committee stated in one report that "they number in the thousands annually." Mobile land units maneuver in West Germany, while Soviet army units are in the field, exercising in East Germany or Czechoslovakia. In South Korea similar units operate. The United States Navy keeps twelve to fifteen spy ships, such as the *Pueblo*, afloat around the world on extended cruises.

Another form of signals intelligence is known as ELINT—for Electronics Intelligence. This is information collected by NSA from foreign noncommunications, electromagnetic radiations, such as radars. Eighty percent of the take of shipborne and airborne collection platforms is ELINT. The age of electronic warfare dawned after World War II, when sophisticated radar and rocket systems came into their own. War planners at Strategic Air Command Headquarters were concerned with the ability of United States bombers to penetrate the Russian radar network undetected. They began to fly missions along the periphery of Russia trying to find the points at which a certain radar set was unable to detect an incoming bomber. Analysis of the pulse rate of the Russian radar would provide data on which the radar set's range and height-finding capability could be estimated. Eventually, war planners made maps pinpointing the location of all Russian radars, and from this were able to project cones or umbrellas of radar coverage outward from the sites. Routes of penetration could then be planned.

The arena of electronics has been a tremendously dynamic one, however, and a deadly game of defensive measures and countermeasures ensued. American planners developed a jammer to block out Russian radar sets; the Russians developed an antijammer. The Americans came up with a false-image projector, and the Russians developed a way to filter that out. The battle goes on today and is not confined to radars. Missiles and rockets which emit signals are very vulnerable to what is known as ECM—Electronic Countermeasure.

A dangerous game of routinely tickling the enemy defenses was begun in the mid-1950s and continues today. Mock raids would be mounted by United States military units in Turkey, for example. A flight of ELINT-equipped bombers would fly at minimum altitudes across the Black Sea toward Russia, hoping to stimulate a defensive response. More often than not, the Russians would scramble MIGs and alert other forces, only to have the American flight veer off immediately toward Turkey.

There have been many less fortunate incidents which date back to the mid-fifties. A United States "cargo" plane was shot down near the Turkish border by Russian fighters; an RB-47 was downed by MIGs in the Barents Sea; several "weather" flights have been shot down by Chinese Communist MIGs in the past decade and a half. Near Hainan Island, in the South China Sea, my unit ran into trouble. The incident grew out of the situation I described earlier, in which the enlisted men in the rear of the plane oftentimes had to tell the pilot which way to fly. As the Super Constellation with the camelback radar dome on its fuselage neared the territorial limits of Hainan Island, the troops in the rear of the plane picked up Chinese MIGs on voice communications. It was evident that they were coming after their plane. The buck sergeant in the back told the pilot to reverse his course and get the hell out of the area. The pilot, a newly assigned lieutenant commander, resented being told where to fly by an enlisted man and refused to change course. The MIGs intercepted the recon plane and shot it up badly, destroying the radar dome and wounding two of the men in the rear of the plane.

Bombing raids over North Vietnam were supported by airborne ELINT stations which would advise American pilots when a North Vietnamese SA-2 missile site activated its radar. They could also determine when it fired a missile because of the shift to another type of radar to guide the SA-2 toward the incoming United States aircraft. Devices which would detonate the North Vietnamese missiles prematurely were experimented with, and the North Vietnamese, under Soviet tutelage, countered with changes in their style of radar operation.

The result of this collection effort is a massive store of technical data. In Vietnam the emphasis was on the immediate situation; nevertheless, the data collected was fed into the analytical process stretching up the military chain of command throughout the Pacific area to NSA headquarters at Fort Meade, Maryland. The daily take from Europe and other areas is also funneled back up the chain of command.

The men in this field of work—mostly enlisted technicians—are referred to as RAVENS. They are trained to operate oscilloscopes and calibrating machines and to recognize and record the signals emitted by various radars, missiles, and fighter aircraft under vector. Confined to a cramped position either in an aircraft or aboard ship, their world is a frenzy of warbling headsets and dancing green scopes.

Another field of technical intelligence that receives fairly wide publicity is photo-intelligence. The scope of this effort by United States intelligence is far broader than the spy-in-the-sky satellite programs. SR-71 high-altitude aircraft and the infamous U-2 back up the satellite program. Equipped with Polaroid camera systems, these aircraft fly an average of 120–150 missions a month over various parts of the world. They are aimed against national priority targets—in other words, the hottest items in Washington at the moment. The furor in the press in early 1971 about the Russians building a submarine base in Cuba was the type of flap a U-2 or SR-71 would be assigned to cover. This is not to say that these aircraft are reserved solely for crisis situations. They are employed on regularly scheduled missions, such as the routine surveillance of Cuba, and on overflights of Communist China.

More routine targets are covered regularly by the military services, who fly hundreds of photo recon missions a month. Each military unit abroad has its own peculiar photo-intelligence requirements. In Western Europe the Army must be prepared to maneuver against any potential ground threat by the East European or Soviet armies, and their photo-intelligence needs run the gamut from the conditions of the roads and rail networks and the location of possible enemy defensive missile units and airfields to the possible enemy's logistic and communication system. Naval fleets in the Mediterranean and Pacific have a wider range of targets to cover, including not only the ones described above but also detailed information on coasts, landing beaches, port facilities, and tidal data. To err on the safe side is the prevailing philosophy among intelligence staffs. If the aircraft and ships available for photo collection work, they are kept busy collecting. The photo-intelligence game has become just that, a game. It is common practice for an American recon unit to scramble into the air to take pictures of a Soviet recon unit taking pictures of the American unit. A classic photo that passed through the intelligence community right after the USSR started overflying United States carrier fleets in the Atlantic shows a Soviet reconnaissance bomber flying over a Sixth Fleet carrier task force. The close-up shot of the bomber allows you to see the Soviet intelligence officer in the plastic photo bubble on the side of the bomber. He is in the process of giving the American intelligence officer in the jet fighter the classic middle-finger salute.

These programs constitute the lion's share of technical intelligence collection. Others, of limited interest, are carried on. The Atomic Energy Commission equips many military aircraft with radioactivity filters for detecting the atmospheric presence of nuclear particles adrift on the air currents flowing across Communist countries. One friend of mine assigned to Hong Kong routinely collected liver samples from cattle raised on mainland China from an elderly woman butcher in a Hong Kong slaughterhouse. The purpose was to detect nuclear fallout over mainland China. I accompanied him one evening to a meeting, where he was handed a quivering bloody hunk of meat that he and I wrestled into a Baggie. We returned to the

American consulate, stapled it to a report form, packed it in dry ice, and shipped it off to Washington for analysis.

Technical expertise is relied upon for a variety of lesser collection programs geared normally to operations. CIA's Technical Services Division (TSD) staff has an unusual collection of men skilled in lie-detector tests, phone-tapping, bugging, and an assortment of other trade-craft skills such as lockpicking, safe-cracking, and what is known as "flaps and seals" for men skilled in opening mail. One of their feats, often spoken of in training sessions at CIA, was the stealing of the Soviet Sputnik. On a world tour after its successful launch, the Sputnik display was stolen one night for three hours by a CIA team which completely dismantled it, took samples of its structure, photographed it, reassembled it, and returned it to its original place undetected.

Another is the story of the CIA team that stole a sample of King Farouk's piss. The object of the exercise was to determine his exact state of health. To achieve it, they rigged up the men's room of one of the gambling casinos in Monte Carlo with a device that captured the urine flowing through the urinal to the sewer. All of this was done without the knowledge of the owners of the establishment. When Farouk was at the gaming tables, one CIA officer stationed himself on a toilet in the men's room with a peeping view of the two urinals. He gave a coughing signal when Farouk entered and another coded cough telling the men on the other side of the wall which urinal he was peeing into.

The field of human intelligence collection is, of course, the classic arena of the spy. Little has changed in this area of activity since the dawn of time, when intelligence collection became a requirement of tribes or nations. The goal is to find out what's going on in the minds of one's potential enemy. In the United States intelligence establishment there are five elements involved in working with human sources of information. Most active is the CIA's Deputy Director of Plans (DDP). The three military services have their own collection elements, and the Defense Department also runs an elaborate and separate military attaché system. The armed services and the CIA jointly operate Defection Reception Centers and other programs at various locations around the world, and the State Department contributes indirectly to the intelligence process through its routine reporting of contacts with foreign government officials.

The DDP employs all those people who "don't work at CIA." Its staff is all covert with various forms of cover. Most common among CIA's clandestine service is what is known as official cover. I was the Army librarian when I first joined CIA. Other members of my training class had covers ranging from an agronomist with the Department of Agriculture to an educational specialist at HEW. Even this light form of cover requires some fancy double-dealing. I had an office number and telephone number at the Pentagon to back up my cover story. If anyone called me on the number, CIA had a special switchboard set up to monitor the incoming calls. The girls would see what number lit up on their board and answer the phone accordingly with either "Department of the Army Library," "Agriculture Department," or whatever was appropriate. They would then dial my regular CIA office and connect me with the outside caller only after informing me that it was a cover call

was receiving. I suffered a few embarrassing moments when former service acquaintances or school friends would call me on their way through town for lunch. One guy, an Air Force captain, called me for lunch from the Pentagon. I had to pretend I was in the Pentagon too, rush out to the CIA parking lot, ride twenty minutes to the Pentagon, find a place to park, and then meet my former colleague, excusing my tardiness by complaining about a heavy workload at the library.

Wives must play the cover game, maintaining in the most trivial circumstances that their husbands work somewhere other than at CIA. When I first went to work at CIA, the guy who lived in the apartment above me was a captain in the

Army, and my wife, over coffee, told his wife that I worked at
the Pentagon. So the natural thing happened. The guy came
down to our apartment that night and asked me if I wanted to
form a car pool, since he too worked at the Pentagon. Ridiculous! How do I tell the guy I don't really work there? Well, I
played the game and made a flaming ass of myself. I replied
with something like, "I'd love to, but I can't predict when I'll
get out each evening. Some nights I have to stay in the office
for an hour or so to clear up the work." The guy gave me a look
of utter disbelief. He couldn't imagine the Army library doing
such a brisk trade that its librarians had to stay late to "clear
up the work." It all could have ended there, but this guy was
desperate. He was sick of the Washington traffic and his wife
wanted to use their car during the week so they could avoid the
crush of traffic in the Virginia shopping centers on Saturday.
My wife had the same complaint. So the guy then volunteers
to stay late and wait for me. He even sweetened the kitty by
telling me that we could duck over to the Fort Myer Officers'
Club and grab a cold one each night, allowing the traffic to ease
before we started home. Now that really appealed to me. Fort
Myer is the last bastion of the five-cent large draft beer, and I
was making only fifty-five hundred bucks a year at the time. So
what does superspy say? I tell the guy that I really don't care
for car pools, that I'd rather drive myself, and that I just
wouldn't feel right letting him stand around for a half-hour or
forty-five minutes waiting for me. The guy leaves my apartment
muttering something about "damned civilians." To make matters worse, we both came out of our apartments every morning
for the next year at exactly the same time and returned at night
within two minutes of each other. I used to keep track of him
in my rearview mirror each morning, hoping to elude him in
traffic before I made the turnoff to CIA instead of staying in the
mainstream of traffic heading toward the Pentagon.

This form of cover holds up well in Washington, but has to
be supplemented when clandestine service officers go overseas.
They usually retain "official" cover by being placed in the State

Department, the Agency for International Development, or another appropriate federal agency. When I went to Vietnam I was an economics officer in the embassy. This creates a good deal of friction among State and AID employees who don't appreciate the CIA interlopers and whose wives generally question how the "spooks" always manage to get the best housing for their families. In CIA stations such as Saigon, where the staff numbers in the hundreds, cover all but falls by the wayside and usually is the source of much local humor. CIA staffers in Saigon were given their own jeeps. Problems arose when the overzealous CIA motor pool officer painted them all metallic blue. Driving down Tu Do Street one day in Saigon in one of the blue jeeps, another fellow and I stopped at a red light. A partially drunk American GI standing on the corner looked at us, then at our jeep, and snarled, "I wish I worked for CIA instead of the lousy Army." We drove off congratulating our motor pool officer.

In Taipei, Taiwan, where CIA's official cover was the United States Navy Auxiliary Communications Center, or NACC, my wife and I caught a cab and told the driver to take us to the NACC office. The driver slammed his Toyota into low gear, laid rubber, and, as he swerved into the mainstream of traffic, turned to me, gave me a thumbs-up gesture, and bellowed, "CIA, number fuckin' one."

Commercial cover is also used in selected cases. Men with a particular skill or background are found regular employment with American firms abroad. This is always done with the agreement of the firm's top management. A friend of mine, a geologist, went to work for an oil company in the Far East, another with a major American bank in one of its Pacific offices. They worked a regular eight-hour day for their employers and did their CIA chores at night and on weekends. CIA had an arrangement with the firms whereby salary differences, if any, were made up either by CIA or the firm, depending on the man's position. Men with independent skills, such as doctors and lawyers, are also set up in private practice abroad.

Lastly, CIA uses what they call "deep cover." Men usually accept such tours for seven- to nine-year periods, and all traces of American governmental or commercial connections are kept to an absolute minimum. They blend into the local landscape and perform only discreet tasks for the Agency. They receive no pay while serving abroad—it's banked for them in the United States or Switzerland. They are prohibited from mixing with whatever American community exists in their area of operation. Two classic cases spoken of frequently in CIA training sessions involved guys who found they could do better for themselves by severing their CIA connection. One man managed to start an automobile-battery manufacturing plant in Western Europe. Most of the funding came from CIA's coffers to help the operation get rolling. In a few years, however, he found that the business was quite profitable, so he paid CIA back their original investment and quit to run his CIA-sponsored business. Another guy got CIA to set him up in a plywood manufacturing business on a Pacific Island, and he, too, cut the cord once on his feet financially. The Agency was very angry but powerless to do anything about it because of the potential embarrassment to the United States government. Deep cover knows few bounds. CIA has a surprising number of Mormon Church members in its employ, and the fact that many of these men had spent two years in a Mormon mission in Latin America or the Far East is not overlooked by CIA. A friend found himself back in the Mormon mission in Hong Kong after his training.

The size of CIA stations abroad varies from two-man stations in places like Chad to stations of several hundred men, as in Saigon. On the average, however, most CIA stations number about twenty-five or thirty people. They are all organized along the same lines, with the station chief reporting directly to the United States ambassador as his special adviser. Beneath him the station is organized into an operations branch, a reports branch, and a support branch. The operations staff usually engages in three activities—counterintelligence, political action, and foreign intelligence. The counterintelligence team is primarily concerned with protecting whatever collection programs CIA has underway in the particular country. They focus on keeping tabs on the host government's intelligence arm to see that they don't find out what targets CIA is working on. Political action runs the gamut of dirty tricks that have made CIA famous. I witnessed dozens of stunts by the political action arm of CIA in Saigon. During the Buddhist riots of the summer of 1964, political action officers dispatched several dozen South Vietnamese into the crowds of Buddhists with itching-powder bombs. Egg-sized, these capsules were dropped onto the ground and stepped upon by the agent. The fact that most of the Buddhists wore no underwear was taken into consideration before the devices were used. The powder floated upward and effectively defused the revolutionary spirit. The political action arm also noted that heavy rain had a tendency to break up student and Buddhist demonstrations, so they arranged to have planes on standby with silver iodide bomblets on board. Frequently the atmosphere over Saigon was liberally salted with these crystals during the 1964 troubles.

During that period a political action officer assigned to the Bien Hoa Air Base to keep tabs on General Ky's "coup bombers" was quite active. Ky's unit of A-1 Skyraiders was stationed near Saigon to thwart any move by Army or Marine Corps commanders who might think of moving on Saigon to topple the government. When Premier Hoang outlived his usefulness and a coup was imminent, the CIA political action officer at Ky's headquarters managed to slip a potent laxative into the pilot's meal at the air base, incapacitating the entire squadron and allowing the military to topple the civilian premier. The man who came up with this idea had also used it to great advantage in 1960 in Laos, when he had averted a coup by rightist Lao forces by slipping the same concoction into the drinking water of an entire battalion guarding the capital of Vientiane.

Foreign intelligence means simply the collection of positive information of use to the United States government. The greatest portion of a CIA station's effort is directed against such collection. Men in these jobs work closely with all elements of the host government and society, collecting the kinds of information needed to determine what the government is planning. In Saigon, for example, we wined and dined every province chief and batallion commander in the South Vietnamese governmental structure, trying to keep abreast of what particular group might be plotting a coup. In Western nations these kinds of operations are subtle and sophisticated, unlike the CIA operation in Vietnam. Agents are cultivated over a period of years and carefully developed as reliable sources of information. The inducements for such work are rarely the kind of patriotic motives some Americans would suspect. Seldom, if ever, will you find a CIA agent who is a dedicated anti-Communist or a man who believes that the American form of democracy is the only form of government worth having. Normally, CIA tries to find the human weaknesses in a man in a position to supply it with information. In today's modern world this usually involves money or a tendency to chase women. Many agents accept CIA employment and risk treason for reasons as fundamental as keeping up a mortgage payment. CIA has many ways of enticing its agents, from arranging to have the man's children attend college in the United States with all expenses paid to arranging to have the man promoted within his own government by devising situations in which he can be made to look good for his superiors.

The reports section goes through all of the information that the CIA case officers develop in the course of a day's work. Every contact, every phone call, and every conversation must be recorded by the foreign intelligence case officers. These reports filter through a three- to five-man reports section, and the meat of the day's developments is selected for dispatch to Washington by air mail pouch carried by the diplomatic couriers. While the emphasis in all of CIA's training is placed on the careful development of a good agent, the real world operates differently. Case officers are under tremendous pressure to get out the reports. The result is that many of them spend little time developing and cultivating new agents, but, instead, focus on getting a high number of cables sent back to Washington. When promotion time comes—despite all efforts to change the system—the men in the field are judged by the number of cables sent to Washington. Quality doesn't count, just quantity. We all learned this shortly after arriving in Saigon. If a contact furnished us with some decent-sounding information, we'd feed it slowly to the reports machinery, peeling off a tidbit a day for several days, rather than filing it all as one report.

The support branch carries on the normal personnel and finance chores necessary to any large organization. Their job, however, is not all that mundane, for operational requirements sometimes require them to come up overnight with a surgeon to tend an ailing head of state, a completely armored limousine for an important government figure, a quick plane trip out of country for an agent about to be burned, or a safe haven for an agent to hide in.

Despite the seemingly adventurous tinge to the job of collecting intelligence abroad for CIA, it should be stressed that the work routine abroad is considerably duller than one would suspect. The typical case officer with CIA spends an entire career without ever actually recruiting a new agent. Rather, he is assigned those already on the payroll when he arrives at a new station. He spends most of his time filling out innocuous contact reports and keeping his operational files up to date with the trivia of intelligence that the bureaucracy requires, such as making weekly assessments of his agent, his problems, his job, and his accessibility to target information, and providing justification for continuation of his agent on the payroll. The typical case officer, too, is somewhat frustrated in terms of promotion and assignment to a level of responsibility commensurate with his age and experience.

The military has been involved in the field of human intelligence since the days of World War II. Its reports have the unique reputation among intelligence professionals as "garbage." Today, somewhere on the order of thirty-five hundred United States military intelligence specialists operate abroad, collecting what they deem to be needed intelligence. The Air Force and the Army have two major collection units, one each in Europe and the Far East. Broken into small detachments, they are scattered throughout the areas where United States military units are assigned. The Navy maintains similar units operating out of each of the major fleet headquarters. A goodly portion of their efforts is devoted to the counterintelligence activities necessary to protect the military security of United States bases abroad. It is when they get into the area of collecting positive foreign intelligence that their amateurish methods are most noticeable.

To start with, they are easily identified in a crowd, as most have a tendency to adhere to American military-length hair, wear their GI shoes and T-shirts, and look generally uncomfortable in PX-purchased civilian garb. The military custom of short tours overseas never allows for the development of operatives solidly based in their areas. Their language ability is usually limited, and the rotation policies contribute to the continuation of marginal and even useless sources of information. One Army agent in Tokyo regularly supplied "inside" information on the Chinese Communists by simply reading the daily Peking press and selecting items he thought were salable to his Army case officer. In my years of scanning intelligence reports I noted a pattern to American military reports. Any noteworthy event such as the death of Ho Chi Minh or a change in the Chinese Communist power structure would be followed within a week or ten days by a rash of reports from United States military agents, purporting to have the real meaning of the latest development. Most were merely rehashes of the general editorial interpretations of the world press on the subject. The agents, however, claimed they got the information from a party member who got it as the official gospel at a recent special meeting of his party cell.

A lingering anachronism in the field of human intelligence collection is the military attaché system. The United States has more than eleven hundred military personnel assigned to eighty-five embassies around the world. The custom of exchanging military attachés, which dates from the eighteenth century, has long outgrown its usefulness in the field of military intelligence. In Communist countries, particularly the Soviet Union, the attachés are confined to living a ritual in which every one of their days is a staged event. They rarely, if ever, make contact with useful sources of information, and their reports are filled with the cocktail party gossip of a group of Soviet military officers who serve as their counterparts and whose every action and word is carefully designed ahead of time. Their big day each year in Moscow is the filming of the May Day parade of Soviet weaponry, hardly an event worth the expense of maintaining a staff of high-ranking military officers, considering that the Western press covers the event also.

In countries such as Laos, Cambodia, and the African and Latin American countries, the attachés have more flexibility in moving around the country and observing its military forces. The information collected, however, could be gleaned at considerably less expense by a well-paid clerk at the embassy who was trained to understand military tables of organization. The concept is that the attaché can "get next to" the military hierarchy of the host country and thus learn all its deepest secrets, its war plans, and its military capabilities and intentions. As pointed out above, this does not work in the Communist countries, where the United States is threatened most directly. In underdeveloped countries the attaché's training does not generally provide him with the ability to understand the local military situation. He is inclined to judge military capabilities and intentions by the classic methods of adding up a nation's infantry, tanks, and airplanes and from there deducing its intentions. The attachés in Laos and Cambodia, in particular, have made little if any solid contribution to the base of knowledge about the military situation in those countries. If anything, my experience in reading United States attaché reports from Laos points to the fact that they confuse more than they enlighten by applying the Army War College standards to the ragtag Pathet Lao and concluding that the Royal Army, equipped with jeeps, radios, and modern weapons, can easily defeat the less fortunate Pathet Lao. They never seemed to understand the tripartite nature of the Laotian government and were thus unable to tell the good guys from the bad. Their short tours of one year never afforded them the opportunity to get to know the Laotian military hierarchy, so they took everything they were told by Laotian officers at face value and dutifully reported it to Washington.

My strangest experience with military attachés happened in Paris in the spring of 1968 during the student strike. The American attaché, an Air Force general, felt compelled to be on the scene. I entered his office in the United States embassy one morning at the height of the student demonstrations and found the portly general standing on the window ledge five stories above the ground. He was peering across the Seine through binoculars and calling out staccato items for the Army captain standing in the office with a pad and pencil. "There go three more garbage trucks down the Left Bank heading toward the university," he snapped. The captain wrote it down. "Here comes a six-by-six truck with four policemen in the rear," he snapped again. This went on for well over an hour. When the commotion died down on the Left Bank, the general had the captain type it all up for cabling to the Pentagon as his contribution to an assessment of the 1968 student strike in Paris.

A lucrative source of first-hand human intelligence has developed since the mid-fifties with the flow of political emigrants from east to west. Starting with the Hungarian Revolution, CIA established Defector Reception Centers in Europe to process refugees in a systematic manner. Today, three major Defection Reception Centers operate in Bonn, Miami, and Saigon. There, escapees and emigrants from the Communist world are processed thoroughly and debriefed in detail on their former lives. It is difficult to single out any one source of information that has contributed mightily to the intelligence base from this process, but the cumulative effect of these thorough debriefings has been to add immeasurably to the feel and understanding of Washington analysts for the country under study. From reading thousands of debriefings of North Vietnamese or Vietcong defectors I gained a solid understanding of the attitudes, personal difficulties, life style, and overall environment of the Communist military apparatus in South Vietnam.

The staffs of these centers are fairly experienced interrogators in most cases, familiar with the political, economic, and social system from which the emigrants are traveling. The greatest volume of traffic through these facilities consists of "low-level" defectors—individuals who simply elected to leave their homeland. Occasionally there is a "high-level" defector—one who has either made arrangements beforehand with a CIA case officer in his home country, has flown out a military aircraft, or has somehow managed to escape. These men are also processed through the reception centers and given a more thorough and detailed debriefing, sometimes requiring Washington to send a team of experts to conduct the debriefing firsthand. Usually these men are granted diplomatic asylum and established financially in the country of their choice. The director of the CIA is authorized to grant such immunity and financial assistance if the intelligence to be gained is considered of sufficient value to the United States government.

The Saigon Defector Reception Center was located at the South Vietnamese Navy Headquarters in the center of town.

We visited it once and were proudly shown around the entire facility by one of the CIA psychologists manning it. It was hideous. Here headshrinkers were experimenting with their notions about how to get a man to talk. Our guide showed us one room through a slit in the door. It measured about five feet by five feet with a normal ceiling height. A Vietnamese kid around nineteen or twenty sat on a wooden stool in the center of the room. The walls were white. With a rheostat on the outside of the room the shrink gleefully showed us how he had been changing the lighting in the room, gradually going through a spectrum of colors that started with black, became purple, then blue, and finally went into greens, yellows, and reds. The shrink claimed he could change the guy's moods from happy to sad merely by regulating the lights. Another room of similar construction had controlled heat and cold, and prisoners were forced to sit through the rude temperature fluctuations to satisfy the whims of the shrink. We discovered that all of this was simply an experiment that he had been authorized to conduct. It had no practical application to the war. The only thing the shrink was interested in was the accumulation of sufficient data so that he could write a detailed report of his findings and, perhaps, substantiate a long-held theory of his. The victims? They were just handy.

CIA has an element set up to monitor the outside immigration quotas because of the value of information they provide of defectors allowed to emigrate to the United States. Known as the Contact Division, this unit engages in a wide variety of human collection programs, which are simply a housekeeping operation for the defectors.

More important, Contact Division runs a program of collection which relies entirely on volunteers. They have thirty-five field offices throughout the United States, and the staffs of these offices maintain accounts files much the same as an advertising agency. They contact the presidents of major corporations who travel widely or individual scholars and scientists who travel abroad in line with their work to attend seminars or other international gatherings. If the men are willing to volunteer their services, CIA will provide them with a detailed list of intelligence requirements from the Washington elements of the community interested in their field of study. These sources are not paid for their services and are not expected to put their lives or their professional reputations in jeopardy. Many of the "students" nabbed by Soviet police are people trying to collect tidbits for CIA.

The intelligence community relies heavily on the official reporting of the United States State Department and other federal agencies conducting business abroad. Their daily reports, counted in the tens of thousands, are routed to the intelligence community and are screened by the analysts along with all other sources. These reports provide an insight into the day-to-day workings of the government under study. More importantly, they provide some knowledge of the thinking of the individuals within that government.

Today, two kinds of material are collected in the primary source category—commercial and radio broadcasts and documents such as those picked up from underground headquarters of the Vietcong by American soldiers.

CIA maintains fourteen listening posts around the world to monitor the radio broadcasts and press of target countries. They publish a daily compendium of the transcripts of these broadcasts under an arrangement with the Commerce Department. The collection program is known as the Foreign Broadcast Information Service (FBIS). The fourteen overseas listening posts in places such as Cyprus, Liberia, and Panama operate around the clock. They are staffed by some three hundred CIA editors who oversee the work of local native translators. All fourteen of the listening stations are linked by teletype to CIA headquarters; as the editors scan the daily programming, they select worthwhile items for immediate teletype dispatch to Washington.

In Washington, where the daily report is put out, the FBIS is broken down into geographic areas, with editors selecting the most important items of the day's take for publication. They also maintain an office known as the Radio Propaganda Analysis Branch, wherein men who have been following a particular country for some time scan all of the daily take and put out analyses of the radio broadcasts. This includes the amount of time that Moscow, for example, might devote to the SALT talks and the Middle East situation. Since the Communist countries have a controlled radio and press, the relative importance of a subject to the Communist government can be seen by the weight of radio and press play the subject is given. More detailed studies of lengthy speeches by Communist officials are rendered, saving the users of the information the agony of reading through a three-hour Castro speech, for example.

FBIS has become a very important source of intelligence in the past twenty years. It was over FBIS that United States intelligence first learned of Khruschev's ouster, of the Czech invasion, of most Latin American coups, of Ho Chi Minh's death, and of Nasser's death. All of the FBIS listening posts are able to send CRITIC messages to the White House and have done so on many occasions.

The Vietnam War has resulted in an overwhelming number of Communist documents coming into the hands of United States intelligence. The volume was so great that it was measured in tons in 1966–67. This necessitated the establishment of a document exploitation system so that tactical and long-range intelligence could be extracted from the mass of paper in a systematic and reliable way. Despite the efforts of more than fifteen hundred persons assigned to this awesome task by the United States Army, the problem was never mastered. The variety of documents covers the entire range of paper that you would expect any army to maintain in the field—from medical records to personnel and finance rosters, to the awarding of medals to individuals, and to the detailed studies of battles won and lost. Orders from higher up the chain of command and treatises on how the war was going were also included. At best, the Army was able to provide a one-paragraph summary of any particular document unless someone up the line determined that it should be translated in its entirety. The volume was simply too great for reasonable exploitation of the material, and scholars of Vietnam will have a rich area for research when and if the documentation is released.

It can be readily seen that intelligence collection knows almost no bounds. Every angle is covered. There are major problems throughout, primarily problems of coordination. It is difficult to establish adequate control once collection gets started because of the complex layers of bureaucracy. That is why the United States Army is having difficulty assuring Congress that the files of information collected on American citizens in 1968 have been destroyed. Despite several direct orders from the Assistant Secretary of Defense, the files are still active in several branches of the Army intelligence structure.

III

The Paper Mill

If the intelligence picture seems to be a little confusing at the collection phase, the second phase—processing—holds little hope for the emergence of a clearer situation. Rather, it is at this stage that the crisis of intelligence exists. The United States is capable of collecting infinite amounts of data; its ability to process and manage the data with reasonable efficiency, however, is severely limited. Two trends of bureaucratic thinking have an impact on the processing stage of intelligence. The first, called the "Pearl Harbor syndrome," is concerned primarily with getting all tidbits of intelligence to Washington in the shortest possible time so that the top level of government can be aware of possible surprise developments and not get caught short in a fast-breaking situation, as happened at Pearl Harbor when a dozen or more pieces of intelligence were floating around in different channels. Because of this attitude, an elaborate warning and indications network has been established on a worldwide basis. Today, it operates as the funnel through which the major portion of intelligence flows. The second trend is the "Church of What's Happening Now syndrome," which pervades the entire intelligence apparatus. Everyone aware of the existence of the intelligence process wants to be cut in on what's happening. In the military, commanders from the battalion level on up want a daily intelligence briefing. All United States ambassadors, AID administrators, Treasury officials, and others working abroad believe that they too can benefit from the intelligence process. This desire to be current has necessitated the lateral dissemination of raw intelligence collected in the field and a staff of intelligence specialists to process it and make some sense out of it for the colonel, the general, or the ambassador. These daily intelligence briefings usually prompt more questions than they answer. So the small overworked staff in the field must interrupt the work routine of the next higher headquarters with questions from the general or the ambassador before the headquarters staff has had a reasonable chance to process the same information. As a result, the elaborate information-processing system becomes a frenzy of jangled nerves, with requests for interpretations of raw data sometimes arriving before the raw data.

On July 24, 1965, the intelligence community went into a tailspin because the North Vietnamese fired their first SA-2 missile at American aircraft and downed one. The word that an American plane had been downed by a missile ricocheted up the chain of command to Washington in a matter of minutes. The Secretary of Defense was on the phone to DIA wanting to know all the details before we had any of the electronic evidence to analyze. We just stood there with our mouths open.

The intelligence professional unfortunate enough to be caught in this crossfire must be able to roll with the punches. We used to have a slogan with which we'd greet one of those "urgent" requests—"If you want it real bad, you gonna get it real bad." The entire atmosphere becomes charged with unnecessary excitement and the men in the processing cycle react like a Chinese fire brigade, charging off to put out nine brushfires at once and expending their creative energy on all but their primary job of analysis. I credit my years in this arena with one duodenal ulcer.

To understand the processing of intelligence, visualize two separate information-handling systems—the first being the warning and indications network established to avoid another Pearl Harbor and the second being the routine flow of information between the collector in the field and the Washington agency charged with that particular collection program.

Since Pearl Harbor situations are likely to unfold only between the United States and the Soviet Union, one might think the warning system was simply an hourly check with Ballistic Missile Early Warning Radar networks, the North American Air Defense Command, and United States military units in western Europe. It doesn't work that way anymore. The system was set up worldwide and regardless of the fact that it is highly improbable that the Communist Vietnamese could launch a surprise attack on the United States homeland, vast amounts of detailed information concerning Vietnam are fed into the warning system simply because it exists. The same holds true throughout the rest of the Far East and other geographic areas of the world. The original concept of the system has become distorted, and it now serves as the main viaduct through which fast-breaking intelligence developments find their way to Washington. Originally, there were seven warning centers at the major area commands, such as Commander-in-Chief, Pacific, in Hawaii; and Commander-in-Chief, Atlantic, in Norfolk, Virginia. At this level, it was reasoned, analysts could screen all intelligence and operational data from their respective areas and earmark any unusual items for the National Indications Center in Washington. Burgeoning United States military command hierarchies throughout the world brought with them an expansion of the warning network. In the Far East, for example, there exist today no less than nine major warning centers and a dozen minor ones, where one sufficed fifteen years ago. In Honolulu alone, there are four—one at the Commander-in-Chief Pacific Headquarters, one at the Pacific Army Command Headquarters, one at the Pacific Fleet Command Headquarters, and one at the Pacific Air Force Command Headquarters. Beneath them, American military commanders in Vietnam, Thailand, Korea, Taiwan, and Japan each have their own warning centers. In Vietnam the services further subdivided the responsibility, and the Army, Navy, Air Force, and Marine Corps each set up their own centers. Similar centers are in operation in Taiwan, Korea, and Japan.

The staffs of the warning centers are primarily oriented toward moving the paper along and are not deeply versed in the substance of what they deal in. The result has been the necessity to maintain a staff of intelligence specialists to handle substantive issues that arise. The worldwide warning centers are furnished with elaborate walnut consoles, leather chairs, dim lighting, and world situation maps showing the disposition of the world's Communist armed forces on all four walls. Secure telephone and teletype lines keep them in touch with all other warning centers. The men there scan all intelligence and operational reports produced in their area of responsibility. The National Indications Center in Washington provides them with an elaborate check list of items to look for—items which might serve as preliminary indicators that a nation intends to take hostile action against the United States.

The routine flow of information between the collectors in the field and the Washington agencies is not a simple system. Multiple layers of command exist in certain collection programs to narrow the flow of raw data to Washington.

In the photographic field, the satellite programs are the only ones that go direct to Washington for processing. This is necessitated by the unique camera systems on board the satellites. The film can be processed only at the Washington Navy Yard in the National Photographic Interpretation Center (NPIC), a sub-element of CIA. When a film capsule is received and developed, the entire reel is scanned immediately for "quick and dirty" developments—such as those anticipated by analysts working on the Soviet missile test ranges, for example. The analysts sent a list of things to look for to NPIC when the satellite was being programmed. Within twenty-four hours of arrival, NPIC normally has a preliminary assessment out to the interested analysts in the Washington intelligence community. This includes military intelligence analysts at CIA and the Pentagon and those at the National Security Agency. The men who scan the film are photo interpreters with a generalist's approach. They do very little detailed analysis, but merely look for things anticipated.

Many copies of the photographs are made by NPIC, and these are sent out to the specialists in the intelligence establishment for comparative analysis of new developments. Again using the Soviet missile test activity as an example, men at DIA and CIA who follow the range activity closely are able to compare the new photographs with previous shots and determine what changes may have taken place at the range.

NPIC also produces detailed charts showing where each satellite orbited the earth and distributes these to interested analysts, who then send in requests for detailed examination of a particular set of pictures. An industrial specialist may be anxious to find out the status of a particular Soviet steel mill or truck manufacturing plant. Agricultural specialists might be following the Soviet wheat crop and desire photographs of the present crop to see if they can spot blight or other indicators which will help them in estimating the wheat output.

All other photographic intelligence is processed through the many layers of military command that exist between the field and Washington. All collecting units are obliged to give a "quick and dirty" assessment of every roll of film, but this is always gone over in more detail by the unit's next higher authority. In Vietnam, for example, the Air Force files scores of tactical photographic missions daily. As soon as the planes return to their base the film is developed and scanned for new

developments. It is then shipped to Seventh Air Force Headquarters in Saigon, where it is gone over in more detail, checking out the initial assessments and looking for additional developments of interest to the entire Air Force Command structure
within Vietnam. From Saigon the film is flown to Honolulu
where photo interpreters at the Pacific Air Force Headquarters
go over it again, checking the work of both levels below them
and performing whatever detailed analysis the intelligence staff
at Honolulu needs. The staff in Hawaii might be trying to
conduct a detailed study of the infiltration trails through the
jungles of Laos. They have a longer-range interest in the subject
than the fighting units in Vietnam, so they take a more leisurely
approach to the study, drawing on a year or two's photography
to put together a detailed analysis of the trail network. The film
is then shipped to the Defense Intelligence Agency in Washington, which checks the work of the other units and performs its
own detailed analysis to support its own research projects. This
constant check-and-double-check process normally generates
considerable debate within the intelligence community. Often
the initial assessments—which are cabled to the whole intelligence community—are proven wrong, and a process of retrac-
tion has to take place because units up the chain of command
to Washington have reported the initial developments to their
superiors and now have to tell them that the preliminary readout was in error. The constant bickering within the community
about the accuracy of a photo readout, known affectionately as
"pissing contests," has spawned the creation of photo-intelligence shops within each and every component of the intelligence structure, since no one element wants to rely entirely on
the judgment of another unit's analysts. This means tremendous duplication.

The volume of communication intelligence (COMINT) intercepted daily around the world is beyond the imagination of
most laymen. As a conservative estimate, I would judge that
upwards of a hundred tons of paper a day record the radio and

Morse codes of other nations' communications intercepted by the National Security Agency. Because of the enormous daily take, the NSA maintains a multilayered structure reaching out from Washington around the globe. Every syllable intercepted is recorded and translated by language specialists. It is then scanned at the site of intercept by analysts working on the detailed structure of that particular target. At one military airfield, for example, a day's activity could involve an hour of morning signal checking between the tower, the firing range controller, the taxi strip monitor, the bombing range controller, the weather station, the aerial intercept controller, the ground safety crews, and the radar operators. Morning flight activity could see a squadron of twenty-four MIGs conducting aerial intercept practice, another working on the ground attack firing range, and still another working on the bombing range. Afternoon activities could see the same units alternating among the various activities described above. The constant air-to-ground and air-to-air conversations in one day's activity at one airfield are likely to require upwards of 150 man-hours of translation time.

Each day's take is gone over for any subtle changes in communications patterns by the men at the site. They then forward the take to the next higher headquarters, which is responsible for monitoring and analyzing all of the take from a larger geographic area. In the Far East, I worked at an intercept site in the Yellow Sea monitoring Communist Chinese activity at several airfields in Manchuria. We sent our take to an NSA unit in Japan, which monitored the take of all air, ground, and naval units in northeast China. They in turn sent their product to another NSA unit on Okinawa, which processed all of the daily take from Communist China. At each level reports were produced on, say, the activity at each airfield in a particular day. When the unit in Okinawa got the daily take, it would produce a daily summary of all military activity in Communist China and forward it to NSA Headquarters in Honolulu, which would issue a report summarizing all Communist military activity in North Korea, Communist China, and North Vietnam gleaned from all the units reporting to them.

As a double check, all the original tapes and translations are forwarded to NSA Headquarters for storage and retranslation of any significant sections. The translations are gone over in detail by NSA analysts working the same problem against the national requirements of daily reports to the rest of the intelligence establishment in Washington, which must keep abreast of day-to-day developments.

The ELINT daily take is no less impressive than is the CO-MINT take. It is all on tape and is processed through the same chain of command as is the voice and Morse traffic. From the daily intercept, it is possible to render a detailed analysis of what radars and missile sites were active. Changes in equipment can be detected also. Any new developments are checked and double-checked as the tapes proceed up the chain of command. At NSA in Washington, comparative analysis and computer studies of the intercepted signals are made to assist electronic countermeasure planners in developing equipment concepts and design features.

A large portion of NSA intercept sites' daily take consists of enciphered radio messages that cannot be broken. It is all shipped back to NSA Headquarters, where the two thousand employees of the Research and Development Office ransack the domains of statistics and higher algebra for ever more sensitive and more powerful tests to solve these complex ciphers.

The processing of human intelligence reports is far less empirical than that of technical data. Disseminated simultaneously throughout the field collection area and to all interested agencies in Washington, these cables require an intrinsic feel for the politics and personalities of the country involved. They are not processed in any set pattern. An analyst at CIA might read a cable from the CIA station in Ankara about developments within the Turkish Foreign Ministry, disbelieve it, and toss it aside. An analyst at the State Department, however, might be inclined to believe the cable and file it as documentation of a particular point he is trying to make in a paper he is writing on United States–Turkish relations.

IV

Spreading the Gospel

回回回

It is difficult to divide clearly the processing and reporting stages of the intelligence cycle. The speed with which information is disseminated throughout the governmental structure frequently results in raw, unprocessed intelligence serving as a finished report which is snatched up by the policy level of government and used as the basis for key decisions. This was the case in 1964, when President Johnson retaliated against the alleged North Vietnamese PT boat attack on United States destroyers in the Gulf of Tonkin.

The formal structure of the Washington intelligence community militates against this happening too frequently. On paper, CIA is the only member of the ten-agency intelligence community responsible for reporting directly to the President and his cabinet each day. Informally, however, each of the agencies in intelligence sees that its daily reports find their way to top policy advisers in the National Security Council and the White House. And there are the raw reports filtering into the White House Situation Room hourly.

Much is made of the kinds of intelligence reports that are produced. Finished reports are those that have gone through the analytical process and represent a distillation of the best knowledge on a particular subject. Raw reports are unevaluated individual pieces of information picked up by a collector in the field.

Three kinds of finished reports are produced within the intelligence community—current assessments, basic or encyclopedic studies, and estimates of future developments. Here again, another major crisis exists because of the sheer number of finished intelligence reports circulating in official Washington.

There are no less than ten official summaries of the previous day's activities. The CIA's Office of Current Intelligence puts out three separate reports. The most important is known as the President's Intelligence Checklist (PICKLE). It usually runs about ten pages in length and merely skims overnight developments touching on perhaps five or six major items known to be on the President's mind. The PICKLE is delivered to the White House in time for the President's first morning reading. When he is out of town on a trip, it is cabled directly to him from CIA. This report is not coordinated with the other members of the intelligence community, but care is taken to ensure that the community view is provided.

CIA also produces a top secret daily intelligence bulletin, which is delivered to the White House and to all cabinet members each morning. Lower officials with a need to know in any of the executive agencies are also provided with copies. This report normally runs about fifteen to twenty pages and includes graphics and maps when appropriate. Its closest parallel in the news field is the News Summary and Index in *The New York Times.* Here again, only major items of interest are included in the bulletin, but the range of material is broader than what is personally delivered to the President. Known as the Central

Intelligence Bulletin (CIB), this report is fully coordinated within the Washington intelligence community at a committee meeting each afternoon. Agencies disagreeing with the interpretation of a particular item have an opportunity to show their dissent by footnoting the particular sections with which they disagree. The report is also cabled to all CIA stations and American embassies abroad to keep the men in the field apprised of official thinking in foreign developments. Its distribution, however, is limited to those with top secret clearances.

To ensure that intelligence officials and other federal civil servants with a need to know but without top secret clearances are kept abreast of developments, a secret report is issued each day by CIA. Known as the CIA Digest, this report usually covers the same topics as the top secret one, but with the top secret material "sanitized" from the final version. It, too, receives wide distribution throughout official Washington and to CIA stations and embassies abroad.

The military establishment is kept abreast of daily developments by the Defense Intelligence Agency, which issues three daily reports. The intelligence summary is a top secret version of the CIB, with the major difference being that DIA goes into considerably more detail in its reporting. The DIA report normally runs about thirty to forty pages and covers a far wider spectrum of events than CIA's top secret report. It is primarily to inform the Secretary of Defense and his immediate staff and the Joint Chiefs of Staff of military intelligence developments which affect United States policy. It is also cabled to all the United States military command headquarters and attachés around the world to be used as the official Washington briefing each day.

DIA also issues a secret version of its daily top secret report. Known as the Intelligence Bulletin, it is disseminated throughout Washington and by cable to the major United States military commands abroad and to all United States attachés. Its contents are similar to CIA's secret report—it contains sanitized versions of the top secret items.

A third DIA daily report is known as the OP-INT and consists of ten or more pages tying together operational and intelligence matters for the Secretary of Defense, his staff, and the Joint Chiefs of Staff. This report originated early in the Vietnam War and has since grown to include operational and intelligence developments around the globe. The idea behind it is that an American military operation often prompts an action by another country not reported in its entire context by the intelligence community—which is not always aware of exactly what United States military operations are underway.

Aside from the many daily detailed reports that the National Security Agency issues to other members of the intelligence community, the agency also puts out a Daily Intelligence Summary, which reports highlights of overnight COMINT developments and presents its findings in layman's language, so as to be understandable by policy makers outside of the intelligence community. It also issues daily regional summaries, which report specific developments noted within a geographic region such as the Far East or the Soviet Union. These summaries play down the esoteric technical aspects of COMINT which characterize all of the agency's other reports and translate the technical findings into understandable events. The reports are designed for the information of men in the regional bureaus at the State Department or in the International Security Affairs Offices of the Defense Department. They contain such information as detailed reports of a Soviet field army on maneuvers or a naval and air defense exercise.

The National Indications Center in the Pentagon, which sits atop the vast Warning and Indications network, also issues a daily report to the intelligence community and to the policy-making levels of government. It sifts all the raw unevaluated reports that come in during a twenty-four-hour period and selects eighty to a hundred of the most significant. Excerpts or the whole text of the reports are then printed and distributed around Washington in a thirty-five- to fifty-page daily report called the NIC Watch Officer Notes.

The State Department issues a daily top secret intelligence report called the Diplomatic Summary. It covers intelligence developments with a direct influence on foreign policy and is distributed via cable to embassies abroad and by official mail to the Washington agencies.

The Foreign Broadcast Information Service, as already mentioned, issues a daily compendium of the entire text of significant radio broadcasts of the past twenty-four-hour period. This receives very wide distribution in government and the academic world.

These written reports constitute the backbone of the intelligence community's efforts to keep government informed of day-to-day developments. They do not include all of the attempts by intelligence to present its views to the policy-making level of government. More widely used in Washington are the "dog and pony shows"—the official briefings presented to various levels of government, a specialty of the Defense Department. Each morning the department dispatches a half-dozen polished briefing officers to give a fifteen- to thirty-minute oral presentation to select congressional subcommittees, working groups in the National Security Council, and top officials in the Defense Department. The State Department's Bureau of Intelligence and Research is perhaps the second busiest in this area. It presents its views to the Secretary of State each morning at his staff meeting and also are called upon frequently to brief members of Dr. Kissinger's staff at the National Security Council. Both the State and Defense briefings are accompanied by elaborate visual aids, color slides and, in some cases, motion pictures. The impact is like that of the NBC, CBS, or ABC evening news.

Official Washington is also treated to a daily barrage of cabled versions of the Daily Intelligence Summaries prepared by the various military commands around the globe.

The current intelligence reporting does not end with the daily reports. CIA issues a top secret version of *Time* magazine each week. It runs about thirty-five to forty pages and explores in greater depth the past week's developments in each geographic region of the world. Photos, maps, drawings, and other graphics adorn the weekly summary. A secret version of the report is issued for those without top secret clearances. This well-bound glossy report is circulated throughout Washington and pouched overseas. The text is cabled ahead to all CIA stations and American embassies, as well as to all United States military units abroad.

The National Security Agency puts out a weekly report covering global COMINT developments in a broader context than the daily reports. The regional reports are also issued weekly to all offices in Washington handling COMINT material. Cable versions of these reports are also disseminated to NSA's field stations and all embassies and United States military commands.

The Foreign Broadcast Information Service issues a weekly analysis of trends in the content and format of Communist radio broadcasting. These are circulated widely throughout the government and to selected college libraries.

The Air Force Chief of Staff for Intelligence in the Pentagon presents a weekly film to all interested officials. It normally runs about forty-five minutes and would put any of the evening news shows to shame for its style of presentation. It uses devices such as color film from gun cameras to portray a United States fighter tangling with a MIG over North Vietnam and other official classified Air Force films of operations underway around the globe.

Lastly, the current reporting scene in Washington is supplemented with official "think pieces." These are issued on an ad hoc basis by each of the agencies involved in intelligence. Normally one or two a week appear from each agency. Devoted to a thoughtful analysis of a current problem, they provide the reader with an in-depth look at the problem in its historical context. Topics are all-inclusive. An in-depth study of the militant and moderate factions on the North Vietnamese Army General Staff might be prompted by a current upsurge in the fighting in Vietnam. A new development in the field of Soviet foreign aid might prompt a review of the entire Soviet foreign aid program. A coup in Latin America would doubtless stimulate a report on Latin American governmental stability. These special reports are disseminated in a number of ways. The State Department might elect to send one only to the Secretary of State and the White House staff. The Defense Department might send one to all United States military units via cable. CIA might elect to disseminate on to the members of the National Security Council. There is no set format for distributing these reports, but they do represent a potent force in the policy-making arena, since they step back from the day-to-day nitty-gritty and try to place a current development into its broadest context.

The Foreign Broadcast Information Service provides very useful reports under the title of World Reaction Report. Any major United States move in the field of foreign affairs is assessed in terms of the press and radio reaction it stimulates around the globe. The initiation of the bombing of North Vietnam, the opening of the Paris peace talks, and the decision to go ahead with the ABM are topics FBIS would focus on for such a wrap-up report.

The need for basic intelligence was never more graphically demonstrated than during the invasion of Tarawa during World War II. Inaccurate data about the tides put the invasion force ashore on a coral reef some fifteen hundred yards from the beach and resulted in the slaughter of thousands of American troops. Motivated by a desire not to let such an event occur again, United States intelligence set out with the formation of CIA to establish a system to collect basic intelligence information. One of the offices assigned the responsibility was the Contact Division, which sought such seemingly trivial items as tourists' road maps. The program was further expanded to a point where the United States State Department has men assigned as geographic coordinators, whose duty it is to photograph such things as roads, bridges, beaches, telegraph poles, power stations, rural and urban homes, and police and army uniforms the world over. These are all passed back to CIA, whose Office of Central Reference keeps an elaborate photographic file on every country in the world.

An important product of basic intelligence research is the National Intelligence Survey (NIS), a sixty-chapter encyclopedia on every country in the world. Starting with basic terrain studies which highlight and examine military geography topics such as coasts and landing beaches, roads and rail networks, ports and harbors and weather data, it continues with basic information on the social and cultural heritage of the people, their demographic distribution, their politics and government, their urban and rural life styles, their economy, their military forces, their medical and health facilities, and their internal security apparatus.

The NIS studies are updated at intervals by all of the agencies in the intelligence community. Normally each volume is completely revised every four years and is distributed throughout the United States military establishment and to all other federal departments with activities abroad.

Another major area of basic intelligence reporting is the economic sphere. Those most intimately involved in this kind of research are CIA, DIA, and NSA. Each produces quarterly, semiannual, and annual reports on subjects such as a nation's foreign aid, its trade, manufacturing, agriculture, transportation, and communications. During the height of the bombing of North Vietnam, DIA produced a monthly report known as the Bomb Damage Assessment, which would try to reconcile the number of trucks, bridges, barges, and rail cars reported destroyed or damaged with the remaining national inventory, and would attempt to assess the impact of the previous thirty days of bombing.

The scientific field is another important basic research area in which CIA, DIA, and NSA, in particular, are very active. They regularly publish technical studies and analyses on all weapons systems, large and small. They produce monthly, quarterly, semiannual, and annual reports on the Soviet and Chinese missile and space programs, as well as Israeli aircraft production, and on a variety of other scientific topics such as the Japanese electronics industry and space research. These basic reports are disseminated throughout the intelligence community to serve as background studies for the reading of analysts with a generalist's approach to an entire country. More importantly, they go to United States military planners concerned with keeping abreast of the state of the art in the Communist countries.

The study of the leading personalities in other countries is another important segment of the basic research area of intelligence. DIA and CIA keep extensive dossiers on political, social, and military leaders. These dossiers contain not only biographical information but, more important, as much as is known about the leaders' views and attitudes as reflected in their writings, public addresses, or other sources. DIA regularly publishes a Biographic Register of military officers, and CIA routinely issues reports on political and social leaders. Perhaps the Biographic's biggest moment occurred at the time of John F. Kennedy's funeral, when heads of states of dozens of countries descended upon Washington. A booklet describing the individual members of each country's party was prepared and disseminated to harried State Department officials responsible for the protocol of the event. These studies are particularly needed when a change in government occurs suddenly and an assessment of the direction the new leadership might take is needed.

The disposition of a nation's military forces is another vital facet of basic intelligence. United States war planners are constantly updating plans and need to have daily and weekly changes in the disposition of a potential enemy's forces. CIA, DIA, and NSA, as well as the four service staffs, are actively involved in keeping abreast of minute changes in the combat forces of all potential enemies. They produce daily, weekly, monthly, and quarterly reports for United States war planners to use.

The third major facet of intelligence reporting is the estimative projection of future developments. The process normally begins when the President or one of his close policy advisers poses a question for the intelligence community, such as "What direction is Chinese Communist foreign policy going to take?" Such a question is turned over to the Board of National Estimates—a group of twelve senior intelligence officials, retired ambassadors, and military officers whose combined wisdom and experience, so the theory has it, enables them to preside over this most difficult of intelligence tasks. The board defines the problem more precisely, divides it into feasible components, and assigns it to the appropriate intelligence agencies. This first step is known as drawing up the terms of reference. Each of the participating intelligence agencies then prepares its contributions to the estimate and sends it along to the staff office at CIA —the Office of National Estimates—for a first draft. Once the draft is completed, it is circulated to all the intelligence agencies and they get together with their various experts in a series of working meetings to hash out whatever differences may exist in the draft. Normally three or four such meetings occur before tentative agreement at the working level is reached.

When the board member in charge of the particular estimate is satisfied that all of the agencies have had their chance to comment on the draft, he submits the new draft to the United States Intelligence Board. This group, which is composed of representatives of all the intelligence agencies in Washington, sits as the board of directors of the intelligence community. They are presented with the working draft, which normally contains several dissents and conflicting opinions of the various agencies. The USIB members try to reconcile these conflicts and produce a consensus report for the President and the National Security Council, but they are under no obligation to come up with a totally agreed-upon final estimate. More often than not, however, all of the dissenting views are compromised at this final stage.

An estimate produced on an ad hoc basis as described above

is known as a Special National Intelligence Estimate (SNIE). Another type, known simply as a National Intelligence Estimate (NIE), is produced on a regular basis. Every year, an estimate of Soviet military capabilities and intentions is undertaken. Selected countries are reviewed regularly with a view to providing policy planners a complete picture of the direction of the country's foreign and domestic policy, its governmental stability, and the likelihood of changes.

The production of estimates is not confined to the rarefied atmosphere of the upper echelons of the intelligence structure. The Defense Department, always eager to have estimates of potential enemy capabilities and intentions, has devised a system to sidestep the formal processes just described so that they can continue their weapons planning in a routine manner. The Joint Staff elements responsible for planning ahead have established a standing requirement with the Defense Intelligence Agency for the regular production of what is known as Joint Intelligence Estimates for Planning (JIEPs). DIA and the service intelligence staffs get together and produce projections of future enemy capabilities in the weapons areas without alerting the rest of the intelligence community. This saves considerable time and friction and allows the regular planning for less glamorous weapons systems to proceed. It also has more sinister implications, in that it allows Defense to move ahead into weapons procurement without an objective appraisal of the DIA force projections by intelligence agencies with less vested interest.

Most critical commentaries on United States intelligence raise control as a crucial issue. The myth of CIA being an invisible government has never been dispelled, and many are quick to conclude that the CIA simply needs to have its wings clipped and not be allowed to wheel and deal so freely in the volatile arena of intrigue. The problem with this prevalent attitude is that it automatically assumes that things are very well organized and well run within CIA and the rest of the intelligence community.

Such is not the case, however, as even a cursory glance at how the intelligence process is controlled will reveal. The word "control" is really a misnomer. "Management" is a more proper word. For what we are talking about is simply the day-to-day management of a complexity of intelligence collection, processing, and reporting functions.

Starting with the collection phase, a variety of instruments are used to monitor what intelligence is collecting and what needs to be collected. Within each of the intelligence agencies, under various names, exists a staff whose function it is to guide collection programs. In theory, CIA's collection guidance staff acts as a middleman between the analysts and the collectors. They allegedly sit back and take a broad view of what is going on and direct collection toward targets that need to be exploited more fully or developed anew. The concept is that, by constantly talking with the analysts, they are aware of exactly what kinds of information they are lacking to complete whatever particular puzzle they are presently working upon. They then impart this to the collection components of the agency in order to keep the intelligence cycle active and in tune with current and long-range needs.

NSA has a similar staff, which keeps abreast of the COMINT targets and the needs of the technical analysts working on the individual problems of signals intelligence. DIA does the same sort of thing for the only collection program they directly oversee, the attaché system. Indirectly they are also supposedly monitoring all of the individual service technical collection programs to ensure that they not only fit in with the services' needs but also are contributing to the national needs of the Department of Defense.

The system doesn't work as it should. In CIA the collection guidance staff is used as a dumping ground for intelligence officers who, for a variety of reasons, do not fit well on either the operational or analytical sides of the business. The men are generally elderly officers awaiting retirement or temporarily exiled to the collection staff of office politics in their career service. This escapes any formal investigation of the system.

Added to this is the reality that the diversity of collection programs and the variety of analytical needs are so broad that the paperwork the guidance system generates is vast enough to swamp the procedure and turn it into a vicious paper mill which pays little or no attention to the broader aspects of collection requirements. A collection program, once initiated, has a very high potential of continuing ad infinitum. The staff is too busy keeping up with the daily flow of paper between the analytical and operational sides of CIA.

Examples of how this operates abound in later chapters. The basic problem of effectively managing the diverse programs stems from the basic compromise made when the central intelligence concept was bought in 1947. Essentially, it was a compromise between the desire of the individual services not to give up an inch of their intelligence responsibilities and the recognized need for some form of central control. What emerged was a loose confederation of agencies designed more around political and vested interests than around a functional concept of a smooth-running intelligence gathering and processing arm of government.

The problem is compounded by the existence of collection guidance elements in each of the collecting agencies. They theoretically coordinate all of their actions, but, again, it doesn't work that way in the day-to-day world. The intricacies of one program such as the airborne ELINT collection program are so vast that the staffers at DIA responsible for blending it into the national requirements picture are unaware of the validity of the actual mission put forth by the services. They do not have the technical competence to judge the proposal, nor do they have the authority to effectively challenge a proposal put forth by the services. In effect, then, they merely act as paper brokers for the service program. They send it over to a committee at CIA, whose technical competence is also questionable, and they defend the service requests if any suggestions are made to cut back in a certain area.

The interagency coordination of the various collection programs is superficial at best. As long as the requirements for new programs and the continuation of existing programs fall within the budgetary limitations of the entire intelligence budget, then no serious or fundamental objections arise. It is another example of the system looking good on paper. The chart depicting the detailed interagency balancing of collection requirements against national priorities is a masterpiece of hairsplitting. Each facet of the detailed procedure falls into its proper place, and a balanced picture of exactly how the collection programs are managed emerges for the naive observer.

Almost as an admission of the frailty of the existing management tools available to United States intelligence, the United States Intelligence Board over the past twenty-five years has established special committees to oversee individual troublesome areas of intelligence management. Today, there are approximately one dozen USIB committees in existence. Of course, within each agency special subcommittees have been set up to respond to the requests of the master committee—another classic example of bureaucratic layering. The Committee on Overhead Reconaissance, for example, supposedly sits back and takes the long view of all aerial and satellite reconnaissance missions. In reality, it simply serves as a place for the director of CIA to point his finger when a hot situation arises. It allows him to sidestep the established procedures (an admission, of course, of their ineffectiveness) and get a job done quickly and effectively. Another committee watches worldwide missile and space developments. Another is wrestling with the introduction of computers into the intelligence business. Supposedly, they are to ensure that all ten agencies are going in the same compatible direction with purchases and installation of very expensive computer equipment. The Watch Committee was the first instituted, representing the institutionalization of the Pearl Harbor syndrome. Yet another committee is charged with overseeing the efficient allocation of human resources within the ten-agency intelligence community whose duplication of effort is staggering.

In the processing stage of intelligence there is simply no central management of men or material. So long as each of the ten agencies adheres to its own budgetary restrictions, then the whole is assumed to be functioning well and in concert with national requirements and priorities. Despite the existence of a USIB committee of intelligence resources, the individual agencies shift personnel and balance their own workloads more in accord with the day-to-day crush of events than with any national plan.

A review of the sheer number of reports emanating from the various members of the intelligence community stands as silent evidence of the degree of management exerted in this area. That they duplicate one another, prompt incestuous bureaucratic battles, and slow down the entire production of intelligence throughout the community has not been raised previously as an issue. However, it is, perhaps, one of the major problems confronting intelligence today.

I have not presented a complete picture of the organization of United States intelligence. A detailed rendering of the community would leave most readers cold and somewhat numbed —as it did me while I sat through four solid weeks of such a drill as a CIA trainee. Only the broad outlines have been discussed. They nevertheless represent the kinds of organizational chaos that exist in intelligence, and they explain why I think of it as the intelligence maze.

V

Technology:
The Tail Wagging the Dog?

In intelligence, as in many aspects of American life, the reverence accorded technology is open to serious questioning. The mere development of a new gadget should by no means be the criterion for its introduction into the intelligence toolbox. Regrettably, this often is the case. The intelligence community's thirst for new information is an unquenchable one. The vaguest hint that something new will afford an opportunity to open another peephole into a potential enemy's domain prompts the loosing of intelligence money and the approval of "feasibility tests"—which invariably lead to "further developmental tests" and finally implementation of a new collection program.

Critics of these efforts are few, for few wish to confront "the national security" argument flaunted by supporters of intelligence. Even a House Armed Services subcommittee hedged its criticism of technical intelligence by bowing to the national

security idol. Fortunately they were not overawed by this argument in their conclusions on the *Pueblo* seizure and the *EC-121*
reconnaissance plane shootdown. "The subcommittee con-
cedes," they wrote, "that reconnaissance activities of this type
must be conducted by our government to ensure the availability
of information essential to our national security interests. However, the subcommittee is not convinced that the magnitude of
this intelligence activity is completely justified, nor is it persuaded that the many millions of dollars that are expended
annually to support our individual intelligence activities are
fully and properly utilized."

The irony of this report is that the House was only looking
at two isolated incidents—one a shipborne collection program
and the other an airborne collection program. Both types of
collection programs are supplemental to other technical intelligence collection programs in effect. Together they provide less
than 10 percent of the total technical intelligence take used by
the United States government. These two programs are relatively more efficient than the other varieties of collection programs. Were a full-blown investigation conducted of all United
States intelligence-gathering programs—particularly the du-
plicating ground-based sites—it is certain that the House would
soon forget the national security syndrome and call a spade a
spade. In intelligence, technology has allied itself with bureaucracy, and together they ride roughshod over reason and logic.
The result is a maddening, self-perpetuating chaos which has
distorted the entire intelligence process to the point that technology has become the goal rather than the means to a goal.
Cloaked in "relevant" language such as "the information explosion," the technical intelligence collectors have aided the evolu-
tion of a system that continually expands and never contracts.
Our almost limitless ability to collect information has prompted
only a few to question the utility of the information that is
collected—and those few are treated as heretics for raising such
questions. The results are frightening. More and more information of less and less value is collected. The worthless items are

stored, against a slim hope that their value will increase when more technology affords added meaning to them. The expansion of technical collection attracts intelligence professionals to that side of the business—for it is there that promotions are more rapid. The analyst who is supposed to make sense out of all the information has been forgotten, almost shunted aside. As the programs expand they defy rational management and we have international incidents resulting from collection programs designed to provide information that will allow the United States government means to avoid such incidents. Intelligence today is almost the ultimate irony.

Perhaps the most sinister aspect of all this is the attitudinal changes the technology revolution has wrought among the upper echelons of the intelligence leadership. Beginning with the U-2 incident and moving forward through the sixties, the dozen or more technical intelligence goofs that have received public attention prompted at first a defensive attitude among intelligence leaders called to task for these failures by the Congress or the President. As the number of failures have increased, initial defensiveness has taken on a paranoic tinge. Today all who question intelligence are automatically branded an enemy. And this means even the President. The result is the great "C. Y. A." (Cover Your Ass) attitude that prevails at such investigations. Half-truths, distortions, and acts of omission characterize the answers put forth by the intelligence community when called on the carpet. They respond directly to a particular question and will not elaborate on any aspect of their answer unless directed to by the investigators.

The House Armed Services subcommittee investigating the *Pueblo* incident was furious with the Pentagon for its obvious attempt to hide the facts. In one instance regarding a message from NSA that could have prevented the seizure, the subcommittee report stated: "The incredible handling of the NSA warning message on the *Pueblo* mission is hardly looked upon with pride by responsible authorities in the Pentagon. It obviously is a proper source of considerable embarrassment. However, the subcommittee is as much concerned with the demon-strated lack of candor of witnesses on this subject as it is with the actual incident itself.

"Pentagon representatives who testified or briefed Congres-sional committees immediately after the *Pueblo* incident and up until March, 1969, never hinted that such a message ever ex-isted. As a matter of fact, there appeared to be a deliberate effort to bury and obfuscate the fact by discussion solely of 'warnings' allegedly issued by the North Korean government.

"The subcommittee inquiry was specifically designed to un-cover areas in Pentagon policy and procedure that require cor-rective action. It is the opinion of the subcommittee that Penta-gon authorities have done very little to assist in attaining this objective. Responses from the Pentagon on this matter and others raised by the subcommittee have sometimes been less than forthright. Responses to subcommittee questions which are 'technically' correct but constitute 'half-truths' are hardly calculated to engender confidence in the professed desire of the Pentagon to correct any shortcomings in established policy or procedure."

I have taken part in the preparation of testimony for the DIA director and have fielded some of the questions that the House committees wanted submitted for the record. The dominant attitude among the colonels and generals reviewing the submis-sions was all-out hostility toward Congress. A review of all public congressional inquiries fails to reveal one single instance in which any intelligence official stated, "Congressman, the only realistic answer I can provide is that we made a mistake." Rather, congressional hearings on intelligence over the past six years that I researched show only very lengthy, detailed, and specious explanations of why one particular agency in intelli-gence was not at fault.

Three incidents I witnessed in the Pentagon underscore this defensive attitude and reveal the extent to which some intelli-gence officials will go to cover their own tracks. On the day the USS *Pueblo* was seized by North Korea in January, 1968, the

Far Eastern Division of DIA was in turmoil. The seizure had occurred shortly before midnight, Washington time, and men were called in to work as soon as the first cable arrived. Added to that was the fact that division resources were stretched thin because the Vietnam branch had been beefed up in anticipation of a massive North Vietnamese assault on the United States Marine Corps base at Khe Sanh in South Vietnam.

The crucial questions being asked about the *Pueblo* were, Where was the ship when she was seized? and Had she violated North Korean territorial waters? The most important person asking was the President. His national security staffers in the White House situation room called DIA at about 8:00 A.M. and said the President wanted a straight answer on the *Pueblo*'s location.

All of the evidence was reviewed, and a conflict emerged immediately. All of the United States Navy operational reports indicated that the *Pueblo* had stayed outside the Pentagon's 13-mile limit. COMINT sources watching North Korean air defense and naval coastal radars, however, indicated that the *Pueblo* had violated North Korean waters on four occasions in the three days prior to the seizure. The Far East Division chief, when informed of the nature of the evidence, remarked, "Bullshit, I'm not believing the Communist radar. Those bastards were probably sending false radar tracks. Until we get something better than that, give the Navy the benefit of the doubt." While there was a degree of logic to the colonel's suspicion of radar trickery, the record of accuracy of Communist radar tracking did not support it. Their radar networks, like ours, are primarily concerned with accurately keeping track of potential enemies, alerting their defense forces, and, if necessary, guiding them to any hostile penetration. The colonel should have provided the White House with a balanced appraisal of the facts on hand. The briefing team dispatched to the White House relied exclusively upon United States operational reports. This briefing resulted in the proclamation of the official line that the *Pueblo* had not entered North Korean waters. Secretary of

Defense Robert S. McNamara was not so certain of the facts involved. Some days later, in an interview with Max Frankel of *The New York Times*, he remarked that he "couldn't say for certain that the *Pueblo* never entered North Korean waters."

During that same day the White House posed another embarrassing question for DIA. What was to be gained by this particular mission? The request was taken by telephone at the North Korean current intelligence desk by the Army major running the shop. He thought it would be an easy one—but a fifteen-minute search of his office couldn't turn up an answer. He called the DIA collection requirements staff and asked them. An hour later they called back confessing that they, too, had nothing in their files to indicate what take was expected. "All we do is process the paper. We don't keep track of all the details. Why don't you see if the Navy staff can help?"

The Navy staff was called, and they had to call NSA for the answer: the *Pueblo* was targeted against three items. It was a new program justified by the Navy staffs in the Pacific. They claimed that it would be working on a new effort to "(1) determine the nature and extent of naval activity at North Korean ports, (2) sample electronic intelligence along the east coast of North Korea, and (3) keep a surveillance on the Soviet fleet operating in the Sea of Japan."

The briefing team for the White House then put together a briefing to highlight the new and very important targets the *Pueblo* was working against. Tony, an analyst familiar with the programs in the area, raised an objection with the division chief when the final briefing was given a dry run before going to the White House. He pointed out that one COMINT station in South Korea and two in Japan were already providing daily and detailed reports on the nature and extent of naval activity at North Korean ports. Further, he questioned the need to "sample the electronic intelligence" along the east coast of North Korea when the Air Force flew an average of sixty missions a month in the area, collecting more than enough ELINT to accurately portray the electronic order of battle for all of North

Korea. Lastly, he pointed out that two COMINT stations in Japan provided detailed daily reports on the composition and movements of the Soviet fleet in the Sea of Japan. The division chief brushed Tony's observations aside. "It's too late for all that detail to get cranked into the briefing now. They have to be at the White House in a half-hour. Anyway," he added with finality and a smile, "we don't want those politicos over there thinkin' the mission wasn't necessary. No, we ain't gonna make those kind of waves this late in the game."

The fact that the *Pueblo* was totally unnecessary from an intelligence point of view has never been admitted by the Pentagon. In testimony before the House Armed Services Committee investigating the *Pueblo*, Defense officials stated that "the *Pueblo* was a vital element in the development of plans for contingencies which we must expect to face and in the development of new weapons systems needed to prevail against potential enemy military and technical advances. The failure of responsible authorities to guard against this possibility would constitute a dereliction of duty to the American people." This remark is a classic example of United States intelligence waving the "national security" flag, and it is a lie. Intelligence officials would have Congress believe that had the *Pueblo* mission not sailed the United States would somehow have lost out in the arms race. Yet, since the *Pueblo* seizure no United States intelligence ship has ventured into those same waters, and we somehow seem to be keeping abreast of the Communist world despite the dire warnings of "dereliction of duty" put forth by the Pentagon. Perhaps the saddest aspect of this avoidance of the truth is that it was perpetrated first within the government. Intelligence officials waved the same national security flag under the President's nose in an attempt to ward off any close investigation of the incident. And they succeeded.

When it was discovered in DIA that NSA had sent an unsolicited warning message about the potential risks involved in the *Pueblo* incident another internal crisis developed. The director called for a copy and the North Korean desk couldn't find it.

They finally found a copy in the message center and got it up to the director's office—but they failed to tell him they didn't have it on file in their office. Instead they acted as if they had had it all along and told the director it had been considered in their own assessment of the risks to the *Pueblo*.

At issue in these situations is the form of control exerted on the technical intelligence collection programs. High intelligence officials insist the system works well, but an examination of how the *Pueblo* and other missions get started shows that the majority of such collection programs rise imperceptibly out of the bureaucracy, gain their own momentum, and persist simply because it requires too much paperwork to stop them.

In 1961 I was working as an intelligence analyst at the Strategic Air Command Headquarters in Omaha, Nebraska. There they have an organization known as the Joint Strategic Target Planning Staff (JSTPS), whose responsibility it is to program all of the targets for nuclear attack and divide the targeting pie among missiles, Polaris submarines, or B-52 bomber attack. To assist in this awesome responsibility the commander of SAC had the 544th Reconnaissance Technical Wing, which mounted airborne intelligence missions to monitor Soviet, East European, and Chinese Communist air defenses and other military targets.

The target staff at that time was concerned that we were not getting a complete electronic picture of Soviet air defenses of the Novya Zemlya area adjacent to the Kara Sea. The intelligence staff was ordered to write up a proposal to institute a new airborne collection program to cover the region. It was quickly approved by the Pentagon, and SAC was ordered to establish the program at an air base in England. An RB-47 unit was set up there and began to fly routine patrol missions in the area. At the end of the first year of operation the intelligence staff at SAC had to review the year's intelligence take and assess the utility of the effort. The review disclosed that the missions had indeed collected considerable amounts of new intelligence on the defense systems in the area. The director of intelligence at

SAC was pleased. But additional research by the staff indicated that during the same year NSA had opened two new intercept positions in West Germany with new intercept equipment that collected the same information at considerably less expense than the airborne program. The director of intelligence was not pleased. At that time SAC was having a bit of a morale problem. With the introduction of missiles into SAC's arsenal the number of command pilot slots was being cut back. Men with years of flying experience were being retrained and transferred to missile silos underground as launch control officers. They chaffed at being pulled out of the wild blue and getting stuck underground.

An old bomber pilot himself, the director of intelligence was in sympathy with the pilots. He ordered the intelligence staff to write up a proposal for continuation of the reconnaissance program on the basis of what the program had collected. He specifically ordered that no mention be made of the new NSA intercept positions in West Germany. "If they are all that hot," he said, "the boys who review our proposal at the Pentagon will know about them. Let them make the decision to kill our program." Of course he was fully aware that the "boys" who review the programs at the Pentagon merely rubber-stamped the services' requests and would make no effort to see how this one program fit into the overall national collection effort. The program was approved. In 1968, seven years later, I was working at DIA. My curiosity got the best of me one day while reviewing the monthly reconnaissance schedule that had come to our office for approval. I leafed to the section covering recon programs against the Soviet Union and sure enough the old SAC outfit in England was still in operation, using the exact same flight plans that we had put together in 1961! They had new planes and a much larger complement, however; the "boys" at the Pentagon had by this time apparently assumed that the program was worthwhile simply because it had been flying for seven years without cessation.

A similar incident occurred after the U.S. Navy *EC-121*

recon plane was shot down off the coast of North Korea in April, 1969. The intelligence community's nerves were raw over this incident, coming, as it did, on the heels of the *Pueblo* incident. President Nixon was furious, and the word came from the White House to make a thorough review of all recon programs to see what could be done to avoid another such incident. In the course of this review it came to light that the Air Force had been flying a routine intelligence reconnaissance mission over Albania for twelve years. Digging back into the files it was then discovered that the mission had never been approved by the Pentagon. Its original flight plan took it across Greece and the southern tip of Italy. In 1959, however, a new flight plan taking the patrol into Albanian air space suddenly appeared in the file without comment by anyone up the elaborate chain of command that supposedly "carefully reviewed" these programs. DIA brought this to the attention of the Air Force intelligence staff. They quickly ordered the mission stopped, but failed to inform the JCS, the Secretary of Defense, or the White House that such an error had even been made.

The *Pueblo* incident is perhaps the best publicly documented intelligence fiasco in the past twenty-five years. The reams of testimony and the books that have been written on the incident all conclude that, at best, "the system" was at fault. No one individual can be singled out for the multitude of mistakes that were made. The *Pueblo* incident is not unique in terms of how the program started. The elements involved in the origin of the *Pueblo* mission are common to all the technical intelligence collection programs in effect today. It bears out my contention that the technical intelligence collection tail is wagging the entire intelligence dog. The *Pueblo* mission started only because the Navy had a new ship to play with. The rest of the *Pueblo* story is simply a sad chronicle of the Navy bending over backwards to justify its decision and to put the *Pueblo* into operation. The House Armed Services subcommittee investigating the incident didn't miss this subtle point either. In their report they stated: "The subcommittee suspects that Navy enthusiasm and support for the AGER program [of which the *Pueblo* was a part] was, not in small part, prompted by the prospect of acquiring its own fleet of surface intelligence collecting vehicles, independent of control by MSTS or the National Security Agency."

The *Pueblo* incident underscores the manner in which many reconnaissance missions are planned. Once the Navy had the boats to start a collection program of its own, it was faced with the question, What shall we collect with them? Since the *Pueblo* was being assigned to United States naval forces in Japan, its area of operation was limited to the northern Pacific.

According to Trevor Armbrister's detailed investigation of the *Pueblo* incident in *A Matter of Accountability,* the next decision—the actual planning of the mission route—was reached by a seemingly unusual method, but one I have seen many times. A young Navy lieutenant assigned to the intelligence staff at Yokosuka, Japan, was given the job of selecting the route. He had been in regular correspondence with a friend of his—a Navy lieutenant commander—working on the intelligence staff in Hawaii. The lieutenant commander was concerned because the military staffs in the Pacific were focusing all of their attention on Vietnam. He wrote a personal letter to the lieutenant in Japan bemoaning this fact and also claiming that no one was interested in China or North Korea. The lieutenant was impressed with his friend's sincerity and thereupon decided that he would direct the *Pueblo* against North Korean targets.

Two additional critical issues emerged from the *Pueblo* investigation. The Navy's claim that the risks of reconnaissance missions are carefully evaluated is, at best, a polite fiction. The second is that intelligence effort is damaged by the severe compartmentation that plagues the intelligence structure. Responsibility is so fragmented that men charged with crucial decisions are almost completely out of touch with reality.

On paper the elaborate mission approval process works like a charm. The command originating a recon mission and all intervening commands, including the Defense Intelligence Agency, independently evaluate and establish the risk involved for each mission proposed. The Joint Chiefs of Staff has promulgated a list of fourteen specific criteria to assist in evaluating the risk of any recon mission, but the evidence indicates that these were completely ignored in the case of the *Pueblo*. The only criterion that was applied was a judgment on the part of the Navy lieutenant in Japan, who believed that since the *Pueblo* was to sail in international waters the risk was minimal. This judgment was not subsequently questioned by any higher authority. Even CIA and the State Department agreed with it. From my personal experience, once a mission is proposed and given a "minimal risk" evaluation no one up the chain of command questions it. Despite all the high-sounding rhetoric to the contrary, each unit above the first merely rubber-stamps the proposal. The attitude common at all levels is, "The guy who proposed it must have done his homework, so there's no sense in me diggin' into this." I've seen this happen with U-2 overflights of Communist China, SR-71 overflights of North Vietnam, and scores of other reconnaissance proposals. Added to this is the harsh fact that at the time of the *Pueblo* mission proposal, the unwritten policy in the Far East was, "If the risk on a mission is anything other than minimal it won't get approved." This policy was instituted because American forces throughout the Pacific were stretched disastrously thin because of Vietnam. If an honest risk assessment had been made on the *Pueblo* mission, it would have been disapproved. This would have meant that the ship and her crew would have had to sit idle at a dock in Japan. And the Navy being what it is, it would have chaffed at this expensive inactivity. The Navy wanted to put *Pueblo* to work.

The second point about intelligence staffers working in a vacuum was never more clearly demonstrated than in the *Pueblo* incident. Despite the elaborate communications flow of intelligence information throughout the community in Washington and abroad, the sheer amount of paper in the system forces men to single out only those pieces that directly pertain to their individual tasks. The Navy lieutenant in Japan who drew up the route for the *Pueblo* was the surface reconnaissance staff officer. He therefore busied himself with intelligence paper that directly involved that subject. He obviously was not tuned into the political and diplomatic realities surrounding North Korea at the time that he chose to sail *Pueblo* up the east coast.

The first item on the apparently ignored JCS list of criteria for assessing the risk of reconnaissance missions is "the political climate." The second is the "sensitivity of the target country." Beginning in October, 1966, the North Koreans had adopted a decidedly belligerent diplomatic stance. They backed this up with military actions. Kim Il Sung, the North Korean premier, announced in an uncompromising speech that he was intent on reunifying the Korean peninsula by force if necessary. President Johnson shortly after that speech paid a visit to South Korea to reaffirm American support to the South Koreans. This apparently infuriated Kim Il Sung, for in the next ten days North Korean troops ambushed and killed more UN troops along the DMZ than they had in the previous thirteen years.

Incidents of ambushes and sniper fire along the DMZ between North and South Korea rose dramatically in the following months. In 1966 there had been a total of 37 such events. In 1967 there were 445! During the same time the North Korean navy became belligerent. It captured 50 South Korean fishing boats and detained 353 crewmen. In early January, 1968, after the *Pueblo* had set sail, the North Koreans pulled off their most dramatic gesture in mounting an assassination attempt against the South Korean president, which ended up in a street gunfight in front of the presidential palace in Seoul.

Added to these widely known public events was a growing list of secret intelligence indicators that the North Koreans were planning increased belligerence. In the infamous warning message that NSA sent out concerning the risks to the *Pueblo* they pointed out: "(1) The North Korean Air Force has been extremely sensitive to peripheral reconnaissance flights in this area since early 1965. This sensitivity was emphasized on April 28, 1965, when a United States Air Force RB-47 was fired on and severely damaged 35 to 40 nautical miles from the coast. (2) The North Korean Air Force has assumed an additional role of naval support since late 1966. (3) The North Korean Navy reacts to any Republic of Korea Navy vessel or fishing boat near the North Korean coastline. This was emphasized on January 16, 1967, when a Republic of Korea Naval vessel was sunk by coastal artillery. (4) Internationally recognized boundaries as they relate to airborne activities are generally not honored by North Korea on the east coast of Korea."

The leaders of the intelligence community would have the public and Congress believe that in cases like the *Pueblo* all of the established procedures were followed. The working world of intelligence, however, is a far cry from the rosy picture of dedicated professionalism that the upper echelons project. The *Pueblo* incident, because it was an isolated event, is sometimes judged out of its proper context. In reality *Pueblo* was only one of close to four hundred reconnaissance missions that were scheduled during the month of January, 1968, and its handling should be assessed with that in mind. The singular acts of the Navy lieutenant in Japan and all of the others who supposedly evaluated the mission were simply routines of paperwork that, in most cases, represented one of hundreds of similar acts performed in the course of any work week.

When all of the individual proposals finally filter into Washington from military commands around the world, they are compiled into one large monthly reconnaissance schedule. It normally runs about the thickness of a Washington phone book. Once assembled it is sent around the intelligence community for coordination and approval. The speed with which the January, 1968, recon schedule containing the ill-fated *Pueblo* mission was approved by all of official Washington—three days —bears moot testimony to the "careful scrutiny" allegedly given the missions. Month after month this thick volume would come into our offices at CIA. Normally the man from the collection guidance staff would drop by with the book at 9:00 A.M. and say he'd be back at 10:30 to pick it up. Since that was the busiest time of the day for us, we would all try to avoid getting stuck with the chore of going through the recon schedule. Moreover we were always uncertain as to what we were supposed to do with it. We'd normally leaf through it, remark about how nice the cover was, and sign off on the memorandum attached to it. The man would return from collection guidance, and we'd say we had no problems with it. One of the reasons we had no problems is that we didn't understand the computer language in which it was prepared. Under the risk category there would be one of four letters—A, B, C, or D. Nowhere was there an explanation of what they meant. Was "A" a high risk or a minimal risk mission? Pressed by our other duties we'd give the recon schedule as little time as possible and get on with our work. The situation at DIA was worse because the pace of the daily work routine was faster. There the book was normally dropped off in our office for no more than fifteen minutes or a half-hour. Analysts at DIA had the same aversion to checking the schedule as they did at CIA.

Now, let's consider the testimony of the former director of DIA, Lieutenant General Joseph Carroll, when describing how the *Pueblo* mission was checked by his staff. "The complete monthly reconnaissance schedule for January, 1968, was distributed on December 27th, and it included the proposed *Pueblo* mission. Its area of operation and its evaluated risk category had been known to DIA for at least ten days. During all this while, as I have described, there were daily considerations of changes in the military or political situation, increased sensitivity and reactions to other reconnaissance missions. There was nothing in these considerations to cause us in DIA to alter the risk assessment which had been assigned the mission."

General Carroll no doubt believed he was accurately portraying the work environment at DIA. Plagued with a bad back, he rarely if ever left his office, and his only contact with the working level was through the half-dozen hard-charging colonels who served as his deputies. If they were familiar with actual conditions at the working level they'd never relay these truths to the general.

General Carroll further amplified his testimony before the subcommittee by stating that he did not recall any instance in which DIA had disagreed with a minimal risk assessment on an individual mission after the monthly reconnaissance schedule had been formally prepared and circulated throughout the intelligence community.

General Carroll was queried at length concerning the specific and detailed criteria used in risk evaluation. He stated categorically that each of the criteria was considered in the risk evaluation process by his agency. He conceded, however, that he could produce no written evidence or supporting document indicating that these criteria had been reviewed in the case of the *Pueblo* mission. When asked, "How do you know that your staff people have done this?" General Carroll replied, "Because they are charged with doing it, because they are professionals."

From my vantage point at DIA I know of no one who engaged in the "daily considerations of changes in the military or political situation" of which General Carroll spoke, and if such daily monitoring took place it would have been done in the division where I worked. The Army major who headed up the North Korean desk was fresh back from a tour in Vietnam, green on the subject of North Korea, in the throes of a drawn-out divorce action, and also involved in vigorous handball playoffs then underway during working hours at the officers' athletic club at the Pentagon.

Another aspect of the inefficient control of United States reconnaissance programs stems from a community-wide insatiable appetite for more information. All of the agencies are guilty of this. Once a program uncovers anything new, say the appearance of a different pulse rate on a Soviet radar, then all of the analysts working that problem want to know more about it. They submit special intelligence collection requirements, and the system takes over from there with additional ammunition to continue many programs. Requirements are normally highly technical, and the persons processing them do not have the technical competence to thwart the over-eager analysts who claim that the information is essential to their work. During the bombing of North Vietnam it was discovered that the North Vietnamese had changed the guidance radar on their SA-2 missiles. This sent the scientific analysts at CIA, DIA, and NSA into a tizzy. They wanted to know more about it. In their justification for laying on additional recon missions they stated that this information would enable them to determine more precisely the range of the SA-2 missile. They were correct, but the difference they were trying to reconcile was a mere two-tenths of a kilometer. A group at DIA was convinced that its range was 27.5 kilometers. Had the men on the committees massaging the requests been technically competent they could, perhaps, have questioned the expense and risk involved in collecting information to settle a long-standing internal feud within the intelligence community of such trivial consequence. They didn't have that competence, however, and the additional recon missions were approved. The difference in range estimates never affected actual United States flight operations. Knowing that such a dispute existed, tactical planners merely assumed that the range of the missiles was 32 miles and drew up their flight plans accordingly.

The old "continuity argument" is another long-standing favorite of analysts for extending reconnaissance programs. It works like this: Photos pick up evidence suggesting the beginnings of construction of, say, a new SA-3 missile site in East Germany. COMINT sources are immediately diverted to investigate the problem and determine if new missiles are in fact being deployed to East Germany. Once the case is established, the intelligence community demands that twenty-four-hour tabs be kept on this new adventure on the part of the Soviets. Justification is provided which no one will argue with. They claim that we don't want to be faced with any surprise developments. The introduction of SA-3s must be closely monitored.

Daily flights are mounted and ground-based resources are diverted to watching the emergence of the new SA-3 system in East Germany. A day-to-day chronicle is kept and an accurate history is recorded. The specious aspect of this approach, which costs considerable sums of money and intelligence collection effort, is that the Soviets, like us, are unable to spring a new weapons system into being overnight. Like us, they must first go through a predictable pattern of installation, checkout, and testing. In my fourteen years' experience I never witnessed the overnight appearance of a new weapons system. Every new system introduced followed the expected timetable, and the reams of intelligence collected during those months were actually quite useless to the intelligence community. This same logic applies to Communist China, a nation whose technical and industrial capabilities makes the sudden appearance of anything new even more remote than in the Soviet Union. In cases like this a weekly check on new developments would suffice.

The same continuity argument extends to all routine aspects of technical intelligence. NSA feels compelled to be intimately aware of the innards of each and every target it covers—be it an air defense radar or a mobile radio van. It wants to know when a tube is changed in each radar set and it religiously chronicles and highlights such developments in its reports. While it is certainly nice to know such details, no one has asked if such information actually contributes to our knowledge of potential enemy capabilities. Moreover, no one outside of intelligence has balanced this off against the costs in money and in the international tension that monitoring these developments causes.

The layer of control above the working level of intelligence is superficial. The Joint Chiefs of Staff, civilians close to the Secretary of Defense, and high-level officials at the State Department all, theoretically, have equal voice in the United States reconnaissance effort. The *Pueblo* incident underscores just how effective this control is. All of the above people supposedly checked the January, 1968, recon schedule. The record indicates that each of their offices signed off on the schedule; it also points out that it took only one day for this so-called "final high-level review." You can imagine how closely the mission schedule was checked when you consider that it is a logistic marvel for the book to have been physically passed to all of those offices in one day.

The dilemma of this elaborate control system stems from the age-old bureaucratic penchant for passing the buck. The working levels of the intelligence community think of themselves as mere processors whose job it is to dish up the menu for the policy level of government to consider. Decisions on a mission proposal are deferred for the consideration of the policy makers. The policy maker, on the other hand, lacks the technical familiarity with the collection programs. Moreover, his span of attention, given the vast array of other duties and decisions he must make, is necessarily limited. He must depend on the judgment of the technical specialists feeding the proposals to him. And they are not doing it. The result is that the tough decisions —those requiring not only a knowledge of technical collection, but also a total familiarity with the political, military, and diplomatic environment—are not brought forward in a recognizable manner for top-level consideration. The size of the collection efforts each month is such that the administration of these efforts has reached a dangerous level of routinization.

The absence of control over the technical collection programs creates another major problem—what to do with the vast amounts of material collected. Rather than questioning the utility of the information, the community has assumed it is of value and enlisted the aid of the computer. This has created a new subculture within intelligence, injecting a broad new layer of bureaucracy into the system and delaying, perhaps avoiding altogether, the need to grapple with the question of scaling down United States collection efforts. It seems the computer will prompt additional collection as it demonstrates its ability to ingest ever-increasing amounts of information. The rising tide of statistical data allegedly of intelligence value prompted by Vietnam prodded the intelligence community into action as far as introducing computers was concerned. In 1966 it spent a little over one million dollars on a system whereby CIA, DIA, NSA, and State could query the internal files of one another. This program expanded to the point where ten million dollars had been invested in it by 1971.

Judging from the testimony of intelligence leaders before Congress, the computer has found a home in intelligence. No manager worth his salt in intelligence would argue against the use of computers. General Donald Bennett, the director of DIA, spoke optimistically of the computer in the 1971 appropriations hearings. "In addition to linking the files of CIA, DIA, and NSA," he said, "we are developing another program to handle overhead reconnaissance programs . . . another to design a plan for photo-intelligence . . . another to support requirements in the ELINT area." I am certainly not one to totally discredit the use of computers. I do harbor deep concerns, however, for their blanket application to intelligence. As already noted, the vital area of collection guidance for reconnaissance is slightly out of touch with reality. The computer may help solve some of the problems in handling the voluminous paperwork that surrounds these programs, but I fear it will further dehumanize the process to a very dangerous degree.

Within the Pentagon most military men stand in awe of the computer. Time and again I have seen generals and admirals rely on the computer as a substitute for human judgment and intelligence. Computer readouts somehow gain significance simply because they come from a machine.

Near lunacy prevailed at the upper levels of the JCS during the heyday bombing of North Vietnam, largely because of the computerized reports coming from Air Force and Navy units. Daily they would file detailed lists of the number of trucks they had (1) sighted on North Vietnamese roads, (2) damaged, and (3) destroyed. These were fed into the great mother computer at DIA which also held the figures on North Vietnamese truck inventory—an elaborate mathematical equation which included what intelligence knew of truck imports and Hanoi's repair capabilities for damaged trucks. Out of all this, intelligence allegedly could fathom that magic day when Hanoi would run out of trucks—thus ending the war!

North Vietnam ran out of trucks at least seven or eight times while I worked on the North Vietnam desk. Each time this happened the JCS demanded to know why we were still seeing trucks in North Vietnam. An Air Force general on the J-3 operations staff berated me loudly and lengthily at one briefing session about "how fucked up you intelligence types are." I reminded him that our estimates were based largely on what his operations staff provided. American pilots flying at five to six hundred miles per hour over North Vietnam would sight a half-dozen trucks speeding along a road and immediately attack them with rockets and bombs. Pulling out of his attack run, the pilot would look back over his right shoulder to see what damage he had inflicted. In nine out of ten cases all he was able to see was the billowing explosions of his own bombs. He'd write down on his clipboard, however, that he had destroyed four and damaged two. His wingman would also take a chunk of the glory and write down that he had zapped three and damaged three. The man flying cover for the mission would write down that he had sighted six trucks.

When the day's bombing was over and the reports were filed, Washington would be told that eighteen trucks had been sighted, seven had been destroyed, and five had been damaged. In many cases the original six trucks involved had pulled quickly off the road and watched as the American bombs missed their mark by a half-mile or more.

The J-3 staff would not accept reasoning which suggested the possibility of error in American pilot reporting. In reverent tones such arguments were rebutted with, "The data base indicates that the truck kill for 3 June was 182. Can you disprove that figure?" This kind of thinking prevailed in all aspects of the war which could be quantified—body count, North Vietnamese infiltration, MIG sorties, SA-2 missile firings, weapons captured, and pacification statistics.

The ready availability of such minutiae about the war provided the generals and admirals an opportunity to avoid the kind of strategic thinking they were being paid to do. Instead, they could immerse themselves in the tactical nitty-gritty of the war and, in effect, serve as rather high-paid company or squadron commanders. One Air Force general, provided with a detailed assessment of North Vietnamese SA-2 missile defenses, set his staff to working out a flight plan through the defenses. This plan required that DIA provide intelligence support in an effort requiring upwards of two hundred man-hours of work. Once completed, the study was used by the Air Force general whenever he had an opportunity to discuss the air war with a returning squadron or wing commander. Marine Corps and Army generals in the National Military Command Center became obsessed with the North Vietnamese siege of Khe Sanh in January, 1968. They insisted that DIA provide them with daily drawings and photographs of the intricate web of trenches the North Vietnamese were digging toward the base. Again, they had no need for the information in the performance of their jobs; it was simply a matter of personal fascination for them and it relieved the tedium of shuffling papers.

All these complex technical developments are not without major impact on the intelligence community as a whole, especially the attitudinal changes technology has wrought at the working level. As Henry Howe Ransom so perceptively pointed out in *The Intelligence Establishment,* "Since 1957 emphasis has been shifting from the social sciences to the physical or hard sciences—from ivory tower research towards operations, from theoretical analysis towards technical means of interpreting data. Once the social scientist occupied the center of the stage in intelligence work. Now he is being displaced, for better or worse, by the electronics expert, the physical scientist and the specialist in technical means of collecting and collating and interpreting data."

This displacement has taken place slowly and bureaucratically over the years. An intelligence official working in the Secretary of Defense's office told me, "The only place to be in intelligence these days is in collection. There is a ten-to-one leverage between a collection program and the production of intelligence. In collection you get the opportunity to manage many different collection programs and rise to the top quickly. If you look at the organization charts you can see where all the high grades are today. Any smart guy in intelligence today will get out of the production side as soon as he can. He's on a dead-end street if he doesn't." His statement checked out. At the Defense Intelligence Agency I looked into the manning structure. The proportion of high grades is three times as high on the technical side as on the production side. Thus the weight of intelligence's reliance on technology has truly reoriented the central thrust of United States intelligence. Careerwise, the production analyst—the guy who interprets and reports on the "data" collected by technical intelligence—has been left behind. His colleagues on the technical side, who theoretically exist to support his efforts, outrank him and thus effectively control the direction of intelligence collection. The technocrats reign supreme.

VI

The Culture of Bureaucracy

Viewing CIA's impressive office building in the Virginia country-side, one notes with some apprehension Parkinson's law. Professor Parkinson has suggested, with as much validity as wit, that organizations tend to achieve architectural magnificence and comfort at a point when institutional effectiveness declines or signs of deterioration begin to appear.

HENRY HOWE RANSOM

Very little is publicly known about the inner working of CIA and the rest of the intelligence community. Those in the press who claim to have some knowledge seem purposely to overlook the problems within, almost as if they believed that CIA is a superagency, immune from the bureaucratic foibles and weaknesses of other departments of government.

Professor Ransom's point, as quoted at the head of this chapter, underscores the fundamental problem of intelligence today. The intelligence community is a bureaucratic morass, a fragmented, disjointed effort in which no one seems responsible for momentous decisions, where vested interests are coldly played off against one another, where men of varied expertise stifle the unorthodox and opt for wretched half-measures or compromises so weakened by consensus that they would be better not taken at all.

It is very difficult to pinpoint the exact reasons why the state of affairs within the intelligence structure is this chaotic. Two major contributing factors, however, are the unusual, almost idiotic, reliance on the committee approach to even the most routine chores and the staggering amount of duplication of effort that has been allowed to persist for nearly three decades. The CIA is very well protected from official and unofficial scrutiny, and its officers have devised seemingly sound arguments in defense of the committee system and the duplication of effort. Most reasonable men in official positions charged with looking into CIA's problems are warded off with these arguments. The difficulty here is that these men never have had the opportunity to dig beneath the surface, to see for themselves how extensive and how ineptly these bureaucratic mechanisms operate.

There is an understandable, but not pardonable, explanation of why these devices are employed. After Pearl Harbor the major problem confronting the United States in the field of intelligence was the total lack of coordination of effort within the government. The State Department had its select crew of men ferreting out information abroad. Each of the three armed services had its own intelligence corps. All of these entities treated their counterparts as rivals, perhaps more dangerous than any foreign potential enemies. They never shared any intelligence take among themselves. They had no organized method of presenting their findings in a balanced or objective manner to the nation's leaders. If the Army or Navy intelligence officers came up with a relevant piece of intelligence, as happened when they were listening in to Japanese diplomatic codes, they would never consider sharing this information with the State Department. The episode of Pearl Harbor itself serves to highlight the gross inefficiencies that existed: the dozen or so sources of independent information pointing to an attack were never brought together.

During World War II, a series of patchwork solutions were applied to this problem and the concept of unity of effort earned a place in government intelligence circles. After the war it was realized that a centralized approach to national intelligence was needed as a permanent aspect of government. Such an instrument finally evolved after considerable infighting among the services, the State Department, the Office of Strategic Services, and the Office of War Information. The Central Intelligence Group, authorized by President Harry S Truman in 1946, finally evolved into the Central Intelligence Agency, which was created in 1947 with the passage of the National Security Act.

The intelligence system which evolved was, like the national defense establishment, the product of compromise between the competing organizational concepts—centralization and decentralization. And, as in the case of most such compromises, it left unsettled the issue of how much control was to be exercised by the central agency and it opened the door for great duplication of effort. Since that time the expansion of the community into many functionally fragmented compartments and their increasing involvement in detailed activities has resulted in the establishment of a profusion of management information systems and reporting requirements. The excessive detail and duplication of reporting requirements have generated such a mass of information that relevant and important facts are often obscured. Efforts at reports control and limitation have proved largely futile and have added to the already significant cost and load of paperwork.

In the substantive field today the intelligence community looks good on paper. Men from all components of the community labor diligently and manfully to develop and maintain the integrated approach to national intelligence. The representatives of each of the agencies working as committees are nothing more than a series of individual protective societies sent to the CIA by their bosses to ensure that their organizations yield on sovereignty.

The formal organization of intelligence proudly displays

committees at the top of the structure. The United States Intelligence Board is adorned with approximately a dozen offshoots, committees reporting directly to it. There is the Committee for Overhead Reconnaissance, which purportedly sorts out the monthly programs for overhead recon and provides the intelligence leadership with a strategic view of this problem. The Guided Missile Intelligence Committee interprets the volumes of worldwide data on this problem and affords the intelligence board a panel of experts to aid their investigations. The Watch Committee, the first to be created, massages the daily message traffic from around the world in order to ferret out any indicators that a nation is possibly considering overt military actions against the United States. It came into being as a result of the official investigations of the mishandling of information during the Pearl Harbor episode. The Joint Atomic Energy Committee seeks to keep the intelligence leadership abreast of worldwide developments in this field. The list includes a committee to oversee the implementation of computers in intelligence, one to coordinate clandestine collection efforts around the world, one to ensure that intelligence resources are being used efficiently, and one to keep abreast of just what intelligence information the United States is sharing with its allies.

With the existence of such creatures at the very top of the structure, each intelligence component has evolved a duplicate set of experts to handle the reports and support asked for by the Olympian master committee. The shadows of the master committees extend deep within the community. Experts advance through this filmy structure hoping to cap off their careers as staffers at the top. At the working level the different agencies share analytical data. During the bombing of North Vietnam the intelligence community began to receive a trickle of unverifiable reports that the Soviets might provide North Vietnam with surface-to-air missiles better than the SA-2 system. The military also was concerned that surface-to-surface missiles capable of destroying Seventh Fleet ships in the Gulf of Tonkin would suddenly appear. The Watch Committee therefore ordered that a Project Lookout be set up to monitor this problem. They were to meet as often as necessary and report weekly to the supercommittee at the top. Tapped for this task were the analysts on the Vietnam desks at each of the agencies working on the problem. They first met thrice weekly to set up the operating procedures and reporting requirements. After that they met twice weekly to go over the evidence newly emerged and draft a report for the top committee.

The major criticism leveled against the committee system is the fact that the committees develop a particularly limited perspective of the problem they are dealing with and the context in which the problem should be judged. This seems to be particularly true among the many committees that deal with technical data or complex paper procedures. The method in which the route for the *Pueblo* was selected is a good case in point. When the request reached Washington, the various committees that reviewed the risks for the mission failed to take into account the political and diplomatic environment into which the *Pueblo* would be sailing. Instead they focused their attention largely on the fact that the ship would be outside the twelve-mile international limit and paid no attention to the fact that the North Koreans were growing increasingly hostile toward both the South Koreans and the United States.

Another intelligence committee during the early days of the bombing of North Vietnam unnecessarily sent the crew members of a C-130 Air Force transport to their deaths because the committee was concerned with the technical aspect of an air-dropped mine. At the time the operations branch was toying with the idea of seeding mines in the waterways and estuaries of North Vietnam because intelligence had come to the conclusion that a great deal of war matériel was being trans-shipped south from Hanoi to South Vietnam via waterways. The technical committee charged with finding a way to cope with this problem got caught up in the intricacies of the Navy's concern with air-dropped mines and the Air Force's alleged capability to reconfigure five-hundred-pound bombs to serve as delayed-action mines in the many streams and rivers of North Vietnam.

The committee worked out a compromise to resolve this interservice fight to deliver the ordnance: the Air Force would deliver the Navy's mines. An air intelligence commando unit operating in South Vietnam was chosen for the mission. It was to fly a C-130 turboprop transport at night to a preselected area north of the city of Vinh. When the night for delivery arrived, the mission was dispatched, despite bad weather conditions. The crew erred in navigation and delivered the mines to the general vicinity, but failed to drop any of them into the waterways. Intercepted North Vietnamese communications indicated that the local militia forces had recovered the mines intact from dry land. A flurry of official radio traffic between Vinh and Hanoi indicated that North Vietnamese ordnance experts were quickly dispatched to the area to have a look at this latest American trick. Moreover, the North Vietnamese air defense system the next day was noted alerting the antiaircraft and missile units to the route the C-130 had flown into North Vietnam. They were told to be especially watchful for low-flying large aircraft in the future.

The failure of the first mission saw some embarrassed faces at the committee level in Washington. The Navy claimed that only they could deliver them. The Air Force rejoined that it still was their mission. To avoid a real donnybrook and the necessity of passing the problem to the Joint Chiefs of Staff for decision, the committee decided to have another go at the mission as soon as possible. Intelligence representatives from DIA objected on the grounds that another site for delivery should be selected because the North Vietnamese were fully aware of what we were up to and would be prepared to down another aircraft flying the same route. It was argued that time would not allow the replanning of another flight route, and the decision to try again against the same target was agreed to by all parties, including the DIA representative. The C-130 was dispatched two days after its original mission to the same target area. It was shot down on its first delivery approach.

Closely related to the problem of committees having a limited perspective of reality is the fact that it is difficult if not impossible to assign responsibility to any one individual or agency within the intelligence community for its failures. Each component expends tremendous amounts of energy on covering its own tracks whenever a crisis situation emerges. It is not so much the substance of what is transpiring that worries the individual agency heads as how their particular agency is going to look in the final analysis. There is so much overlapping of responsibility among the various components that in reality no one has the responsibility.

In 1968, Vice Admiral Vernon Lowrance, the deputy director of the DIA, perhaps unknowingly provided moot evidence of the prevalent attitudes at the top of the intelligence community when he was being chastised by a House subcommittee about DIA's lack of initiative during the *Pueblo* crisis. Congressman Jamie Whitten and the admiral had the following exchange:

> Whitten: The South Korean Air Force was within fifteen to twenty minutes of the *Pueblo* but nobody had thought to get the approval of the United Nations for this force to come to the rescue of the *Pueblo*. Is that a failure to properly act or is that a failure to obtain information?
>
> Lowrance: I do not think that this is in the intelligence field.
>
> Whitten: Intelligence would not know where the South Korean Air Force was?
>
> Lowrance: Certainly we would.
>
> Whitten: Intelligence would not know that an unarmed ship was loitering around in close proximity to antagonistic forces such as those of North Korea?
>
> Lowrance: Yes, sir, intelligence knew she was there.
>
> Whitten: Intelligence would not know that there might be some reason to feel that attacks might be made

when runs at this ship had been made repeatedly? Intelligence would not know that?

Lowrance: Certainly intelligence would know that.

Whitten: Intelligence would not know that if they did attack we would need somebody to come to their rescue? Intelligence would not know that?

Lowrance: Certainly intelligence would know that.

Whitten: And if the South Koreans whom we support to a great degree had an air force, you would be aware of that?

Lowrance: That is right.

Whitten: And you would be aware as to where the *Pueblo* was and the only forces close enough to come to its rescue in time would be the South Korean Air Force. You would know that?

Lowrance: Yes, sir.

Whitten: And you would know that the South Korean Air Force was within fifteen to twenty minutes of the *Pueblo* when it was captured?

Lowrance: That is right, sir.

Whitten: But intelligence would make no recommendations that anything be done to make the South Korean Air Force available, which would call for an approval by the United Nations. This would never have dawned on you?

Lowrance: That intelligence would have made this recommendation?

Whitten: Yes. What does your system call for under such circumstances?

Lowrance: The operational commanders knew this as well as anybody else, Mr. Chairman.

Whitten: Do you have statements showing that you called these various facts to the attention of operations?

Lowrance: Sir?

Whitten: Operations would be those who would get clearance from the United Nations to use these forces?

Lowrance: Yes, sir, this would not be an intelligence matter.

Whitten: Did you call these various facts to the attention of operations?

Lowrance: They had this information. They knew where the *Pueblo* was. They knew where the South Korean Air Force was. They knew where the North Korean Air Force was.

Whitten: This is an Alphonse and Gaston act . . . and let Harry do it.

In the technical sense Admiral Lowrance was correct. This was not a matter for intelligence. But the alarming aspect of this and many other such situations is that many separate units within intelligence can sit back and watch horrendous situations develop but feel no compunction to intervene. They assume someone is in charge of the matter, and so long as it is not them they are not going to interfere.

This attitude at the top has been passed down to the lowest level within intelligence. In DIA on the Vietnam desk we had an army major whose job was to monitor in detail the infiltration of North Vietnamese army regulars into South Vietnam. His specialty was the movement of troops within North Vietnam. He was to analyze and report on the positions of army units within North Vietnam. Another major was assigned the task of keeping track of these units once they left North Vietnam. During the buildup period preceding the seige of Khe Sanh in December, 1967, the major responsible for monitoring North Vietnamese army units after they left North Vietnam was on leave. One weekend the major who watched them within North Vietnam was on duty when three divisions of the North Vietnamese army deployed from their garrison areas north of the demilitarized zone into Laos and South Vietnam, surrounding the base and obviously preparing for further military action.

The major merely reported the fact that the units had moved

The major merely reported the fact that the units had moved from their garrison areas. He failed to speculate where they might be going or to point out that their movements in the north indicated they were heading for the Khe Sanh area. On Monday morning the Secretary of Defense's office and the White House Situation Room wanted an explanation of why they were not told of this development over the weekend. The major argued to his boss, a Navy commander, that his job description only required that he report on movements within North Vietnam. The commander, surprisingly, accepted this explanation and went to bat for the major with the general. Frustrated, the general was forced to reply to the Secretary of Defense that the vital facts had been reported. Here again the general was technically correct, but the importance of the vital facts was never interpreted for the Secretary of Defense or the White House. Given the swirl of facts and the volume of daily reporting on Vietnam, in particular, the importance of singling out and highlighting the interpretation of the facts has increased even more.

It has been argued that intelligence systems are, after all, works of art, and whoever heard of a great work of art created by a committee? In compromising differences of opinion on difficult questions—say, the future capabilities and intended use of Chinese nuclear weapons—it may be that the intelligence estimate will be so watered down by committees as to diminish its validity and usefulness. The size of United States intelligence organizations gives them a great capability for research in depth, but their size also imposes limitations, for subtlety of thought is not the most noteworthy trait of a large organization. Special efforts are needed to see that thoughtful, unorthodox views and individual insights are encouraged rather than stifled by the system.

The decision-making process in the intelligence community is similar to that employed by the military services. This is so largely because the military plays such a major role in intelligence, and is its chief consumer. An objective, factual study of the Joint Chiefs of Staff's decision-making process by the President's Blue Ribbon Panel revealed the basic flaws in the military system. The same flaws exist within the intelligence committee system, and the findings of the Blue Ribbon Panel apply with equal validity and weight to the intelligence community.

The Blue Ribbon Panel reported that "the JCS procedure for decision-making is ponderous and slow, but its most serious deficiency is the incentive created for unanimity, compromise, and mutual accommodation of the views of the military services. So strong are the pressures for unanimity that in 1969 the JCS were unanimous on all but eight-tenths of one percent of the issues considered. And in 1966–68 the JCS split on only two-tenths of one percent of the issues considered. This process militates against the likelihood of the JCS facing up to clearly difficult and potentially divisive issues. The repetitious committee negotiations tend to reduce issues to a level of compromise which will either avoid the potential conflicts or substitute a solution that can be accepted on a quid pro quo basis. Lost in the process is the advantage of a joint staff which, ideally, should be able to provide a more national viewpoint than staffs which are service-oriented. This is because the procedure injects the joint staffer into the process as little more than a coordinator of the views of the several services."

Vietnam serves as the most prominent arena in which unorthodox views were stifled within the intelligence community. By unorthodox is meant, in this case, any view or opinion that the United States was not winning. Within the military intelligence structure, "unorthodox" translated into any view that disputed General Westmoreland's view of the war. General Westmoreland and his air staff aides were convinced that the key to success in the air war against North Vietnam lay in the bombing of the port of Haiphong. To them this represented the classic military problem of finding a "chokepoint" where the flow of war matériel could be effectively severed. Soviet and Chinese Communist merchant ships made routine calls at the port. Many East European flag vessels also stopped there. It was the opinion of General Westmoreland's staff that these ships simply had to be carrying war matériel. The best intelligence information available disputed this contention. Reports from agents in Turkey, deck hands in Singapore, overhead photography, and COMINT all indicated that the Soviets were shipping war supplies, not via sea, but overland via China to avoid a confrontation on the open seas with the United States. The administration bought the view of the intelligence community and established restricted bombing areas around the port to lessen the possibility that a Soviet or free-world merchant ship would be attacked by mistake. The operations staff at the Pentagon chaffed under this restriction, and they never really bought the assessment of the intelligence people on the issue. They came to the Far East Division in DIA with a request for intelligence support for stepping up air attacks in and around the port of Haiphong. DIA refused to present an appraisal clearly stating that intelligence could not support the contention that war goods were coming in via Haiphong. Instead they described Haiphong as "a major point wherein war goods are transferred." It read very ambiguously, as if the goods came across the Chinese border and then somehow ended up in the port of Haiphong for further shipment south to the war zone. DIA then came up with a list of several hundred small, insignificant targets in and around Haiphong, listing them as crucial and suggesting that the cumulative effect of hitting all two hundred or more barge and ferry landings, rail spurs, bridges, and road intersections would be the same as flattening the port of Haiphong—again a triumph for the art of compromise and no doubt of great comfort to the many pilots shot down in that heavily defended area.

Another case of the stifling of unorthodox views occurred well before the Tet offensive of January, 1968, when the enemy buildup at the United States Marine Corps base at Khe Sanh became obvious. Several of us who had been studying enemy tactics and strategy for four or more years by reading all that the North Vietnamese army general staff wrote or spoke publicly and comparing it with actual battlefield developments wrote a paper that concluded the enemy was planning a feint at Khe Sanh. We outlined a likely enemy course of action designed to draw American forces to the Khe Sanh area so that the populous coastal plains would be left thinly defended. The paper concluded that it would be unwise to react to the enemy buildup at Khe Sanh. This, of course, was in direct contradiction to General Westmoreland and his staff, who at the time were saying that the enemy was pulling together for another climactic battle like Dien Bien Phu. The findings were presented to the deputy director of the DIA at a briefing at which it was suggested that our views be shared with the JCS and General Westmoreland's staff in Saigon. This recommendation was the cause for much laughter in the room, first by the general and then in cadenced order by the six colonels present. "How could you possibly know more about this situation than General Westmoreland?" we were asked. We suggested that perhaps our perspective would add to his own and at least allow him to entertain a different point of view from what his staff was feeding him every day. The paper never left DIA. The general stated that he was not in the business of contradicting field commanders, but rather was there to support the commanders in the field. As events later unfolded, the North Vietnamese never did assault the base at Khe Sanh. They drew a considerable number of American combat battalions off from the coastal plains and, instead, launched the Tet offensive which swept through the cities and towns of the coastal plain of South Vietnam.

The arena of vested interests is at best always a tawdry one. No one within the intelligence community is immune from criticism on this point. Some who have written of CIA have loudly defended it as being the one agency in Washington without an ax to grind, the one that can be counted on to present an impartial view of things. Well, however true that may be, I nevertheless have witnessed CIA officials playing the game with gusto equal to that of the most vociferous Army colonel defending a budget request. *The New York Times* pointed out that CIA was the only agency in the intelligence structure with the guts to bring to President Johnson a true picture of pacification in South Vietnam. CIA did foster and promote a National Intelligence Estimate on the subject of pacification which concluded it was doing very poorly. It is noteworthy, however, to recall that the CIA did not make this move until after the United States Army won its fight to take charge of the pacification program in South Vietnam. While CIA ran the show—from the early 1960s until late in 1967—there was not a single "things-going-poorly" estimate done on pacification. Instead all the estimates came to the same nonconclusions: on the one hand, things are not going too well; but on the other, we are doing great.

In addition, CIA successfully kept from view the abortive commando raids against North Vietnam that it began in the early 1960s. It was not until the Gulf of Tonkin incident in August–September, 1964, that any public light was shed on the maritime operations CIA had been running. Its failures far outnumber any successes it had. The staff at the Pentagon charged with overseeing paramilitary operations such as those against North Vietnam was purposely kept in the dark about CIA's commando ventures against North Vietnam until after the Gulf of Tonkin flareup.

Another incident in which CIA opted to protect its own vested interest occurred in a Washington conference room in early 1967, when Stokely Carmichael, the militant black leader, was en route to North Vietnam. A clandestine services officer related to me that a meeting was called by the FBI to discuss the possibility of contriving a situation in which Carmichael could be publicly discredited. They wanted to stage such an operation while Carmichael was in Hong Kong. CIA squelched the venture—not on the grounds that you might expect, but rather because the incident might endanger some of their ongoing operations in Hong Kong, a city in which CIA is constantly at war not only with the forces of Communism but more directly with the British intelligence service.

Tales of military self-interest are numerous. Often the military's primary concern in intelligence is to bend the intelligence to support military budget requests. The public record is filled with many such tales. During the Vietnam War, another facet of military self-interest has blossomed. The intelligence reports and assessments issued in Washington have become, in effect, report cards for the services. And the lengths to which all of the services go to look good are what one might expect from schoolchildren.

During the early days of the bombing of North Vietnam, for example, the Army, which was pushing for a large buildup of American ground forces, wanted to show that North Vietnamese forces were pouring into South Vietnam at unprecedented rates. At the same time the Air Force wanted to prove that its bombing campaign against the North was an unqualified success. The resolution of this basic contradictory situation was left up to a committee in Washington composed of DIA intelligence officers and representatives from the intelligence staffs of each of the services. They were to go over all the reports and come up with an agreed-upon monthly assessment of progress. Manned about equally with Army and Air Force officers, DIA never really admitted that a conflict existed. Each month a standard phrase was added to the report to please both the Army and the Air Force. It read: "Enemy infiltration continued at a rate higher than last month; however, the cumulative effect of United States bombing has seriously degraded his ability to mount a large-scale offensive." It didn't really matter that there was no evidence that the enemy was considering a large-scale offensive.

Another fight between the Air Force and the Navy occurred when the North Vietnamese sprouted an air force of their own with Soviet MIGs. The division of labor between raiding Air Force and Navy units had been devised so that the Navy, which operated from carriers in the Gulf of Tonkin, attacked targets along the coast and inland to the Hanoi area. The Air Force, which flew its missions largely from Thailand, was responsible for targets further inland and west of Hanoi. Approximately three months after the North Vietnamese MIG force came into being, the Air Force was quite upset because the Navy was bagging considerably more MIGs than they were. The reason, of course, was that the MIG defenses were deployed at airfields near the major cities of Hanoi and Haiphong, where they put up stiff resistance. The Air Force, on the other hand, met little MIG resistance as its planes flew in from Thailand. This situation was finally resolved by redrawing boundary lines from Navy and Air Force operations so that the Air Force could attack targets near Hanoi. The situation then became quite competitive. An intelligence committee in Washington was charged with keeping the official score on MIG kills. It was composed of men from DIA and each of the service staffs. They would daily review the operational and intelligence reports from the field units and tally up the MIGs downed as well as record the American losses. It soon became evident that the North Vietnamese had a fairly proficient crew of pilots. Their kill rate of American airplanes was impressive. The services then began another competition to see who lost the most planes to MIGs. Of course the service with the lowest score looked best in this competition. This made the work of the committee next to impossible. Since the daily bombing runs against the North ran into conventional antiaircraft fire, SA-2 surface-to-air missiles, and MIGs, it sometimes was difficult to tell exactly which defense system had downed a United States jet. The committee meetings became regular cat-and-dog fights, with the Navy representative insisting that a Navy plane was downed by a missile rather than a MIG—missiles being deemed the more respectable manner of being zapped. The Air Force representative would disagree, insisting that his evidence showed that the Navy jet was downed by a MIG. Once he had established his case, the Air Force officer was put on the hot seat, for he had to defend the loss of Air Force planes, and he found himself being fought every inch of the way by the Navy officer. What finally evolved was a trade-off system, wherein the Air Force and Navy men would agree before the meeting just what percentage they'd allow each other for official record-keeping purposes.

Perhaps the greatest flaw in the committee approach to thorny problems is that the committees are manned by men of varying expertise. CIA has the upper hand in Washington and thus dominates many of the interagency committees. This is not because its men are any smarter but because CIA tours of duty are stable. CIA men rarely transfer out of town; thus they become skilled in conference techniques and outgun their service or State Department counterparts. One deficiency in the CIA system which usually goes unnoticed by the men at State and Defense is that CIA's intelligence production people normally use the committee assignments as a convenient dumping ground for their less competent officers. Pushed aside to a committee, these men can do little harm to the agency and are kept very busy processing the reams of paper that all such committees generate.

When the Paris peace talks opened in May, 1968, it was deemed advisable to form an interagency committee to review the day-to-day battlefield and diplomatic developments to support the peace mission in Paris. Expectations were running high at that time, so the JCS picked men with the hardest noses possible for assignment to the committee. They faked DIA out by ensuring that their representatives outranked the DIA and service intelligence staffs by at least one grade. The natural result within the Pentagon was the predominance of the JCS view—which at the time was, "We don't want to give those bastards an inch." This war isn't over yet, the JCS believed, and they simply wanted to go on fighting, pretending that the peace talks didn't exist. Each time the North Vietnamese tried to manipulate battlefield events to suit their diplomatic needs at the conference table, the JCS representatives screamed and prevailed with the opinion that the current lull in groundfighting had no diplomatic significance whatsoever. Rather, they insisted that it was further evidence that the North Vietnamese and Vietcong were on the ropes because of the aggressive United States ground actions. This kind of thinking suited the preconceived notions of men like Walt Rostow, President Johnson's National Security adviser, and it had a direct influence on the instructions sent to Paris from the White House. At least three major episodes such as this occurred between May and September, 1968, and three chances for an earlier settlement of the war were lost.

DIA sensed early that the Paris peace talks committee within the Pentagon could be an arena in which a lot of friction could develop between themselves and the Joint Chiefs of Staff. They chose men who they knew would play ball with the JCS staff. In our shop an Army colonel was picked to present the intelligence evidence gleaned from sources aimed at North Vietnam. The man had just arrived at DIA from a seven-year tour of duty with the infantry in Western Europe. I was asked to give him a rundown of what went on in our shop so that he'd be familiar with the business. One of the first questions he asked was, "Where the hell is Vietnam anyway? I don't know shit about that part of the world. Closest I ever came was Japan when I went there TDY in 1952." Needless to say this man never once raised a dissenting voice at the committee meetings on the peace talks.

One of the more outlandish cases of a committee in action concerned the problem of the strength of the Vietnamese Communist forces in South Vietnam—a controversy which raged for five years in the intelligence community.

It could be brushed aside as simply another bureaucratic battle except for the harsh reality that it had a direct influence on American military strategy and, ultimately, on the number of American lives lost in Vietnam. Had the problem been handled intelligently, about twenty thousand American lives could have been spared.

In early 1964, when enemy forces were an estimated 35,000

strong, the issue was an academic one delved into lazily by a few American specialists in Saigon and a few in Washington. Traditional United States Army bookkeeping methods were employed, and no one was concerned that enemy losses, for example, were not being considered. Once an enemy battalion was identified from PW interrogations, it was simply "carried" as a full-strength unit of 500 riflemen, despite the fact that it had tangled with South Vietnamese units and sustained losses. The truth of the matter was that it was too much trouble to do otherwise, that the "traditional way" didn't allow room for it, and frankly, that the United States government wasn't all that interested.

Things changed drastically in late 1964, when enemy troop strength reached an estimated 61,000 and the United States was weighing the pros and cons of getting involved in the ground combat. A crucial, irreparable compromise took place in December of that year, when the Defense Intelligence Agency acceded to the request of the military command in Saigon to take responsibility for the problem—an unusual request, contrary to past practice, which had proved that a unit in the field is quite likely to "tailor" enemy strength estimates to considerations such as proving the success of United States ground operations or the desire to build up overall United States military strength. From 1964 to 1970 the DIA kept less than a dozen men working on the problem, and MACV geared up an operation ultimately employing 1700 people backed up with computers. Needless to say, DIA simply became a transmission belt for the Saigon view, rather than an active, supervisory participant in the process of informing the President of the enemy's strength and capabilities as their charter requires. But it was reasoned that this was a strange war requiring strange approaches.

Several incidents will illuminate the effect of this compromise, which was "hammered out" by a committee in the Pentagon in late 1964.

The Washington intelligence community during 1965

formed a committee to review enemy strength monthly to keep abreast of developments. The committee immediately found that MACV was the only source of information. To compensate for this, the committee avoided the hard decision of having Washington reassume responsibility for the matter and, instead, devised a series of requirements for detailed studies on enemy unit histories, recruitment practices, training, and logistics. General Westmoreland's intelligence staff officer, a Marine Corps general with no great fondness for the Army, agreed and turned his men to the task of supplying Washington with studies and the raw evidence on which they were based.

The estimated troop strength by this time was 221,000, an alarming increase of 160,000 in less than a year and a figure on which the boosting of United States troop strength from 23,000 to 180,000 was predicated. When the studies and evidence arrived and were reviewed, glaring errors—double counting, use of code names to represent three or four battalions for the same unit, and reading the 48th battalion, erroneously listed as the 84th, as two—allowed CIA to conclude that troop strength was perhaps 120,000 and not 221,000.

During the ensuing paper and cable melee the Marine Corps general at MACV was replaced with an Army general. Soon thereafter requests for studies by Washington were answered with cables stating: "Current requirements in support of United States ground units exceed staff capabilities. Your request, however, will be given high consideration." Of course Washington requests were not given high—or any—consideration thereafter. The studies abruptly ceased flowing from Saigon.

By 1967 MACV estimated the enemy to number about 282,000 men. DIA agreed with this figure. CIA, by this time, on the basis of independent studies of documents they purloined from the military in Saigon (an interesting war within a war which saw CIA staffers in Vietnam writing "contact reports" every time they had a beer with a GI), believed the enemy was recruiting far more men from South Vietnamese villages than the United States military did (the reason being that the United

States military now was in charge of pacification). CIA estimated their strength at about 360,000.

During 1967 the breach widened. MACV developed the "crossover point" idea—a computerized rendering of "kill ratio," "body count," "recruitment trends," demographic "facts" about North Vietnam, "captured enemy weapons," and, of all things, a computer-derived "profile" of the combat effectiveness of an American and a Communist GI. Together, these items projected a point in the future (which was defined to be November, 1967) at which the enemy would "cross over" an imaginary divide and begin the slide downward to virtual statistical extinction. On the basis of these computations in early 1967, there began the endless string of "light at the end of the tunnel" utterings, climaxed with Westmoreland's November, 1967, "Victory is right around the corner" speech. By that time MACV "proved" their thesis with estimates which pegged enemy strength at 260,000—an overall reduction of 22,000 in 1967. CIA estimated, on the other hand, that the enemy then numbered close to 500,000 men—a difference which was handled in the community's graphics and color slides with lengthy "explanatory footnotes" showing the "divergent methodologies" and implying that, despite the great difference, this was an esoteric intelligence problem which shouldn't affect the war effort or policy decisions. Key policy makers understandably shrank from probing too deeply into the problem because of its complexity and seeming insolubility. Hawks looked to MACV for comfort, doves to CIA, and decisions were made by horse trading or by taking an average of the two figures. When President Johnson called for a national intelligence estimate in the summer of 1967, the community fought for four months and finally issued one which said enemy troop strength numbered from 200,000 to 300,000. A two-page footnote explained body count, kill ratio, recruitment, and political infrastructure and stated that by following one line of reasoning you could take the figures as high as a half-million, but by following another you could take them as low as 180,000. Nobody seemed upset.

In the meantime the war ground on. The enemy, unaware that they had broached the crossover point, swarmed into cities along the coastal plain of Vietnam during the 1968 Lunar New Year holiday while General Westmoreland had his troops deployed in the sparsely populated highlands area and at the DMZ, where he fully expected a head-on final clash at Khe Sanh. His war-of-attrition strategy—based entirely on his intelligence staff's estimate of troop strength—ordained that by finding, fixing, and fighting the enemy in the unpopulated rugged mountain terrain (where 30,000 American lives were lost) he could force them out of the country and win the war. (An interesting sidenote to this strategy is that it was the major reason the North Vietnamese set up base camps in Cambodia.) Had the strength estimates been more realistic and objective, perhaps both he and the Washington policy makers would have realized in late 1966 that more could have been achieved with less fighting and with about 20,000 fewer American deaths by concentrating on the defense of the populous coastal areas of South Vietnam, where the style of fighting depended mostly on enemy logistic capabilities and where the fighting would have been preponderantly small-unit rather than large-scale divisional clashes.

During this five-year period the performance of top intelligence officials can only be described as childish. If, for example, DIA got wind of the fact that CIA was sending a team of analysts to Saigon to look at new evidence, the general who was the director at the time felt compelled to cable ahead to Saigon to inform them that CIA was on the way. If CIA men came over to DIA to discuss the problem, DIA men were instructed by the director and his deputies to take their charts off the wall, hide studies they were working on, and not to share any information with CIA. The same happened when DIA men went to CIA, where GS-17s and GS-18s, civilian equivalents to generals, issued similar orders.

There is a National Security Council directive that outlines a reasonable division of effort among the various agencies involved in intelligence. The State Department is charged with handling all economic and political intelligence concerning the free world. The CIA is to handle political and economic intelligence dealing with the Communist world. The Defense Intelligence Agency is charged with keeping abreast of worldwide military intelligence matters. The other components of the community, such as the Atomic Energy Commission, the FBI, and the National Security Agency, are to handle their specialized areas.

In implementation, however, the directive is subject to the whimsy of each particular agency head, and, in different periods since 1947, it has been adhered to with varying degrees of candor and honesty. The general trend, however, has been away from the central idea of a rational division of labor. Each agency has developed specialized offshoots which have mushroomed and grown over the years. The natural result has been the blurring of the lines of responsibility within the community. The intelligence pie today is not being shared. Each agency within intelligence has a portion of each slice, rationalizing its involvement with only partially valid arguments.

This process began early in the life of the intelligence community. Lyman Kirkpatrick points out in *The Real CIA* that as soon as President Truman established the Central Intelligence Group in 1946 the duplication of effort got started. "When the OSS had been disbanded in 1945," he wrote, "its large research and analysis branch had been transferred intact to the Department of State to form the nucleus of its office of intelligence research. When Truman established the Central Intelligence Group in 1946 the principle concept was that it would pull together all the research done by the other agencies—State, Army, Navy, and so forth. And it would prepare only the final distillation needed for the policymakers. It would do this with a small cadre of career civilians plus a number of personnel assigned to the CIG by the other agencies. This concept lasted but a short time. General Hoyt Vandenberg, who succeeded Admiral Sidney Souers, who had been the original director of the CIG, and the men he brought with him had different ideas on how the job should be done. When he reviewed the plans for the research side of the CIG, he threw out the modest proposals for an office of about eighty and told the drafters to come back with a table of organization of about eight hundred. He wanted the CIG to be able to research in depth, thereby acting as supreme authority in intelligence. Thus the facetious remark that went about the halls of the research side of the CIA not long after it had graduated from CIG was 'Bigger than State by 48.' "

A look at the organization charts of CIA, DIA, or other members of the intelligence community today will not reveal the extent of the duplication of effort to the casual observer, for it is masked behind a semantic swirl. CIA, for example, boasts of an Office of Strategic Research within its production side. The agency would have you believe that this organization fulfills a peculiarly unique role within intelligence. Its primary subject is military intelligence, contrary of course to the NSC directive on who does what. Glib spokesmen sidestep this by remarking that the Office of Strategic Research with its several hundred analysts takes only a strategic view of military intelligence matters. It came into being, they would have you believe, because the Defense Department was too involved in the day-to-day nitty-gritty of military intelligence to provide the community with the kind of strategic thinking that was required. I worked in both elements within CIA and DIA that deal with military intelligence and can state that this line of reasoning is bureaucratic poppycock. The several hundred men and women at CIA watching military intelligence matters do exactly the same thing that the several hundred analysts at DIA do. They follow the day-to-day nitty-gritty with the same enthusiasm. Their strategic thinking goes no further than DIA's. They provide no special insights that the military cannot. The real reason the Office of Strategic Research was formed (not necessarily invalid) was that the biased reporting by the military intelligence elements had reached such a point that CIA simply did not trust their uniformed brethren to deal honestly with the subject. CIA feels compelled to keep DIA honest, and, of course, the only way to do that is to establish a shop that does the same thing and compare the quality of the results. This same attitude permeates the community. The National Security Agency, for example, is not by its charter to produce finished intelligence studies. It is simply a transmission belt, providing translations of esoteric material to the other members of the community for their analysis. In 1966, however, NSA felt compelled to begin issuing a series of daily, weekly, and monthly intelligence reports which carried the agency into the field of producing finished intelligence—which takes raw data, presents it in a reasoned analytical way, and draws conclusions from it. NSA argued at the time that it was doing this simply to provide policy makers with a thumbnail analytical sketch of what was happening in the field of electronic snooping in Vietnam. This argument did not limit the agency to issuing reports solely on Vietnam. Within a few months NSA had expanded its operation into daily, weekly, and monthly publications on Eastern Europe, the Soviet Union, Communist China, and the free world. They continue today.

No field of intelligence is left out. DIA has on the order of five hundred analysts working on economic matters such as international trade, transportation and communications, agriculture, demography, and industrial development on a worldwide basis. CIA and NSA both have at least an equal number working on exactly the same subjects. The arcane art of photo-intelligence made prominent by the U-2 affair has burgeoned into a full-fledged subculture in intelligence. Every component of the community has its phalanx of "PIs" (photo interpreters) working diligently to catch something the other agencies missed. The subject of interpreting political and diplomatic events, left by charter to State and CIA, is approached with vigor by DIA and the individual service intelligence staffs as well as by NSA. Perhaps the greatest amount of duplication occurs within the "S & T" (Science and Technology) elements of the community. The individual service staffs maintain Washington S & T shops and are supported by massive S & T analysis at the various arsenals and labs each maintains. DIA and CIA both have major sub-elements involved deeply in S & T. NSA expends perhaps one-fifth of its efforts on this complex field. And, as above, there are only very minor differences in what each of these elements studies and reports upon.

The result of the duplication of effort is a continuing form of professional incest wherein intelligence officers at CIA do a study only to have it torn apart and rebutted by intelligence officers at DIA, NSA, and State. They then form a joint inter-agency committee and hammer out their differences. For the plebe in intelligence it is great fun and even somewhat challenging. Until he wises up he has a feeling that he is participating in national policy making. For one no longer enthralled with bureaucratic infighting it seems to be a somewhat sterile exercise, sort of like kissing your sister or listening to two GIs trying to outdo each other with stories of their alleged sexual prowess on their last three-day pass.

For the country as a whole it is productive only in the broadest sense, if you assume that the men at CIA and the other agencies are motivated by a desire to serve the nation's interests and are not simply trying to enhance their own bureaucratic standing.

The official "explanation" for the duplication of effort was provided for the record by Lieutenant General Joseph Carroll, the former director of DIA, during House Appropriations Committee hearings. He said, "As far as duplication is concerned I am sure there is some at the various levels because of the magnitude of the problem. We also must bear in mind that it would be exceedingly dangerous to isolate each major problem to the point where it would be considered and addressed by only one activity. There is strength and enlightenment in having cross consideration, cross checks and balances, dual approaches, as long as they are being coordinated, interrelated. The United States Intelligence Board devotes a great deal of effort to keep abreast of duplication."

This rationale seems rather reasonable. The general is correct in stating that it would not be good to have only one element of the community working a problem as complex as, say, the Soviet ABM threat. But a line has to be drawn. Some official in a responsible position must admit that the duplication has gone too far and take steps to eliminate it, rather than simply clinging to the old explanations and avoiding the reality. The President's Blue Ribbon Panel investigating the Pentagon looked into the military intelligence structure and was surprised to find how many people were involved. The Defense Intelligence Agency was formed in 1961 to eliminate the duplication of effort then going on among the Army, Navy, Marine Corps, and Air Force staffs. The idea in 1961 was to retain only a very small intelligence staff in each service and to concentrate intelligence resources within the DIA. It didn't work out that way. The Blue Ribbon Panel reported that today the four armed services intelligence staffs are considerably larger than they were before DIA was formed. Oh, they went through the cutting-back-of-personnel drill back in 1961. But since then they have slowly crept back up and even exceeded their original staff size. Additionally the Blue Ribbon report indicated that the intelligence budgets for each of the three services had increased manyfold since DIA was organized.

Part of the reason for the duplication of effort that exists outside of the Washington area stems from the military's penchant for keeping itself informed. DIA puts out a daily intelligence bulletin to all of the military commands around the world, which should satisfy the needs of the military commanders abroad. It doesn't. At each of the eight major military commands around the world there is an intelligence staff numbering on the order of 2500 to 3000 men. They receive DIA's

daily bulletin and rewrite it for distribution to their subordinates. Most commanders, too, are very skeptical of relying on
Washington, and DIA in particular, for longer-range intelligence support. So they build their own capability to do such
studies. The intelligence staff at Pacific Headquarters in
Honolulu grew to enormous size during the Vietnam War. At
one point they had more people working on the problems of
Asia than DIA had on its entire staff. After the *Pueblo* incident
in early 1968 DIA was prodded into taking a hard look at the
intelligence staffs in the Pacific area. General Carroll testified
that "the final report concluded that a great deal of duplication
was going on. We ended up eliminating several intelligence
products. This amounted to saving over 44,000 man hours." So,
once again, a crisis-prompted investigation revealed inefficiencies. The regrettable aspect of these is that their effect is only
temporary. By 1969, when I left DIA, the service staffs at
Pacific Headquarters were all back producing the same extraneous reports as they had been before the investigation. The obvious moral of the story is that you can't kill or even impede a
burgeoning bureaucracy with ad hoc special studies.

The frustration of dealing with this problem is that it never
goes away. In 1968 the House investigation of military intelligence concluded that "the evidence disclosed the need for reorganization of intelligence activities in the Defense Department as a whole. The committee is convinced that certain
intelligence operations are overstaffed, duplicative activities are
being carried out, and there is a general inadequacy of management. There appeared to be far too many separate operating
units or intelligence organizations, too many layers of authority, and too much time, personnel, and money being spent on
accumulating a wide variety of information of no immediate
and of doubtful future value."

One year later the House took another look at intelligence.
Its report stated, "The committee noted that the military services are performing functions which were specifically delegated to the DIA and also that the DIA is performing opera-

tions which in some instances could be better undertaken by the services. Sound guidelines should be established for collection and dissemination of intelligence operations and a realignment of operations is clearly needed."

Still, the next year the President's Blue Ribbon Panel concluded, "Duplication results in continued adversary relations between the intelligence departments which although usually confined to the internal paper wars that constitute the community's decisionmaking process severely inhibits the achievement of economy and efficiency required for adequate intelligence within available resources."

No aspect of intelligence is immune from the duplication of effort. Within the Pentagon, mapping and charting activities are done under the auspices of intelligence. Each of the three services has a component responsible for producing the kind of maps it needs. DIA is responsible for supervising the activities of the three services and ensuring that they do not duplicate one another's efforts. The Blue Ribbon Panel pointed out, however, that DIA is in an impossible situation. Only the Air Force maintains its mapping and charting activities under its intelligence staff. The Army and Navy run separate activities outside their intelligence organizations. The result is that DIA, forbidden access by the Army and Navy, has no way to find out what the Army and Navy are doing in the mapping business. Yet, DIA each year must approve their budgets. And the duplication in this business is appalling. The Air Force is interested only in airfields around the world. They'll spend millions flying overhead recon missions over Latin America to produce detailed maps only of the air facilities on that continent. The Navy meanwhile is interested in port facilities, coasts, and landing beaches; it mounts recon missions to photograph the Latin American seaports and coastlines. The Army comes along, and it is interested in everything. It needs to know about the roads, railways, cities, mountain terrain—you name it—dealing with Latin America. It mounts the same kinds of recon missions to gather the information it needs. These separate efforts are not coordinated. DIA can only tell the Air Force what areas to cover. It has no access to the Navy and Army mapping staffs to direct or supervise their collection efforts.

This problem goes one step further. Since the introduction of the U-2 and satellites the CIA has become enamored of the idea of making maps of the world. At the National Photographic Interpretation Center they began the ambitious project in 1961 of remapping the entire world in detail, down to within three or four feet. This project has been going on for over a decade, yet the material will not be shared with the service intelligence staffs until the project is totally completed. It was almost with tongue in cheek that the Blue Ribbon report concluded that "mapping and charting for the United States government should be under the direction and control of one agency."

An even murkier area of intelligence duplication of effort exists in the field of external contracting. This became quite faddish in the early 1960s, when the think tanks gained enormous respectability. The Air Force had its RAND Corporation, and the Army had its RAC (Research Analysis Corporation). Intelligence officials felt compelled to get into the act. CIA went to MIT and Harvard, DIA went to Georgetown and American University, as did the State Department. It became fashionable to have these outside groups produce compendiums of all thorny intelligence problems—particularly those with a social science flavor. Vacuous studies applying mathematical methods to the field of socal science were produced almost in reams. One I read, done for the Army intelligence staff, involved the computation of a mathematical formula showing that the Vietcong attacked most often when the moon was not shining. I have no idea how much the study cost, but it had a three-page summary explaining this most obvious conclusion, which was followed by over forty pages of charts and graphs in support of the mathematical methodology. Another more ambitious project done for DIA by a Washington-based social science research firm attempted to take all of the indicators of insurgency (whatever they are) and devise a worldwide "model" for insurgency. The hoped-for result was a study that would boil down the ethnic, religious, social, and political undercurrents of the world to a point where a program could be fed into a computer and compared with the world's daily events in an effort to show the Pentagon where the next brush-fire war was going to take place. And, if it was able to do that, the expectation was that the computer would "play out the scenario" and tell in advance who was going to win. Pretty neat, huh? We could just sit back in air-conditioned comfort and find out if we should get involved ahead of time. If we were going to lose, then there was no sense getting in the fracas.

One of the annoying facets of intelligence's romance with the social science think tanks was that their analysts used to bother the hell out of us while we were trying to do a day's work. I was delegated on numerous occasions to attend meetings with RAND, RAC, and other think tank analysts to "work out an acceptable methodology" for a particular contract they had. The actual name of the game was that the think tank analysts wanted to pick our brains and have us do most of their spadework for them. At the first couple of meetings I attended I enjoyed myself immensely. The think-tankers provided me with a platform to expound all of my theories and give them supporting detail from my files. They even encouraged me to let them look at unpublished studies I had done. It wasn't until after a few of these sessions that I realized I was being quietly raped. This guy with a Ph.D. sitting across from me didn't know his ass from first base about the problem. Yet he was being paid anywhere from $25,000 to $30,000 a year to produce his contract study, and I was doing it for him.

The House Appropriations Committee finally caught on to the exploitation of intelligence underway by more than a dozen firms in Washington. They looked into it and concluded that no one at the top of the intelligence structure knew how extensive the rape really was. "In our cursory investigation," they said, "we find that the Air Force has three contracts to get the same thing." Congressman Jamie Whitten also pointed out that DIA had a budget request in for forty additional people, additional computers, and additional contract money to carry on the exact same project that the Air Force was paying for three times. Congressman Whitten also discovered that "much of the information in a contract report just completed was just put together and taken out of earlier reports which were done by the intelligence community. . . . It was simply rehashed and turned over to DIA."

These two major problems, duplication and the reliance on committees, are merely symptoms of the disease, indicating that the basic flaw in the entire intelligence structure is an organizational one. So long as the community is structured along departmental lines these problems will persist. The built-in bias of dealing with intelligence by the agencies also concerned with military or diplomatic appropriations ensures that the problems will go on indefinitely. The obvious answer to this bureaucratic mess is a reorganization of the community along realistic, functional lines. Given the proclivity of bureaucracies to perpetuate themselves, however, this is no easy task. It would require bold, decisive action by the Chief Executive.

VII

Intelligence to Please

Within the intelligence community the Defense Intelligence Agency is known as the "taxi squad," the "country club," or the "old folks' home." The intelligence dispensed by DIA is all too often of a quality that makes it more of a hindrance than a help to rational decision making.

DIA today sets the tone for the intelligence gathered and reported upon by the four armed services. By charter they represent the service intelligence viewpoints on the Joint Staff, where intelligence is blended with policy and military operations. Their track record is at best spotty.

The military staff system is composed of six elements: J-1 is personnel; J-2 is intelligence; J-3 is operations; J-4 is logistics; J-5 is plans and policy; and J-6 is electronics and communications. Whenever a military operation is under consideration all of these elements contribute to the decision by bringing their particular expertise to bear. In concept, all of the staff elements are equal and the decisions they reach are balanced ones, with due consideration given to each of the six staff elements. The system does not work that way. J-3 is king. All career servicemen aspire to this role, the command of a combat unit. All of the staffs bow in deference. At DIA the common expression among the working troops is "DIA exists solely to provide justification for whatever J-3 wants to do." During the crucial years of the Vietnam War, from 1966 to 1969, the major strategic military decisions on how the war was to be fought came out of the Pentagon's Joint Staff, where DIA serves in the function of J-2. The J-3 staff never consulted with intelligence about the effect of United States strategy from the enemy viewpoint. Since DIA was studying the enemy and his style of fighting, J-3 could have benefited by asking intelligence what they thought might be the best way to thwart the enemy's plans and the impact of the plans on U.S. operations.

During that period the United States military commanders in the field and the planners on the J-3 staff in the Pentagon became increasingly frustrated with their conventional attempts at beating the Vietcong forces. In desperation they turned more and more to gadgetry to fill the vacuum and soothe their anxiety. Each of the services proposed the use of a variety of technical goodies in the hopes that one would turn the tide. The Air Force was growing increasingly bitter over the monthly bombing assessment reports, which showed that the flow of men and matériel south was continuing. As the air campaign crept northward in 1966, the J-3 staff wanted bigger and better targets. They didn't ask the intelligence people what was worth hitting or what a rational plan of attack might be, they demanded targets that a certain weapons system could attack. They had a TV-guided missile, and wanted to use it. "Pick out a building for us to hit," they said to intelligence. DIA did not tell J-3 that this was the wrong approach. They sent photo interpreters scurrying to their film scanners to find two- or three-story buildings in the areas open to American air

raids. If they saw no signs of military activity around the building they would dub it a "possible military storage area," a
description ambiguous enough to give J-3 the right to go hunting with their TV system.

The raid on the Son Tay prisoner of war camp in North
Vietnam was planned in this same reverse manner. J-3 decided
that they wanted to pull off a coup and snatch some American
prisoners from North Vietnam. When DIA informed them that
they had only a limited and rather old body of evidence on this
subject, they would not back down. J-3 insisted on a target. So
DIA gave them a list. As the planning neared its final stages and
the Secretary of Defense and the President had approved the
idea, DIA was asked to provide an up-to-date assessment of the
Son Tay facility. The only evidence they had was overhead
photography, so they took a look at their recent pictures and
said that it looked like there was activity at the location. They
could not, of course, see any people in the pictures, but they
could see that the grass had been cut and that there were other
signs of life, such as clothes hanging out to dry. They did not
remind J-3 that the only evidence they had which suggested
that this place was possibly being used as a POW camp came
from a captured North Vietnamese soldier who had once
trained in the area before his unit was dispatched to Cambodia.
The last time the soldier had been in the vicinity of Son Tay was
three years prior to the raid. He had heard rumors in his unit
that American pilots were being held in the building with a wall
around it. He had never been inside the building, nor had he
ever personally seen an American prisoner there.

A similar problem occurred in early 1966. The Air Force was
most anxious to destroy the fighting capability of the regular
North Vietnamese Army while it was still in North Vietnam.
They devised a bombing campaign to knock out the divisional
headquarters of the regular army in their home garrisons. Intelligence had a rather complete listing of all of the headquarters
locations—at least they were the headquarters locations before
the bombing campaign started. Once the campaign started in

1965, however, the North Vietnamese Army abandoned all of its identifiable garrison areas and military camps and took to the hills and caves to establish headquarters. This was thoroughly documented in their radio communications and in their own press. The units were praised for following the example of the Vietminh units of the French war by returning to the same limestone caves that the Vietminh had once occupied.

These facts did not deter the J-3 staff when the Air Force reported to it that they had found a division headquarters in recent photos. In one picture they spotted a huge, heavily guarded compound at a village called Quynh Loc. The compound was isolated and ringed with barbed wire, and it included a number of buildings. Inside the compound were areas shut off from each other with more barbed wire. The J-3 and the Air Force concluded that this had to be a division headquarters. The analysts at DIA working on the deployment of the North Vietnamese Army said that they had no information to support the existence of a division headquarters at that location. This did not satisfy J-3, and they insisted that DIA label the facility a possible military headquarters site. DIA acceded to this demand. On May 6, 1966, a heavy bombing raid was mounted against the facility. A few days later the North Vietnamese charged that the United States had bombed a leper colony at Quynh Loc, killing thirty patients and wounding thirty-four. They published photographs of the facility before and after the raid. DIA examined the photos and compared them with those on which they had based the mission. They proved to be the "possible military headquarters site." No public mention was ever made of the incident.

While a considerable amount has been written about the Pentagon and its shortcomings, I have yet to see the work environment there adequately described. The Pentagon is in a constant frenzy of activity. Every project is done on a crash basis. The answers to tough problems are wanted "yesterday," not today, not after adequate study has been done, but instantly. In part, this has come about because in many areas of

Pentagon decision making the computer stands ready to support the generals by providing instant inventories of forces,
equipment, and buying schedules. In the less tangible areas
such as military plans, intelligence, and defense policy, no such
computer exists.

The Pentagon lives largely in the present tense. One crisis
seems to follow another. An unfavorable newspaper report of
a combat unit refusing to enter a fight will see general officers
demanding to know the instant history of incidents like them.
They'll require a staff paper on ways to correct the problem
with recommendations from all of the services. I'm not demean-
ing their desires to correct the problem, only their approach to
solving it. Normally the generals will lay on a requirement and
say they want the results the next morning. This, of course,
requires that about twenty-five people concerned with the issue
will gather for a quick planning conference and then run off to
their separate offices to put together their part of the report.
Then they will all gather again on the subject, usually about
5:00 P.M. The fun begins. The meeting usually degenerates into
a contest between the different parties to show who did the best
homework. About half a dozen people involved in the study will
spend the night sitting around a conference table trying to put
together a study acceptable for all. Army cots come out of
closets, and at different intervals men will lie down for an hour
or so before returning to the fracas. In the morning they normally come up with a finished report that frequently borders on
the incoherent. Decisions are made on such reports.

The "dog and pony" show is also an integral part of Pentagon
life. It is a common belief in the service that once a man makes
general he loses the ability to read. Everything must be presented to him in a briefing. In DIA the staff had the responsibility for briefing the Joint Staff every morning. This necessitated
having one analyst come into work at 5:00 A.M. to write the first
draft of the briefing on overnight developments. At 6:00 A.M.
he had to give the first "dry run" of the briefing to the colonel
who headed up his branch. If the colonel had no objections (and

he usually did), the man had to present the briefing to the division chief (another colonel) at 6:30 A.M. At 6:45 this drill was repeated for the one-star general who was DIA's assistant to the Deputy for Intelligence Production. If he signed off on the briefing, it then went to the "professional barkers" who serve as DIA's talking dogs. These men, all military officers, were selected simply on the basis of their good looks and ability to speak clearly. At 7:00 they presented the briefing to DIA's two-star general in charge of intelligence production. This was done in a fancy walnut-paneled war room that DIA maintains for such events on the first floor of the Pentagon. Panels slide back from the walls, and a slide projection glass screen appears. The "oh-seven-hundred" briefing ranks as high on style presentation as Walter Cronkite's evening show. Color slides, filmstrips, and map projections dance in front of the audience as the talking dog drones on, uncomprehending of what he is presenting. If the general has a question, the talking dog is unable to answer. This 0700 briefing is a must for all analysts, just in case the general has a question. As analysts we spent most mornings scrambling for documentation, explaining an esoteric point, or convincing the general our view wasn't heresy. At these briefings, no unorthodox view was permitted.

At 0730 the briefing officers, the two-star general, and the talking dog march upstairs to the Joint Staff conference room to present their report to the assembled three-star generals along with the talking dogs from J-1, J-3, J-4, J-5, and J-6. Inevitably a question will come up, and, after the briefing, the staff at DIA is sent scurrying to put together an answer for the three-star generals. This entire exercise is repeated at the end of each work day with a "sixteen-hundred" (4:00 PM) briefing. Again there is usually a fallout question or two that must be answered by the next morning, requiring three of four analysts to stay into the late evening hours to provide the answer. Along with this stress atmosphere there is a dictum in the Pentagon that if you don't work on Saturdays you simply are not important. The result? Nearly everybody works on Saturdays. A more relaxed atmosphere prevails, and those who must work are allowed to wear sport shirts and chinos if they desire.

The Defense Intelligence Agency was formed to cut out the competition among the services. The President's Blue Ribbon Panel, which investigated the Pentagon in 1970, concluded that DIA has fallen far short of its intended goal. The Panel stated that "each staff department is still engaged in activities clearly assigned to DIA." The military intelligence staffs justify these activities on the basis that DIA does not have the capability to provide the intelligence needed. The Blue Ribbon Panel pointed out that "it is paradoxical that DIA cannot develop the ability to perform its functions while the military intelligence staffs which supply the manpower to DIA can maintain this capability." This is because the services retain their best talent for duty on their own staffs, sending their least competent to DIA.

A related problem with military intelligence is the fact that intelligence officers in the services are all too often the poor cousins of the other branches, particularly operations. An intelligence assignment has often been viewed as not assisting an officer to advance his career, and there is little incentive for one to make his career in intelligence. The road to high rank is clearly in command and operations. The Army has alleviated this situation to some degree by creating a career intelligence branch. The Navy, Air Force and Marine Corps, however, have not, and the typical intelligence officers in these three services are men who quite obviously would not work out elsewhere.

The pressures on DIA to conform to the views of the military are hard to resist. Take the national intelligence estimates as an example. Everyone in the intelligence business has a chance to assert his point of view on a particular issue, and it is here that DIA's role is crucial. DIA is well aware that many service judgments are biased and don't reflect reality. Its obligation, in these cases, is to assume its responsibility as arbiter among the services and establish a defense position on the issue. It works hard at doing just that, but strong pressures come in through the back door.

For one thing there is something called the "eyes only" cable that is sent "back channel" and is severely restricted in dissemination, usually to no more than five people. I have seen "eyes only" cables come in from the United States military commanders in Honolulu and Saigon to the director of DIA, requesting that he give more than passing consideration to the command viewpoint about this or that. The language is always moving. Such a cable is likely to start off complimenting the recipient for the fine job he is doing and then to work in high-sounding phrases which evoke motherhood, apple pie, the American flag, and, of course, the uniform. It then implies that the sender would like to see a judgment or a particular set of figures changed to conform to the command viewpoint. It rarely offers any evidence to support this request. It is sure to close with a veiled threat that the recipient's career is in jeopardy if he doesn't play the game and "get on the team." Many estimates have been changed or reworded because of an "eyes only" cable from a field commander. In one instance the Air Force chief of intelligence called my boss at DIA about a nearly completed estimate on United States bombing in Laos. He told him that he was sending a team down to change the estimate and that my boss had better remember what color his uniform was. Of course it was the same as the general's blue. The team arrived, and over the protest of the DIA analysts, a compromise was reached.

After the Tet offensive, in the early weeks of February, 1968, the JCS insisted that the offensive was a total military defeat for the enemy—General Westmoreland told them so in his daily cables. DIA didn't agree with this assessment, but it watered down every paper it wrote on the subject so that its position was impossible to determine. Then General Wheeler went to Saigon and came back with Westmoreland's request for 206,000 troops to "clean up" the "defeated" enemy. Suddenly it was legitimate to say that the Tet offensive had really "set us back." Everybody on the service staffs, with DIA leading the pack, started writing gloomy estimates with unaccustomed forthrightness and clarity.

Everyone connected with military intelligence is partially at fault for the mess at DIA. This includes the military who run it, the civilians who staff it, the Secretary of Defense, the JCS, and the individual service staffs. Military men who manage the agency are guilty or incompetent because they are uniformed men with a parent service. Imagine how the prospect of a tour with DIA appears to a military officer. He knows, or soon learns, that he will be thrust into a position in which, on occasion, his professional judgment will vary markedly from that of his parent service. He will be expected to defend a position that could enrage his chief of staff, and officers who do so more than once get known fast and are accorded an appropriate reward at a later date in terms of promotion and assignment. Consider also that a tour at DIA—normally two to three years—is very short when compared to a twenty- to thirty-year military career. And so, most officers assigned to DIA go through a predictable pattern. They come on board as "hard chargers" ready to set the world on fire. They stick to their principles through one or two scrapes. Then they become a little more circumspect, letting individual issues slide by, rationalizing that it wasn't a crunch question anyway. Finally they resign themselves to "sweating out" their tours and playing every situation by ear. They avoid committing themselves or making decisions. They refuse to tackle the agency's long-term organizational ills because doing so would make too many waves.

The shortness of the tours of duty of the military managers of the agency (about nine-tenths of management jobs are filled by military officers) causes some long-term problems. These officers are interested largely in getting good performance out of the staff while they are there, not in building up long-run staff or agency capabilities. They want to impress the general and let him know that he's running a "crackerjack outfit." The general, of course, is normally occupied largely with current problems, so his subordinates gear up to service his needs. This has resulted over the years in the reduction of DIA's long-term research capability to near zero. More than 95 percent of the effort expended in DIA on Vietnam, for example, was and is on current problems. Long-term study groups have been disbanded, and the staff has been reassigned to the current problem areas. Basic intelligence for detailed studies is simply not getting done or is whipped out with a weekend's furious overtime. The managers who choose to cut the long-term staff don't worry about the ultimate effect because by the time it becomes evident they'll be off to other assignments.

Another problem is the "can do" attitude that prevails among the officer corps. It is unthinkable for an officer to tell his superior that he cannot complete a task. It is a form of heresy. Officers accept a requirement for four or six extra hours' work a day when they know their staff already puts in twelve- or fourteen-hour days. Rarely, if ever, does anyone say no, or point out that certain jobs will simply have to wait for a decrease in the workload. "Yes, sir, can do" results in an attitude among DIA staffers that is captured in their motto: "If you want it real bad, you're gonna get it real bad."

There is also the age-old problem of military "time in grade" —the tradition that confers geniuslike powers on the man who's been around the longest. The impact that this has on the efficient functioning of DIA can be illustrated by the fact that I had nine bosses within two years, and that each of them was unseated because someone with more time in grade came along. The game of musical chairs goes on constantly. One Army colonel had been the Commander of Special Forces in South Vietnam before he was assigned to DIA. He came into the Vietnam division and was contributing tremendously until another colonel with more time in grade came along some two months later. Since full-colonel slots were at a minimum, the only thing the agency could do was to transfer the Special Forces colonel to the Latin America division. They assigned the new colonel to the Vietnam division. The new colonel was a graduate of the Army's Foreign Area Specialist Training pro-

gram in Czech affairs—but all the colonel billets in the Eastern
Europe division were filled.

Then there is the civilian staff. It is second rate, particularly
at the middle and upper levels. The military who run the place
have made it that way. They have consistently shown over the
years that there's no room in DIA for truly capable civilians.
They have discouraged original thought, drained the civilians
of initiative, and inculcated them with the "don't make waves"
approach to everything. Very few civilians hold down management slots in DIA, but that doesn't mean they are without
influence. Throughout the agency there are civilian deputies at
most levels of command. They form an infrastructure that
wields a great deal of influence in the day-to-day operation of
the organization. The problem is that the ones who have sur-
vived that long in the bureaucracy are thoroughly bureaucra-
tized. They are the ones who advise a brash lieutenant colonel
to "soften his judgment," "temper his language," and "play the
game." Their strength in many cases comes from their detailed
familiarity with the inner workings of the complicated JCS
paper mill. They know when to delay a paper, when to react
quickly to one, how to kill one, how to ensure that it gets
through, and most importantly, how and where to ensure that
the general's wishes are translated verbatim into the final product, even if those wishes conflict with the evidence on hand or
the views of knowledgeable analysts.

Finally, there are half-breed civilians at DIA—retired military officers. These men are generally capable in their area of
job experience, but two factors virtually negate their experience
and job skill. The first and most important is the fact that they
are retired and looking for an easy deal. Their fighting days are
over, and they want to take it easy. They don't make waves;
they do what is asked of them. The other is that they are heavily
biased in favor of the military, and this colors all their judgments. Their attitudes and actions also have a definite influence
on the other civilians in the agency. For one thing they are hired
at the middle grades and they clog up the promotion cycle for

the younger men. They also have an "in" with the military managers and can frequently be seen on the fairways and greens of the Army-Navy Country Club. Somehow they are always the civilians chosen for the trips abroad.

DIA has always managed to keep investigators at arm's length. With the constant turnover at the top, the agency has been in a continual state of flux since it was first organized in 1961. Thus the managers have a built-in excuse for a curious congressional committee. "We are taking care of that problem, Congressman. See, here are the slides which prove that we are reorganizing our efforts." And DIA has continually been reorganizing since 1961. It sort of follows a three-year cycle in this regard. A new general will come in, take a look at the organization, and decide that it is time to return to the functional approach. So DIA will go through the paper gyration of reorganizing itself along functional lines. The next general will arrive some two or three years later, take a look at DIA, and decide that a geographic approach to the problem would best serve his needs while there. Once again DIA will reorganize itself. Four such reorganizations took place in the first ten years of DIA's life. More can be expected. None, however, will raise the basic questions concerning DIA's ambiguous role within the Defense Department or its inability to serve several masters.

VIII

"I Owe My Soul to the Company Store"

🝓🝓🝓

I was recruited—a Greek who went by the name of Mr. Z called me on the phone and told me he'd like to talk to me about working for CIA. When I said I was interested he said he'd meet me at 2:30 Sunday afternoon at the Chestnut Hill railroad station parking lot in suburban Philadelphia. He said he'd be driving a white Buick.

After a clandestine meeting in which he took hurried notes about my background, he told me he'd get in touch with me. A couple of weeks later I got another call and we met again, this time on the El platform at Sixty-ninth and Market streets in Philadelphia. There he gave me a fistful of forms to fill out and an appointment at Penn State University to take an eight-hour mental exam.

Some weeks later I was invited to Washington for a week of more tests and interviews.

My career in intelligence started off with a bang when I found myself strapped into a lie detector machine in the inner recesses of CIA. The questions started off innocently enough, asking about family, education, and military experiences. Each was posed so that only a yes or no answer was possible. We went along in this vein for about fifteen minutes. The interrogator then eased a question in about my sex life.

"Did you masturbate as a teenager?"

"Who didn't," was my first thought, but then I was gripped with fear. "What's this going to lead to?" I thought. By this time my delay had generated sufficient reaction at the terminal points of the machine into which I was plugged. Apparently my breathing stepped up, my heart rate increased, and my stomach acids started churning because the guy asked the question again —in a tone that told me I had better answer immediately!

"Why—uh—yes," I replied meekly.

"Do you still masturbate?" he retorted almost immediately.

"That's none of your goddamned business," I blurted involuntarily. And I was immediately sorry I said that, for he replied coldly, "I'm sorry, but it is our business."

After this warmup, he asked me if I had ever experienced fellatio.

"What's that?" I dumbly asked.

"Ever had a blow-job," he replied.

With that I sent the needles on the machine scrambling all over the slowly moving graph paper. The shock of that question hadn't worn off when he hit me with:

"Have you ever engaged in cunnilingus?"

Again, I innocently asked, "What's that?"

He reasked the question unemotionally in the argot that made sense to me: "Ever eaten any pussy?"

He then went on to explore my drinking habits, any organizations including the choir and the Boy Scouts to which I belonged, my personal financial situation, my reasons for wanting to work at CIA, and my moral convictions about such things as murder, stealing, and bribery. We closed the session with a rehash of all the questions upon which I had stumbled—and this was a considerable number, for I was convinced about halfway through the test that I was the lowest form of humanity on the face of the earth. I left CIA that day, which was the last in a week of physical, mental, and psychological exams I endured, convinced that I was not suited for gainful employment at CIA—or anywhere else for that matter.

A month or two later I was very surprised to receive a letter which informed me that I was selected for their junior-officer training program and was to report to Washington in mid-May to enroll in the June class.

This was the time of the aura of John Kennedy: the rhetoric; the glitter of Schlesingers, Hilsmans, and Galbraiths; the gay poolside parties and the glamour of Georgetown; mad government service in Washington, the only respectable place for young men to be after college and service hitches. I cried at JFK's inaugural address. His "ask not what your country can do for you" grabbed me and hundreds of guys like me. We came in droves. I first applied for the Peace Corps and was sorely disappointed when they turned me down because of my intelligence background in the service. They wanted the Peace Corps to remain pure—free from any taint of espionage.

Those were heady days in Washington. We drank at Clyde's bar in Georgetown and traded idealistic rhetoric with young lawyers working for Bobby Kennedy at Justice. We were proud young men, and our families in Pennsylvania—Kansas—California—Georgia—were proud of their sons in the Kennedy administration. We were ready "to go anywhere, pay any price" for our country. It was a contagion, an exhilarating time in our lives, a chance to be part of something great.

The seventy-five of us assembled in the auditorium that June day were given the "cream of the crop" speech by a faceless individual from the personnel office. This was a statistically derived speech that let us know how great we were compared to the hundreds of applicants they actually screened to fill the June class. We liked the speech.

Following that they trotted out the king, Allen Dulles. There he stood with tweed sports jacket, leather patches on the elbows, pipe, glasses, and twinkling eyes. We were mesmerized. He launched into the second installment of what we later called "CIA ice cream"—a process in which they pumped us so full of milk, cream, and sugar during the eight months of training that we were shitting ice cream for the next two years. We were embarrassed to take our paychecks because of the high honor of working there.

Dulles really did a job on us. He gave us his infamous "Geneva, 1917" speech. It's a beaut. It goes like this: "When I was a very young foreign service officer I was posted to Geneva, Switzerland. It was 1917. On one particular Saturday I had the morning duty at the American embassy. My mind was filled with only one thing—a date for tennis that I had that afternoon with a very comely young lady. Well, my thoughts of this young lady were interrupted at ten minutes to noon by a phone call from the train station. This heavily accented voice inquired if he could speak with an official of the American delegation. I paused for a second, for the only official available was myself. I wrestled with the idea of talking with this man or playing tennis with the young lady. The young lady won out, and I turned the fellow down."

At this juncture in his story Allen Dulles paused to light his pipe. He scanned the audience, and we all sat there waiting for the punch line and nodding our heads affirmatively—as if we were saying we'd have done the same thing.

"Twenty-two years later," he continued, "I learned that the man who wanted to talk with an American official was named Lenin." We were horrorstruck. The guy next to me muttered, "You really blew that one, Al."

Big Al allowed the effect to sink in before continuing. "Ladies and gentlemen," he went on, "during your careers in intelligence you will be on the forefront of the war for survival. Often the most trivial events are unimaginably important. Don't take any assignment lightly. You will be days ahead of the world diplomatic community. You will be days ahead of the world press. You will be on the front lines of service to this great nation of ours. You will be intelligence officers. And you will do a damned fine job. Thank you, ladies and gentlemen," he closed his talk, turned quickly and slipped behind the curtain.

The eight months' training was an admixture of common sense, insanity, old-time religion, and some of the weirdest lectures you can imagine. The most important result of the training, as far as CIA was concerned, was the attitudes they managed to inculcate among the seventy-five students. We were so deluged with practical and theoretical examples of the importance of intelligence that we became total loyalists. Many among us believed in the intelligence establishment simply because we were a part of it. This attitude lingered for years among us, and today, in middle age, most of us still talk about the mind-bending job they did on us during that training period. I am convinced that this manipulation of attitudes has been responsible for keeping the many men who have left the craft of intelligence quiet. Because of my indoctrination, I still get a visceral twinge—and have qualms of conscience about writing this book.

CIA training takes part in two phases. The first, at headquarters in surburban Langely, Virginia, consists of the kinds of courses you'd expect at any large organization. We had seemingly endless hours of color-slide briefings on the organization and functions of the intelligence community. These were backed up with bus trips to the other components around the Washington area and with guided tours and briefings by the various agencies. We learned how to write in official government language, how to fill out the many forms intelligence officers have to fill out every day, and what resources for gathering intelligence the community had at its disposal. Just in case a nonbeliever slipped through the screening, we were given a ten-week course on Communist party theory and tactics, replete with exercises in which we set up front groups and devised tactics to harass local politicians, labor groups, or a school system.

The second part of the training takes place at "the farm," a secluded, rural enclave in Virginia where we were taught all the tricks of espionage.

We were advised to travel to the farm in private cars, either singly or in pairs. We were given instructions on how to get there and told to arrive after dark on a Sunday evening.

Once on the facility, we drove for nearly two miles along a narrow wooded road, finally emerging into an open area which looked like both a military camp and a small college campus. The one building that attracted all was one whose entrance was lit up; it was called the Club. On entering, the stark contrast was quite shocking. At the bar stood two distinct groups—one, the new arrivals decked out in tweeds and vests; the other, obviously there for awhile, dressed in fatigues, wearing camouflage paint on their faces, and armed with submachine guns, detonating wire, and other paraphernalia. It was an awkward first ten minutes because there seemed to be a reluctance for the new group to mingle with the old. This stiffness broke down, however, when we recognized familiar faces behind the greasepaint. Those first two hours, which turned into a party of sorts, set the mood for the entire stay at the farm. Groups of two or three warriors slipped off from the crowd at intervals, remarking that they had to get back to the exercise. They would be replaced in a matter of minutes with another group of two or three, who would swagger in muddy, sweating, and similarly clothed. In the distance the sounds of small-arms fire and muffled explosions could be heard. As new arrivals, we reacted with the proper amount of surprise, only to be met with matter-of-fact attitudes by the older group.

The following morning we were all roused early by the roar of low-flying airplanes overhead. Looking out the window I noticed that the sky in the near distance was filled with parachutes drifting slowly earthward. On the way to the dining hall, pickup trucks dashed from one end of the site to the other, picking up men who had just landed amid trees, in swampy areas, on the parade ground.

Daylight also afforded a better view of what was to be our home for the coming weeks. Separate buildings were set back among the trees surrounding an expansive parade ground, or common green, the size of a football field. Some of the buildings were obviously classrooms, and others resembled small hunting lodges, housing the instructors and their families. Narrow roads led off from the rectangular field in all directions, and it was down these various avenues that pickup trucks were now speeding. The men who had just jumped were assembling on the green, and I doubt if you'd ever see a more animated bunch. They were swapping tales of horror concerning what was obviously their first jump. We were denied access to them throughout the day by our own schedule, but our lectures were interrupted by the repeated approach of low-flying planes as the group continued jumping. The noises droned on into the wee hours as the fellows were acquiring the dubious skill of night jumping.

The classroom in which we assembled that first day was right out of *The Manchurian Candidate*. It was a cavernous room not unlike a nineteenth-century surgical exhibition pit.

The introductory lectures, as expected, were about the daily routine at the farm, the places we could and could not go, the sights we might see while here, and the details of our course of instruction. While the schedule resembled a typical college program, the contents of the course of instruction certainly did not. Typical of the many lectures we were to hear were "flaps and seals" and "locks and picks"—subjects designed to teach us how to open envelopes and letters and to pick locks. Others included "elicitation," "the dossier," "agent handling," and "agent recruiting."

Within the first few hours we set into the routine of lectures, demonstrations, and participation. It soon became obvious that the course was designed to build to a crescendo of activity in which we'd "put the pitch" to a potential agent. We were to be trained for the graduation ceremony in which we'd have to recruit someone to spy for us. This was to be achieved by first learning and practicing all the tools of the trade, such as surveillance, clandestine meetings, dead drops, letter drops, and field reporting. Once that was completed, we could elect to stay around for several more weeks and learn the fine arts of paramilitary activity—the boom-boom course.

As the weeks went on we finally picked up enough of the fundamentals to be allowed into civilization to practice our devious arts in full view of the public eye. One fine morning we set off in pairs for nearby cities to practice clandestine photography. A class previous to ours had cased certain areas in the cities that were targeted for photographs. The students were not allowed to be so bold as to merely walk up to a building and photograph it. We had to do it the hard way—take the picture without letting it be known that we were doing so. The first lesson to be learned in this exercise was that a picture can be taken with the lens cover on a camera if a tiny hole is drilled in the center of the lens cover. Then we had to learn to operate the camera as it swung idly at the side. The exercise went off as planned, and after developing our photos that evening we had to write up dummy field reports on the subjects photographed. It was amazing how many reports were filed which described in minute detail the asses of scores of faceless girls that unknowingly were the subjects of clandestine photography.

The next time that we were allowed out of the farm was several weeks later, when we had been schooled in the art of following someone. This exercise called for us to operate in fours and keep a close eye and detailed record of where one of the instructors went in a given day. If he as much as laid eyes on one of us we failed. We were told only that he would emerge from a certain hotel at an approximate time of day. Feeling totally conspicuous, we stationed ourselves at intervals a healthy distance away from the hotel entrance at the height of the morning rush in the downtown area of a nearby city. Casually reading newspapers we felt a little silly just lounging around as the rest of the world sped by on their way to work. Our "rabbit" emerged, and we all bolted at once and started discreetly tailing him. He pulled some classics on us by suddenly reversing his course in the middle of the block. Of course we ducked into stores or stooped to tie our shoes or just stood there with our faces hanging out, frozen with fear. The first time he pulled that one, he almost banged headlong into one of our group. He tipped his hat, wished the fellow a good morning by name and suggested that he spend the rest of the day taking in a movie. Crushed, the fellow walked to the nearest bar where we picked him up late that afternoon in fine shape.

The rest of us grew increasingly cautious after that episode and decided by hand signals to give him a long lead on us. He played with us for the next two hours, darting through revolving doors and suddenly emerging from the same door in a matter of seconds. He roamed the lingerie section of a department store fondling the indescribables, as we ineptly attempted to look interested in maternity dresses, fend off curious saleswomen, and keep our eyes on him. He almost caught another of us on an escalator in another department store. He had gone up one side and immediately came down the other, scrutinizing those ascending. Fortunately, we had lost him and didn't realize what his game was until we noticed him standing at the bottom of the up escalator searching the ascending crowd for familiar faces. At the time, I was trying to unpry myself from a particularly aggressive home-furnishings salesman. We visited the local museum and ended up stationing ourselves outside after we discovered there was only one entrance. Of course, we had no idea of what he had been up to in the museum —a facet brought out in our after-session debriefing.

At mid-day he foxed us by selecting the swankiest eating place in town to enjoy his lunch. Being short of coin we elected to subsidize one of our group to eat there while the rest of us munched a hamburger at a nearby stand-up emporium. At mid-afternoon our chase led us into a section of the city under-going urban renewal. The area was level for approximately ten square blocks. We lengthened our lead and progressed across the expanse, which recalled pictures of Hiroshima, with a good fifty yards separation between us, plus one of us on the opposite side of the street. Spread out inconspicuously (as we thought) we advanced slowly, hoping he wouldn't dare reverse his course. He didn't, but as we entered the built-up area, an old gent sitting on the post office steps—who obviously had been watching our advance—called out to him that he was being followed by three fellows.

Perhaps to entice us into the paramilitary activity, we were given some limited exposure to this aspect of agency work at the midpoint of our agent-handling course. It was a pleasant respite from the routine, and we entered our first border-crossing exercise with gusto. Off in the woods a two-mile stretch of border had been erected, similar to what you'd expect to see in Eastern Europe—replete with high barbed wire fences, plowed strips, watchtowers, roving patrols, and searchlights. Our objective was to case the place (undetected of course) during daylight hours and then to slip back there that night and cross the border.

This entailed our learning how to use a compass and find our way through dense woods in an orderly fashion. That was an interesting learning experience, as we circled about in the woods by day becoming more and more lost. Eventually we got the hang of it and set out, after spending an afternoon of casing, to cross the border by dark. Arriving at the edge of the woods, we laid in wait trying to determine a pattern to the patrol activity of the jeeps traversing the road that ran the length of the border facing us. On each side of the narrow road were four-foot ditches, and it only took one venture into them to find that they were filled with the most delightful slime that nature and sprayed oil could concoct. We also attempted to isolate the sweep of the four or five searchlights that panned the area in coordination.

On the other side of the road a six-foot steep incline faced us. After the jeep had passed several times we noted in the glare of its headlights that the incline, too, had been sprayed with oil. (Nice!) The first objective was for a pair of us to get across the road. We'd worry about getting up the hill later. We decided to get into the slime of the ditch and cross immediately after the jeep passed us. As it did, we both attempted to gain the road's edge in one mighty jump from the slime of the ditch. We were spectacularly unsuccessful and ended up sliding right back down it into the ditch, this time tangling ourselves beautifully. By this time the jeep was nearing the end of the road and about to turn around and head back our way, so we waited once more for it to pass us. We then we tried cupping hands and thrusting one of us onto the road. This worked and I sprawled ungraciously onto the hardtop, only to have my buddy grab my ankle to pull himself out of the ooze. On giving a large pull he manage to wrest me from the road (aided of course by my slimy exterior) and we both ended up once more in the slime. At this juncture we both voiced doubts about the efficacy of a paramilitary career, as we obviously lacked that nimble way of James Bond.

Undaunted, we tried once more, after the jeep had crossed, to jettison one of us onto the road. This time my buddy made it and rather than letting me pull myself up by his ankle he crouched, grabbed my wrist, and yanked me up. By this time both the jeep headlights and the panning searchlights were closing in on us, so we leapt into the ditch on the other side, again crashing ungraciously in a tangle into the ooze.

Lying on my back on the bottom of the ditch, I suddenly realized that the wall facing us was about ten feet high. Leaping it in a single bound was out, and we both played with the idea of simply staying right where we were until the exercise was over. It was only the combined smells of the ditch and ourselves that persuaded us to try. Adroitly my buddy stepped onto my shoulders as I crouched splay-legged in the slime. Our plan was for me to slowly rise to an erect position and for him to then do the same. I rose with great effort and announced to him that it was his turn. On flexing a certain set of muscles to arise he cut loose with an enormous fart. I lost all muscle control, and once again we ended up in the slime.

On our bellies we discussed the failure rationally and decided that the system was good; it merely depended on his controlling his bowels. So we tried again. This time he was pinned down by the direct glare of one of the searchlights. It lingered on his figure for awhile, then moved on. We immediately decided that we had been spotted so we broke into a low run down the length of the ditch. It was blacker than the proverbial well-digger's colon, and within forty seconds we collided abruptly with another pair of guys trying to mount the wall. So now four bodies tangled in the ditch, with one bloody nose (mine).

We separated from the other two fellows, who bid us farewell with a string of the finest Scotch-Irish invectives I'd heard in a long time. Within seconds, our attention was drawn back to the other two by the screeching of jeep brakes and the commotion involved in pulling them from the ditch and tossing them curtly into the back seat of the jeep.

It was getting colder in the ditch, and in trying to wipe the blood from my nose I was hard put to find a dry spot on my sleeve or elsewhere. We stopped and rested a bit before once more trying to scale the wall. Once again we tried the one-standing-on-the-other's-shoulders act, but this time I was on top. Standing erect on my buddy's shoulders I was at waist level with the top of the ridge. I scrambled over onto my belly, reached down with one arm, and suprisingly, was able to pull my buddy up. The searchlights passed over our two forms hugging the ground. We felt below us that we were lying on plowed strips paralleling the fence, and any marks that we left would be noticeable by the searchlight crews. With this in mind we rolled toward the fence keeping parallel to it, so as not to disturb the plowed lines. As I rolled over one of the furrows I felt a string or wire against my ear. Before I had time to think about it, we were suddenly bathed in a burst of the brightest light imaginable. I had unsuspectingly set off a trip flare. We sprang to our feet, crashing into one another in the process. I darted off and, in so doing, set off another flare and a string of cherry bombs placed for just such an occasion. I immediately reversed course and crashed into my buddy, who in falling grabbed my shirtfront and pulled me with him. In less than a second we both were in the bottom of the ditch, but, with adrenaline spurting through our bodies, we were up in a flash and tearing together down the length of the ditch at breakneck speed. We collided with another pair of fellows, and by this time the jeep was astride our position shining into the tangled mass of bodies.

On the way to the interrogation shed my buddy confessed that his kidneys had involuntarily functioned when I set off that first flare. He went on to comment that they continued to function until we landed in the ditch. Fortunately the oil, mud, and sweat on our clothes served as an ample screen. The night's activity did not serve as an enticement to sign up for a paramilitary career.

Our next trip to town found us saddled with the seemingly simple job of locating and sketching a place suitable for a meeting with an agent. Knowing the reputation the group was gaining for its evening libations, the staff informed us that bars were not to be cased. A low groan swept the room, but we accepted the restriction in perhaps the same frame of mind that the United States Air Force accepted the restriction placed on their bombing of Hanoi and Haiphong. With one exception, the group succeeded in finishing this assignment without major hitches. Bill, however, was the victim of his own youthful face. At twenty-seven he looked like a well-scrubbed eighteen-year-old. There were times in DC when he'd been asked for an ID card when we'd stop for a drink after work. The drinking age in DC is 18! In any event Bill chose a medium-priced, well-decorated Italian restaurant in the downtown area. He realized after he had been seated by the hostess and given a menu that he only had seventy-four cents on him. Accustomed to a pauper's life in school, Bill of course had never thought of owning a Diners Club or similar card. So he was trapped. His first instinct was to leave, but the waitress hovered over him as soon as he had the menu in hand. He nervously scanned the prices and saw that there was nothing that he could buy for seventy-four cents. To make things more uncomfortable it was lunch-time, and there were people queuing up by the door awaiting tables.

Screwing up his courage, Bill, in his most lackadaisical manner, decided aloud that he wasn't particularly hungry but would like a glass of iced tea. The waitress glanced up incredulously from her pad and repeated his order in the form of a high-pitched question, forcing Bill to confirm it while maintaining the air of dignity he thought he was projecting.

She nodded but began to take away the silverware and napkin. He suddenly realized that he had left his scratch pad in his car and, being loath to go out and get it, decided to ask the waitress for a piece of paper. Of course she was out of normal conversational earshot by this time so he had to raise his voice to recapture her attention. On doing so his voice cracked like the teenager he appeared to be. She detoured to the cash register to bring him his piece of paper. He thanked her in the most officious tone he could muster.

Once she had returned to her chores he set about making a sketch of the interior of the restaurant. It was important to plainly mark all of the exits in the place, including windows in the men's room and the back door. This, of course, entailed a trip to the men's room. Bill decided he'd do it before the waitress returned with his iced tea, and he was just sitting down at his table when she appeared with the tea. She stared at his sketch as she placed the tea in front of him, and he noticed a puzzled look on her face. He failed to notice that she walked over to the cash register to discuss her strange customer with the burly manager of the restaurant.

One last task faced Bill, and as he sipped his tea he wondered how he could learn the layout of the kitchen and whether or not there was a back door. He seized upon an idea, and being consumed with it raised his arm and waved frantically for the waitress. She came over to his table, followed by the manager, who stood at a discreet distance to her rear. With what he thought to be the proper amount of pomp, Bill inquired if he might tour the kitchen, explaining as he puffed up his chest that he was considering embarking on a restaurant career. The waitress turned him over to the manager, who by this time was growing impatient with the kid taking up a table at noon for a crummy glass of iced tea. Unfavorably disposed toward Bill as he was, the manager deflected the inquiry about the kitchen tour and asked him just what the hell he was up to, drawing pictures of his restaurant. Bill, his cool fading, replied with the "going-into-the-restaurant-business" bit once more. The manager was not convinced and reached for the paper on which Bill had been sketching. With his arm he motioned for the maître d' and asked him to call the cops. "I don't know what your game is, kid, but I don't like the looks of it. We got enough problems in the business without letting some creep come in here and draw a layout of the place like this. For all I know, you're planning to bust in here after we close. We'll just let the cops have a look at this."

By this time, of course, there wasn't a soul in the restaurant interested in eating. Their eyes were riveted on Bill, and his blush matched the redness in the eyes of the manager. For a fleeting second he thought of telling the truth. He fumbled in his mind for the right words to tell this guy that he was with the CIA.

He decided to stick to his story, and repeated it, this time with considerably less confidence. "Yeah," retorted the manager, "tell it to the cops. They'll be here in a minute." And they were. Bill was ushered into the kitchen with the manager and the policemen and he went through the same story. Fortunately his youthful face, which had prompted disbelief in the manager's mind, played to his benefit with the policemen. "Look, Tony, the kid doesn't look like a crook or anything. Maybe he's telling the truth," the cop said. Tony, however, was not that easily placated. "Well, I can't charge him with anything, but I'll be damned if I'll let him leave here with that drawing of my place." Bill quickly thrust the sheet of paper into his hand and, clinging to his original story, apologized for the disruption and gladly left. On the way back to the farm he realized that he hadn't even paid for his iced tea. At that we cracked up. Bill was able to remember the layout, and, since the police took him into the kitchen to question him, he was able to sketch in the kitchen as well. He noted on his report, however, that he personally should not be assigned to meet an agent in that place.

During those first weeks we all concluded that the instructors had a pretty easy life at the farm shepherding the uninitiated through the rituals of the trade. As time went on, we realized they had their problems. As in any profession, there are certain occupational hazards. In ours it was either the sauce or the honeys.

For the next trip to town (still unable to carry our guns, however) we were slated to conduct a meeting in a waterfront bar. Our assignment was to debrief a seaman (supposedly able-bodied) who had just returned from the port of Krutch, a commie stronghold denied to imperialist running dogs like ourselves. This was a double team effort, and who did I luck out with but my old buddy from the border-crossing problem. He and I were to meet this guy at about four-thirty in the afternoon at one of the sleazier joints along the waterfront. Of course we dressed appropriately for the occasion, decked out in our dark blue business suits, another masterpiece of planning on our part. This occasioned a glance or two when we entered and also attracted two of the bar girls working the joint. There was very little we could do to impress them with the fact that we were not seeking their attention but were, instead, awaiting a business appointment.

Feeling uneasy in suits among a bunch of guys in dungarees and sweatshirts, we accepted the girls' presence in our booth and bought them a drink while listening to the happy lives they had each spent since puberty. Time passed quickly, and before we knew it, it was nearing five-thirty and no instructor. We ordered our second round of drinks and awaited his arrival.

By six he showed up and, this being the sixth such meeting of the afternoon for him, it soon became evident that he was in the chute. The poor guy was almost out on his feet, but he was determined to go on with the exercise. He bubbled over to our booth and plopped down on my side, careening into the honey on my left, who to say the least was annoyed.

"S'cuse me sweets, I gotta little business to talk over with these two fellows."

"Well, I can take a hint," she retorted.

"Hell no, I don't wantcha to leave. Hell no, stay with us and we'll have a ball after I go over some business with these two guys." He turned and leered at us through red eyes. "Got yer little pads and pencils fellahs? Well, ole Uncle Tommy gonna 'splain it to ya. . . . My ship got in last Thursday afternoon and I watched those bastards unloading tanks from the ship berthed next to ours. . . . Yeah, they was the biggest goddamned tanks I ever saw."

Of course my buddy and I were writing feverishly as Uncle Tommy proceeded to " 'splain it to us." The girls, who at first showed a distinct disinterest in Uncle Tommy's business talk, began to perk up a little.

"Where was that?" one asked.

"Why, right down there in Havana, Cuba, sweetie."

"You were just in Cuba?"

"Not only yes, but hell yes!"

"And you saw tanks?"

"Did I see tanks? Did I see tanks?" (This time louder.) "Christ, there were tanks all over the place."

"Whose were they?" the other girl asked.

"The dirty commie rats', who else's? If they were our's do you think I'd be sitting here in this crummy bar telling these two guys about them?"

Suddenly the lights went on in the eyes of one of the honeys.

"You guys ain't spies, I hope?"

We blanched! With that remark Uncle Tommy burst into hysterical laughter.

"That takes the cake. These guys spies? Christ, they wouldn't make a pimple on a good spy's ass, honey."

"See the way they're dressed?" he pointed at my buddy. "If these guys were spies meeting an agent in this joint, do you think they'd dress like that?"

"Well, I don't know," she replied.

"Well I do, 'cause I'm their goddamned teacher, and I'll tell you, honey, they ain't spies. As a matter of fact they ain't much of anything. As far as I'm concerned they're just a couple of punk kids that I have to put up with. Do you realize that I got over thirty years with this outfit. Yeah, I said thirty years. That's more than those two guys' ages together. And where the hell do they send me for my last tour but to the Office of Training."

"What's with him?" she asked.

"Beats me," my buddy said. "We were to meet this guy in here to check out the latest provisions set down in a recent longshoremen's union strike up in New York and he starts spouting off about tanks."

I mentally applauded him for his quick thinking, but within a second the room reverberated with a mighty "BULLSHIT" bursting from the lungs of Uncle Tommy, who was rising awkwardly to his feet.

"You smart young shits don't know what it's all about! You bastards think I'm washed up, don't ya? Yeah, I can tell it every time I meet one of ya."

Of course the questions (and answers) came from Uncle Tommy too rapidly for us to reply. We sensed that we were in for a good session with him externalizing all his aggressions and frustration. We put up with it for a little while, but got just a wee bit tired of his crap after a solid fifteen minutes, in which he enlisted the verbal aid of a nearby longshoreman with whom he was better able to communicate.

The mockery and derision then came from both of these guys —the instructor damning us because we had never fought in World War II and the longshoreman ridiculing our dress and the fact that all we had ever learned was from books. He then launched into a separate, but related, tirade about how he turned down a commission in the army during the war. This elated Uncle Tommy, who also had been a corporal during the war.

The girls gravitated to our side in the emerging conflict, and, unasked, one of them got up and asked Uncle Tommy to dance. The other forced him to his feet, and while he was being escorted to the dance floor she went over and put some money into the jukebox.

I went over to her at the jukebox, and she asked if we wanted to fix Uncle Tommy's wagon.

Not being the uncharitable kind I replied, "Damn right I do."

"OK," she said, "order a round of drinks for him and the ape there and I'll bring them over. They'll cost you five bucks apiece."

"What the hell are you gonna put in them?"

"Just something to cool 'em both off."

My buddy thought it'd be the greatest thing since sliced bread, and we nodded to the honey to carry on, which she did. When Uncle Tommy came back to the booth we got up and let him sit on the inner side, and as he was about to continue from where he left off the other girl brought the drinks.

"The fellahs here thought you'd like another round," she said.

"They did, did they? They're just trying to brown-nose me, that's all."

"Call it what you will, Tarzan," she snapped, "here's your drink!"

He downed it in two gulps and so did his longshoreman buddy, who by this time had pulled his barstool over next to our booth. He was the first to go. He simply fell forward off his stool onto the table in our booth. Uncle Tommy, who was surprised, began to rise to help him and immediately joined him on the tabletop. We both got up and paid the ten bucks and asked the girls to please get a cab for these two guys and see that they got put aboard a freighter that was sitting at the dock just blocks away.

Back at the farm that evening we witnessed another exhibition of the prowess of one of the training staff. While we were standing at the bar in the club confiding our story to some of our closer associates, we were interrupted by a mighty roar from the other end of the bar. We turned just in time to see a red-faced character in fatigues leap up onto the bar.

"The only way you guys are gonna learn PLF [parachute landing fall] is to practice," he roared.

"Get up here," he said, pointing to one particularly cherub-faced student.

The student mounted the bar, and on his count of three they both fell off. The student landed with a dull thud, but the instructor rolled over a couple of times and sprang to his feet.

"See what I mean?" he exclaimed.

"You guys think a PLF is easy do you? Well, look what happened to him; he went down like a sack of potatoes, and that was just four feet from the ground."

"Come on outside," he roared, as he went through the door.

Outside we watched him scale the railing on the porch and flit up onto the roof. He then pointed at another pink-faced student and told him to get up there with him.

"Sorry 'bout that, coach," he replied.

With that, the instructor fell off the roof and once again demonstrated a PLF. Once again he rolled over a couple of times and sprang to his feet.

We retired to the bar once more, and whiled away the remainder of the evening watching the guys in paramilitary training fall off the bar and listening to the guys in demolition training arguing about the length of fusing required to blow up an oil tank. They, too, were led in their seminar by an instructor

—a big Swede who in the great patriotic war had blown up German plants all over Scandinavia. The evening ended on a dull note when the mousey little instructor who taught the format and procedure of field reporting fell off his barstool and was carried out.

Our training capped off with a trip to Panama in which CIA teams were pitted against Special Forces teams, who were pitted against a regular army unit afield in the jungles on a training exercise. It was followed by a field trip to New York, in which CIA teams were pitted against FBI teams in carrying out a spying mission against the United Nations. The result was the learning of a considerable body of knowledge that few, if any, of us would ever have the opportunity to use. Nevertheless, it was an enjoyable departure from reality in which we learned the subtle art of expense account juggling and savored the questionable night life of several cities.

It is difficult to characterize the work day in the intelligence business. The common denominator is the enormous swarm of paper. It is true in the clandestine services and in the analytical side of the profession. The paperwork has killed more than one man.

Joe Goliash, for example, was thirty-eight years old, a lieutenant colonel of Infantry and newly arrived in intelligence with his tour at the Defense Intelligence Agency. He was put in charge of the Laos desk in the Far East Division simply because he had more time in grade than the man who was filling the job. Joe was not accustomed to the world of intelligence. He took every request for information from the Joint Staff as an order from a superior officer as a good infantryman would. He didn't know that most of us ignored 90 percent of the requests for intelligence that came from the JCS. We did this because they simply reflected the inane game of one-upmanship that is continually being played at the Pentagon. It works like this. The general poses a rhetorical question at his morning briefing to his aide, a colonel. "Wonder what those Pathet Lao are up to?" he might ask aloud. The colonel and two lieutenant colonels leave the general's office and head for their typewriters. Each will type up a request for intelligence support asking DIA to explain, in whatever detail the author desires, what the Pathet Lao are up to. The information desired could range from a short phone answer, through a one-page memorandum to the colonel, on up to a full-blown study requiring several days for completion. The standing procedure among the experienced intelligence hands was to ignore the first such request from colonels and below. If it was really important the guy would come back and ask again. Joe, however, could not bring himself to treat the requests so cavalierly. He even refused to accept the advice of an army intelligence colonel, senior to him, that this was the only way to handle such requests. In such a case, Joe would end up writing three answers to the same basic question —in addition to meeting the deadlines on his own daily reports. To do this, Joe usually had to stay behind each evening until perhaps seven or eight o'clock. Normally, he was at his desk at seven the following morning to prepare for the morning briefing for the general.

Things went along like this for eight or nine months. Joe's wife was a little irritated about his work schedule, but she rarely complained. However, she did put her foot down when the circus came to Washington, because Joe had promised his three daughters that he would take them. She bought tickets for a Sunday matinee. Joe went into the office on Sunday morning but managed to get out in time to take his girls to the circus. They returned about five-thirty. He told his wife he had to go back to the office after dinner to clear up a few things, but he wouldn't be long.

Joe's wife sent their five-year-old daughter into the living room to wake Joe up when dinner was ready. She shook him, but he didn't wake up. She went and got her mother. Together, they discovered that Joe was dead from a heart attack. Joe's death prompted an investigation of his work schedule. It was discovered that he had averaged seventy-five to eighty hours a week at the office for better than eight months. His heart attack was attributed to physical and mental exhaustion. No further action was taken. Joe was awarded a Legion of Merit posthumously and his slot was filled by another lieutenant colonel—from the Armored Corps.

The working pattern for most analysts in intelligence sees them rather busy in the morning hours and in varying degrees of relaxation during the afternoon. Despite the compartmentation within intelligence, analysts are largely oriented toward current events. The morning finds a stack of overnight cables and other reports on each analyst's desk. At the Pentagon on the Vietnam desk this stack normally measured six to eight inches in height because it contained daily contact reports of American ground and air units in the field. This was added to by the steady flow of interrogation-of-prisoners reports that came from the battlefield. The routine saw an analyst going through the mail, sorting and filing it, and writing reports based on the daily developments. We were aided in this by an elaborate secure telephone system which connects all of the Washington intelligence agencies and even reaches overseas. If questions arise concerning the reports, we could pick up the phone in CIA, for example, and talk to the man in Saigon who wrote the report. If it is a very technical report he can confer with the analyst at the National Security Agency who specializes in the subject. Similarly, he can speak with DIA or State Department analysts when the need arises.

The normal work day is often punctuated with a variety of crises. At the time they seem important, but they quickly become irrelevant. I was called into the Pentagon one evening after dinner by the duty colonel, who said two generals in the National Military Command Center were really uptight about the forthcoming visit of the Roumanian foreign minister to North Vietnam, and that I had better come into the office and see what they needed in the way of intelligence support. I asked if he had any idea of what it was they wanted. He didn't but thought I'd better come to work. So, off I went to the Pentagon. When I arrived, I went up to the Command Center and was led into the office where the two generals were conferring. I had visions of having to provide them with a complete rundown of North Vietnamese–Roumanian relations since 1945 or at least giving them a laundry list of how the Roumanians were providing material support for North Vietnam. When I entered and introduced myself, I was asked, "What time is it in Hanoi right now?"

Stunned, I thought for a minute, added thirteen hours to the present time, then subtracted a half-hour. The North Vietnamese refused to set their clocks the same as the South Vietnamese, so there was a half-hour difference. "It's 9:30 in the morning," I replied.

"There, I told you," one general beamed radiantly at the other.

The chagrined general turned on me and scowled, "Are you goddamned sure that's the right time in Hanoi?" I answered that I was and explained the derivation of the time difference.

"OK," they both nodded, "that's all. Thanks for the help."

"But what about the forthcoming visit of the Roumanian foreign minister? I was told you wanted some information about that," I said.

"Oh, that," one general replied. "We just want to update our VIP travel board in the situation room. I was in there after supper and got into an argument with John here about him carrying the times in Hanoi and Saigon as the same. I noticed that when I looked at the scheduled time of arrival for the Roumanian foreign minister on his board. We got into this argument about the right time, so we thought we'd have you guys settle it for us. I knew I was right." End of crisis.

One very busy morning at the Pentagon we got a phone call from the director's office telling us that General Wheeler, the chairman of the Joint Chiefs of Staff, was furious with DIA. We were to report to the JCS briefing room immediately. Two of us went up there and appeared before the assembled body of the four service chiefs and the chairman. They were irritated because the operations staff officer had told them that in yesterday's air attacks against North Vietnam the enemy had fired twenty-seven surface-to-air missiles at United States aircraft. During the intelligence briefing the DIA staff officer told them that the North Vietnamese had fired approximately twenty-one missiles at United States aircraft. This sent them into a tizzy, and they demanded to know the correct number. We explained that duplicate sightings are often reported by United States pilots and that we normally plotted the positions of the United States aircraft and made a judgment concerning the duplicate sightings. This didn't satisfy them. The J-3, a Navy admiral, came out of his chair screaming, "Do you mean to imply that my staff is not properly analyzing the operations reports?" We replied in the negative, but this wouldn't soothe him. Acting as if he'd been emasculated, he launched into a tirade about soft-headed intelligence types who think they have all the god-damned answers.

Intervening in this display, the chairman ordered that we get together with the operations staff, work out the differences, and report back at tomorrow's briefing. Our bosses, quite upset, did not want to have a fight between themselves and the venerable Joint Staff. We analysts were not allowed to handle this matter directly. It took the presence of a full colonel from the director's office to serve as committee chairman. We met in a conference room and spent seven hours wheedling and cajoling the operations staff into arriving at an "agreed-upon" figure. The next morning we presented our findings to the chairman and the Joint Chiefs and everybody was happy. The chairman expressed his satisfaction and lightly said as we were leaving the room to make sure this doesn't happen again. We all nodded affirmatively. Once back in the confines of DIA, our full colonel sat down and wrote up a detailed memorandum of what had transpired. He included the chairman's parting remark. When the director of DIA saw it, he ordered that we set up a joint working committee to ensure that this didn't happen again. So, each and every morning we had to have one man, and the full colonel, of course, come into the Pentagon at five o'clock to sit down at a table with the operations staff and count up the number of missiles fired by the North Vietnamese. This went on for over eighteen months. We never really cared about how accurate we were—only about arriving at similar figures.

Each of the intelligence agencies has a variety of career plans —so many, in fact, that men can shift from one to the other for fun and profit. Within CIA there are half a dozen or so. The man in the clandestine services has his career monitored as closely as a military officer does. He has to have a certain number of tickets punched in order to advance. His training record must show the completion of a variety of "trade-craft" courses, he must have a certain number of overseas tours of duty, and he must look good on his yearly evaluations. The promotions within the clandestine service are considerably slower than anywhere else in intelligence. The official reasoning has it that since the man gets more overseas duty, where amenities such as dislocation allowance, free medical service, and housing are provided, he doesn't need to get his reward in his paycheck. Analysts in the production side of the house, on the other hand, rise faster than their contemporaries in dirty tricks. Men working in scientific areas of intelligence receive several thousand dollars extra a year in what is called scientific incentive pay. This is a source of great irritation among the other intelligence officers, who must spend a great deal of time translating their studies into understandable English before they are disseminated. The best-paying and fastest-promoting agency in intelligence is the Defense Intelligence Agency. This occurs because of a major misunderstanding on the part of the military officers who run the agency. They are not fully aware of how the civil service system operates, and this works to the great advantage of the civilian employees. In the military, when a man acquires sufficient time in grade he is automatically submitted to the promotion board for consideration. This does not ensure his promotion; it only indicates that he has been around long enough to be considered. In civil service, if a man's name is submitted he will be automatically promoted. Unlike the military, the civil service leaves the decision up to the man's supervisor. Many civilian analysts take great advantage of this. When they have the minimum time in grade, they merely approach their military supervisor, tell him that they have the time in grade, and ask if he would please see to it that their name gets submitted for promotion. Most officers comply with this request, thinking it only fair that the man be at least considered.

At the State Department the intelligence bureau is a dumping ground. Many of the staff are not foreign service officers. They are treated as stepchildren at best. The foreign service uses the intelligence bureau as a resting spot for their own staffers returning from posts abroad. They have little grasp of what intelligence is all about and look on assignment to intelligence as a dead-end street. This generates considerable friction among the career intelligence staff who somehow never seem able to advance to the supervisory slots within the bureau.

Cliques exist within all the intelligence agencies. Because of the stable nature of the tours, CIA is renowned for its infighting. It behooves a young officer to join a clique as quickly as possible. On the production side, these cliques normally evolve out of the substance of the work. There was and still is a formal Sino-Soviet dispute within CIA. Sinophiles wouldn't be caught dead having lunch with any of the analysts from the Soviet shop. Their social lives center around world politics. The Far Eastern shops have weekend parties at which Chinese, North Korean, and North Vietnamese analysts get together. The Soviet analysts would never be invited to one of these. They congregate with the East European analysts—with the notable exception of the Czech analysts. Each clique always has a rising meteor, a guy slated by his superiors to go places. Around and behind one of these guys you will see a covey of hangers-on who figure if they support the guy they will naturally rise with him. The loyalties then cross the organizational lines of authority within the agency. A guy on the rise in the Chinese shop will have friends scattered around in various shops, feeding him information on what their boss is up to. They let him know if their boss is planning to come out with a study on a subject that might impinge on his area of expertise. The greatest display of the cliques in action can be seen on the weekends in the shops that must keep a man on duty. With the list of safe combinations for the entire office the weekend duty man can rifle them and find those bureaucratic pearls—interoffice memos. These tell all—what this boss is telling that boss in private, who is and who isn't going to get promoted in the next go around, who is getting a poor fitness report and who is not, who is being groomed for rapid advancement, who is going to be exiled, and who it is worthwhile dropping or clinging to. On a Monday after one has had weekend duty he is lionized by all his colleagues anxious to know what was uncovered.

CIA has a wonderful informal system of rewards and punishments for the faithful and unfaithful. The classic case involved a senior intelligence officer with over twenty years' experience in Vietnam. He had risen to the position of being the director's special assistant on Vietnam, an unusually high position for one on the analytical side of intelligence, since Richard Helms has little time for analysts, preferring the more manly and less intellectual men from clandestine services. Things went well for George until the January, 1968, Tet offensive in South Vietnam, when the Communists swarmed into the cities. George was asked to provide his assessment to Walt Rostow at the White House. He did and concluded that the offensive, while not a clear-cut military victory, was certainly a major political, diplomatic, and psychological setback for United States policy. He even went so far as to conclude that it perhaps was the turning point in the war. This assessment enraged Rostow and President Johnson alike, coming so early in the offensive and being largely a gut analysis with little or no concrete evidence to support it. Well, that was the end for poor George. Within a month he was assigned to the British Army's Defense War College for a year of study. That is the nature of punishment for the men near the top of intelligence who screw up. They get exiled to a cushy overseas post to repent for their sins. The deputy director for intelligence who failed to forewarn the government of Khrushchev's ouster (as if he could) was himself ousted and exiled to Taiwan and then Germany for his misdeeds. The man who called for the cessation of the U-2 flights over the Soviet Union in 1959 was exiled to Australia for a four-year stint. Their intelligence officers' duties at such posts are nebulous at best. The officers are designated as the director's personal representatives, but the substance of their duties is difficult to define. Officially they are to handle those rare but extremely delicate chores the director needs accomplished. What this normally translates into is that the guy is posted to an embassy, given an office, desk, and secretary, and merely spends his tour reading cable traffic and pursuing whatever off-duty delight he fancies.

Rewards come in various forms. Officially, of course, they appear in the form of promotion to a new management slot. Unofficially they take the form of travel abroad on special missions for the director to "coordinate the views of the men in the field with Washington thinking." Such travel is always first class and somehow manages to be worldwide. A trip to Bonn, for example, must also be capped off with discussions in Tokyo. A trip to Hong Kong must be shared with the men in London, and so on.

At the low levels in CIA, men who have spent four or five years on the firing line of daily reporting often begin to show signs of wear through a budding cynicism. If the man is considered worth grooming for bigger things he is sent on an "area-familiarization" tour. If, for example, he works on the Chinese problem, he will be sent to all of the CIA stations in the Far East for a ninety-day tour. If the man is at all cunning, he can expand his trip into a world tour, since he is required to write up his own trip justification. One man managed to visit Latin America and Africa as well as Europe and the entire Far East to familiarize himself with Chinese Communist foreign trade, which was his specialty.

The gripes at the working level within CIA are somewhat unusual. Perhaps the oldest is that of the ethnics. CIA is without a doubt the last solid WASP bastion in government. The State Department couldn't hold a candle to CIA in this respect. Every single top-management position is filled with a WASP, and certain offices simply will not entertain a fellow's working there unless he has the proper credentials. This is not simply the bleating of an Irish-Catholic ethnic. It was the subject of a very close Inspector General Study at CIA in 1964. The Inspector General's office there carries on many selective studies to keep abreast of the undercurrents within CIA. It finally got up the courage to tackle this long-standing problem when many interviews with junior officers revealed their discontent over the sometimes blatant discrimination against a guy from the University of Iowa or Oklahoma State. The study, which I read one day while visiting an Italian-American buddy who made it to the executive suite as a horse-holder for one of the big shots, indicated that the Office of National Estimates had only men with the most proper bloodlines working there, that the first four layers of top management were filled only with "preppies," and that the agency had fewer Negroes in its employ than any other in government.

It is commendable that such a study was conducted, but disappointing that nothing was done about it. It was passed to the director and there it sat. The only results were the selection of a token number of guys with improper backgrounds for elevation to jobs near the top as executive secretaries to some of the preppies.

The agency, today, can claim that this old-school-tie business is no longer in effect. It isn't, as far as recruitment goes. In the late 1940s and through the 1950s the agency recruited only at the Ivy League schools. Its junior-officer training program was designed solely for men with proper breeding. No Jew, Polack, Wop, Nigger, or Mick was in those classes. By the early 1960s, however, with the blossoming of intelligence into a conglomerate, the agency could no longer rely solely on the very best

schools. It simply needed too many men for its ambitious programs, so it broadened the character of its recruitment. Under
these "lowered standards" it got guys like myself.

Another cause of friction at CIA is the "rat pack thesis." The
classic case of this thesis in action was displayed during the
Cuban missile crisis. Bill, a methodical analyst in the economic
shop, watched Soviet merchant and military shipping. In late
1961 and early 1962 he noticed a slow shift of emphasis in the
pattern of Soviet military ships. Prior to that time they had been
involved largely with supplying the Indonesian armed forces
with an arsenal that was the envy of every nation in the Far
East. Bill was the first man to detect this shift when two Soviet
military cargo vessels began routine trips to Cuba. He put in a
requirement for overhead photographs of these ships en route
to Cuba, but it was turned down. Finally a United States Navy
ship sailing in waters near Cuba got a photo of one of these
ships and sent it in through routine naval intelligence channels.
Bill eventually got a copy of the photo. His analysis, based on
how high the ship was sitting in the water, was that it did in
fact contain military equipment. Since communications revealed that the ship's crew was one that had routinely visited
Indonesia, Bill concluded that they were probably carrying
some sort of high-priority military equipment. Bill attempted to
produce an intelligence study on this subject, but it never saw
the light of day because the implications were far too broad.

Finally, when the body of evidence became overwhelming,
the entire intelligence community jumped onto the subject, and
we had the Cuban missile crisis. Bill was allotted several analysts to work with him on the problem. His shop was a frenzy
of activity, and as the crisis heightened Bill took to sleeping on
a cot in the office. In the final stages of the crisis, before the
public announcement, the policy makers at State, Defense, and
the White House required almost hourly briefings on the latest
evidence. Bill, being the most knowledgeable man on the subject, was not called upon to give these briefings. Polished men
from the front office, instead, were chosen. They first went to

Bill, and he gave them all of the details contained in the lat
evidence. They then went about town telling the story. As t
Soviet supplying of missiles and aircraft became more pr
nounced, Bill even developed a methodology to tell what w;
in the wooden crates that were carried on the decks of the ship;
Today it is a science known in intelligence as "crateology," b
which Soviet packing techniques are so well known that a MIC
crate is discernible from a crate containing an Ilyushin fighter-
bomber.

Well, when the crisis finally ended it was time for the intelligence community to celebrate its success. Rewards were
passed out from the White House to all who participated.
The director of CIA and one or two of his top aides were
given a gold calendar with the month of October, 1962, en-
graved upon it. Men beneath the director were promoted,
particularly those who went about town giving the briefings.
The man at Defense who gave the McNamara briefing on
television was promoted from a $12,000-a-year grade to a
$27,000-a-year grade overnight. The managers three levels
above Bill were given promotions, new assignments, and
cash awards of one thousand dollars apiece. Bill got absolutely nothing. His immediate boss felt a little embarrassed
about his own thousand-dollar award and decided to use it
to throw a party for his troops. Bill got smashed out of his
mind, stood up at the after-dinner speech session, and in no
uncertain terms told off four layers of bosses above him.
This was thought not to be a very appreciative gesture on
Bill's part, and he was given a formal letter of reprimand
for his personnel file. There you have it in a nutshell. The
analysts who do the digging in the trenches are all but forgotten when a crisis is over. Out of the woodwork comes a
phalanx of hangers-on—the rat pack—who somehow know
how to get to the right places at the right time—all, of
course, at the expense of the analyst who is doing the hard
work. This is not an uncommon occurrence. It happens with
alarming regularity. I saw it happen during the Gulf of Ton-

kin crisis, during the Arab-Israeli war in 1967, and during the Soviet invasion of Czechoslovakia.

This sort of treatment encourages a goodly number of young analysts to leave the intelligence profession altogether. The exodus of younger men is particulary crucial at DIA, where the military mentality turns off all but the most bureaucratically inclined. After leaving intelligence I published an article about DIA's concern with this problem. In doing research for the article, I was informed by a young man at DIA that the personnel officers were so concerned about the loss of college trainees that they called a conference of those remaining to find out what was on their minds. At this session the personnel staffers informed them that better than 60 percent of college trainees in the past two years had quit. A confidential survey among those remaining revealed that 55 percent of them were actively seeking employment elsewhere. When I published those figures in my article, DIA quickly denied them, rebutting them with a statistical whirl that was beyond comprehension. The DIA spokesmen claimed that the actual attrition figure was about 27 percent—close to industry's norm. I had my sources within DIA do some further digging to find out what happened to the numbers. They found out that the DIA staffers had diluted the issue by broadening the "data base" to take into account all hirings and resignations during the period, including clerks, messengers, and secretaries. They also included in the total only those who quit within twelve months of completion of training; resignations after twelve months were deemed immaterial to the question at hand. They omitted from their figures men who had resigned to return to school for graduate work. They dropped from the total all men who had been drafted and failed to return to DIA after their discharge. They included in the new figures only those men who had resigned while in grades GS-7 and GS-9; higher-grade resignations were not included. The saddest part of this exercise came about a month later. The source who provided me with the basic facts and figures told me that after the personnel staffers had gone through the elaborate exercise of rejuggling the figures, they decided they didn't have a problem with losing college trainees after all. So they dropped any further exploration of the subject.

Many analysts on the production side of intelligence throughout the community are intellectually, if not physically, bold individuals. They are well versed in their subject and, when scratched lightly, will give forth with facts, figures, theories, and strategies. In many cases their thinking on a subject runs counter to the conventional wisdom. In Vietnam, for example, anyone back in 1967 who entertained a notion that we might not be doing well in the war was branded as a heretic. Often the analysts are able to take a shred of evidence and, examining it against their background in the subject, project a likely course of future events. Daily they must deal with several layers of management whose prime concern in life is to not make waves; the management echelons at CIA are rotated frequently, resulting in the men having rather broad administrative skills but little substantive knowledge.

Barry, the Chinese Communist military intelligence analyst at CIA, had long been studying the Lop Nor nuclear test facility. From studying a variety of sources he was familiar with the routine operational activity at the site. Two weeks before the Chinese detonated their first nuclear explosion Barry wrote a paper outlining the recent shifts in activity at the test site and concluded that they were so radically different from years past that they must be preparing for the big test. Barry wrote his paper and was quite anxious to have it published before the event. He was getting a little tired of writing good history that in no way helped the government policy makers.

Barry's supervisor of four months was still getting his bearings on the new job, and he was startled with Barry's analysis. He would not give him permission to publish it, but employed the old dodge of telling him to call an interagency committee meeting to see what the community attitude was. Barry protested, saying that he already knew that the community would not buy such a radical departure from the agreed-upon national estimate without a long-drawn-out fight. The boss insisted. Barry tried one final ploy. He asked that the study be published with sufficient caveats to indicate that it was merely an independent, speculative piece of current thinking at the working levels in intelligence. The boss hemmed and hawed and told Barry he would think that one over. He put Barry's paper in his desk drawer and it sat there until the Chinese exploded their bomb. CIA still managed to look pretty good, however, for on the day it happened it was able to scoop all the other intelligence agencies by presenting a detailed analysis of the events which led up to the explosion, using Barry's paper for background.

Another dimension of this same problem confronts an analyst when he has six to eight years on the desk. Promotions slow down, and if the man is to advance he must leave the substantive desk work for an administrative position in management. This is often a crucial point for an analyst whose interests lie mainly with the substance of a problem. Torn between affection for the work and the realities of a suburban mortgage, most conform and slide into the middle levels of management. Within this system the middle managers, like the bishops in the Catholic Church, must look upward in the hierarchy for further advancement. Their loyalties shift away from the desk and the substance of the problem. The almost inevitable result is the emergence of a layer of corporate yes-men between the analysts and the top. Insecure in their own positions, and uneasy having to deal with men below them who are better qualified, theirs is an unenviable lot.

A humorous gripe within CIA concerns attire. We were subtly made aware of the long-standing CIA clothing tradition during our training period, and we accepted it. A forward-looking intelligence officer simply does not dress like the great mass of the unwashed. We dressed like Choate men, like Harvard men. We wore our regimental ties, our tweeds, and our flannels with distinction. We wore vests beginning in October. We never took our suit jackets off in the office. We never rolled up our sleeves. We never, but never, wore shoes with buckles on them. We didn't go in for rings on our little fingers, because that had definite Jewish overtones. Our cuff links were small and simple. We wore only London Fog raincoats. In the summer we wore Haspel suits and cords. If we were fortunate enough to find a store that still sold them, we were miles ahead of our contemporaries by sporting seersuckers to the office.

This all might sound light and frivolous, but it has its sinister side. In the military shop at CIA there was an older fellow who had been working on the Soviet Army in Eastern Europe since 1946. He could recite the day-to-day events of what happened during the Berlin airlift and was the most competent and respected analyst on the subject in the entire community. During the 1961 Berlin crisis his analyses of events stood head and shoulders above those of the rest of the community. His knowledge of Soviet military thinking was such that several academics who have written on the subject routinely mailed him manuscripts for comment before publication. Ed's major failing was that he wore white socks to work. His newly appointed boss, a Cornell man, recoiled at the sight. But Ed was oblivious to this fellow's little sneers. He merely went about his daily chores. Within three months of the new boss's arrival, Ed was transferred to the training section and replaced by a sartorially splendid young officer from Yale.

This tradition has taken a turn for the worse over the past three to four years. With campus dress no longer reflecting the image of corporate America, styles have slowly begun to change within CIA. Sideburns, beards, and moustaches can be seen in the hallways now on a brave few. And every so often you see one of those wierd amalgams of old and new—a forty-fivish WASP strutting along in his long-familiar tweeds sporting collar-length hair and sideburns, in obvious deference to his own kids.

One gregarious individual at CIA who made his career on the

basis of what he wore was John. A robust six-foot-three, John had all of the proper credentials in terms of bloodlines and schooling. He had served with the Australian Army for a time in the old OSS days, and he took up the habit of wearing an enormous handlebar moustache and outlandishly wild and garishly ornate wide suspenders with his tweeds and flannels. During the quiet years of the early sixties, when crew cuts and button downs were current, John was CIA's walking virility symbol. His bald head lent additional credence to his moustache, and even the director liked to have John along on a briefing trip to the White House or the State Department. He looked like what most Americans would conjure up as a real spy.

It was not until after I left intelligence that I found out about the side "benefits" of having spent the youthful portion of my career in that field. I walked the sidewalks for a time looking for honest work in the field of journalism. I started off optimistic going to the biggies. The reaction of the managing editors of firms like *The New York Times, The Washington Post, Time,* and *Newsweek* was noteworthy. They all expressed more than a passing interest in hiring me, but the only objection they couldn't put aside was that I was "tainted" with intelligence. Max Frankel of *The New York Times* said, "I know that you have left intelligence, but what would happen if we sent you to Indonesia or India and it came out that you had previously worked at CIA. It would destroy our credibility. You would be treated like a spy by the host governments. They'd probably ask you to leave their country." The thought had never occurred to me.

Along the same vein I found it very difficult to convince friends and family that I had actually left intelligence. A year after I had left, my wife and I went on vacation to the Jersey beaches, where a goodly portion of my Irish-Catholic clan waters itself each summer. One afternoon I took a stroll with my uncle. He poked me in the ribs when we were out of earshot of our wives and gave me one of those all-knowing looks. "I know that you are still with CIA. Have they got you on a special assignment? What are they trying to do, set up some kind of deep cover for you?"

A similar thing happened to a friend of mine who left CIA. After more than two years had passed he, too, felt compelled to write of his experiences there, hoping to bring about some change. He went to a congressman from New York State to bring to his attention some of the more glaring deficiencies in intelligence. The congressman was very interested in dealing with him, but he was very nervous about seeing him in his office. He had several meetings with him. Each was set up by the congressman's aide by a telephone call. The aide would not identify himself on the phone. He'd merely give him a place and a time, then quickly hang up.

This all might be lightly brushed off as one of the ironies of modern life. At the same time it might be taken very seriously as an indication of the pervasive myths afoot about the CIA. If a member of the United States Congress harbors fears about talking openly in his own office about intelligence with a former employee of CIA, how much further can it go?

I worked closely with a reporter on the *Los Angeles Times* who was doing a series of articles about military intelligence shortly after the abortive Son Tay prisoner-of-war raid on North Vietnam. He called me at my home, and told me who he was and what he was interested in writing about. I said that I would be glad to talk to him, and I started giving him information I thought would help. He quickly interrupted me. "Look, let's not talk about this over the phone. How about if I meet you tomorrow for lunch?" I said OK, and we met for lunch the next day. However, I thought about his reaction for a long time. What is it about our society that makes supposedly intelligent, experienced newsmen so damned afraid of CIA? They act as if agents are coming out from under every bed. The reporter and I talked about this phenomenon, concluding that a good many American citizens don't think it is absurd. They actually believe that CIA has a big-brother role to play in this country and they are afraid. This cannot be allowed to continue

IX

The Big Boys

🁢🁢🁢

Whatever power in any government is independent is absolute also.

THOMAS JEFFERSON, 1819

Would you believe that Richard Helms, the director of CIA, has the phones of his immediate subordinates tapped? Well, every morning he receives a copy of the transcripts of all the phone calls that his deputies made during the previous day. It is all rationalized as just another efficient manner to keep the director informed of what is going on among his subordinates and within the agency. It is also alleged that only those calls to the White House or other policy-making centers of government are monitored. It is also just a little sick.

The intelligence community was beside itself with joy in 1966 when Richard Helms was appointed director of CIA. "Finally," they said, "we have a professional at the top." Now, with the passage of nearly six years, many have changed their minds. Helms has had time to leave his imprint clearly on the craft of intelligence. His manner and his interest in intelligence are well known within the community. Neither has served intelligence well, in the opinion of many men in the business.

Helms's loyalties today extend upward and outward. He is concerned with keeping the President happy and off his back. Moreover, he is concerned that CIA receive a good press. To these ends he devotes a considerable portion of his time. He does not concern himself with the day-to-day running of intelligence, nor does he exhibit any great interest in sorting out the many problems that exist within the community. First to go when Helms took over in 1966 were all the strong men with power positions beneath him, beginning with Lyman Kirkpatrick, the executive director. In their places Helms put men with all of the proper credentials in terms of schooling and experience. They had one thing in common: none was reputed to be a wavemaker.

Helms quickly let it be known that he would be the man who would represent the agency in Washington. Whenever Congress has a question he goes to the Hill and gives the agency position on the matter. He told his subordinates that he and only he would handle relations with the White House. He also took personal charge of the agency's relations with the press. The results in terms of Helms's public image are just short of fantastic. Helms is a very slick, urbane guy. He can charm the pants off the most sophisticated people in Washington—and he has succeeded in doing just that. His careful cultivation of the big shots of the press corps in Washington has resulted in their having nothing but the greatest admiration for Helms as an individual. That their personal feelings impinge on their reporting on CIA (which is in noticeably short supply) is evident by simply reading what has flowed from the pens of the mighty. Invited to the agency, the select few are whisked to the seventh floor in Helms's personal elevator and treated to a lunch in his private dining room. Then, over coffee, they are afforded a briefing by experts on whatever particular question is alive at the moment. Helms caps this off by dropping a few "inside tidbits," and the reporters leave with feelings of awe over being that close to the center of power. Of course Helms warns them that what he has just conveyed is highly secret information. The overall effect of this routine among the Washington press corps is that Helms has succeeded in keeping the wolves away from his own door by diverting their attention to other departments of government. The Pentagon is his usual patsy. Compare, if you will *The New York Times'* lust to uncover any scandal it can about the Pentagon with its absence of critical reporting on CIA. Those "inside tidbits" he dispenses at his secret luncheon briefings are just the kind of mea a reporter is looking for in terms of what kind of politics at other agencies is affecting national policy. With only a few exceptions, Helms has the Washington press corps eating out of the palm of his hand. This relationship has paid off handsomely—for Helms.

In effect he has merely extended his own spying appartus through elements of the press corps. A former aide in the executive suite informed me that reporters at *The New York Times* have relayed information back to Helms when they have been approached by disgruntled CIA staffers.

Among the staff of the clandestine services Helms is regarded as the absolute king of spies. After all, they will tell you, he made it to the very top of the pile without serving overseas. That, they claim, is a feat just short of a miracle. Helms served one tour overseas during World War II as an OSS officer in London. He has spent the remainder of his career in Washington as a clandestine services officer advancing from branch chief to division chief to chief of the clandestine services, an element of the agency wherein political intrigue and infighting are very highly polished arts. Helms is very skilled in these arts. He keeps his lines open to the men he respects most in intelligence, the overseas operators. He even today spends an exorbitant amount of time influencing the selection of the men on management level throughout the clandestine services. He loves to set one faction off against another. A former executive-suite employee witnessed him playing this game and chuckling aloud at how he had upset a particular division chief in the clandestine services. He would pick up the phone and call the officer working on the desk where he had a question. Helms would have the man come directly to his office without informing his boss. Once done, the man would have to return to his office and inform his bosses what Helms wanted. This would unnerve the bosses right up the line. This way Helms manages to keep them all honest and working loyally for him. They never know when he will tap into the layer below them and find out what kind of politicking is going on with collection programs or paramilitary operations.

Helms's unusual concern with what is going on in the clandestine services is in marked contrast with his interest in what is happening on the analytical side of intelligence. He deals only formally with that side of the house, via the office memorandum. He said publicly at a meeting of the Board of National Estimates that the production of intelligence "frankly bores" him. He said at the same meeting that he doesn't care for "those intellectually bold little analysts who nitpick things to death." He openly nodded at the board meeting when National Intelligence Estimates on Soviet missile strengths were under debate. He left early, remarking to an aide, "I didn't understand what the hell they were talking about."

The role that the director of CIA is to play in government is clearly set down in law and presidential directive. The clearest statement of his responsibilities is contained in a letter signed by President Kennedy which says simply that the DCI "is the government's principal foreign intelligence officer, and it is his responsibility to guide and coordinate the intelligence effort of the United States."

The law states that the director is to report to the President through the National Security Council. Theoretically he has no departmental ties or allegiances and no particular budgetary ax to grind, except, of course, CIA's. As an intelligence adviser to the NSC, the DCI attends each NSC meeting and presents an intelligence briefing. The DCI normally remains silent during these meetings, as he officially has no role in the making of United States foreign policy. His views are often sought, how-

ever, in questions concerning likely reactions abroad to a particular United States course of action.

Those parts of the law dealing with the running of the intelligence community are necessarily vague. The DCI is responsible
for the protection of intelligence sources and methods within
the community. The background to this facet of the law is
interesting. When CIA was being created, the military were
very worried about turning over their secrets to a bunch of
civilians. They had a clause written into the National Security
Act to ensure against leaks by CIA. The law also provides that
the director of CIA has access to all the information of all the
other agencies in intelligence. He is given the authority to in-
spect the files of the other agencies if he desires. But this broad
authority has never been used.

In fairness to Helms it must be said that he is in an awkward
position in relation to the other intelligence agencies. Despite
the charter of CIA, which gives him the authority to oversee
and guide the operations of the other agencies, he simply
doesn't have the clout to do it. First of all he is not of an equal
rank with the Secretaries of Defense and State, who manage the
other components. Secondly, he does not control their budgets.
Eighty-five percent of the five billion dollars a year spent on
intelligence is spent by the Defense Department. Helms has the
weight to influence how they spend it, but if a crunch comes and
the Secretary of Defense insists on spending money on a certain
project, Helms cannot overrule him. Naturally enough, this
causes a bit of frustration for Helms. In the opinion of many
in intelligence, however, it is not a strong enough reason for
Helms to merely allow Defense and State to do what they want
—which is what is happening today. Helms does not take an
interest in administering the entire community. Since he
doesn't, the community simply administers itself.

The day-to-day world of intelligence at Helms's level is not
unlike that of a corporate president. He meets with his immediate staff in the morning after he reads the overnight cable traffic

selected for him by a twenty-four-hour duty staff in the message center. The meetings dwell normally on current developments; each deputy director reports what is up in his shop.

The executive suite is, by government standards, posh. Thickly carpeted and paneled, the set of offices has a seventh-floor view of the rolling hills of the CIA estate on the Potomac River, some four miles from the congestion of Washington. The director is served directly by an administrative assistant who sees to the running of the office. The director's secretary wields a great deal of influence within the executive suite. She determines what paper gets to his desk and what does not. She stays tuned in to the infighting within the suite where some thirty men work. She feeds an assortment of birds each day atop the seventh-floor balcony and employs the director's goons, a threesome of bodyguards who follow him on all official business, to care for the pigeon and small-bird feeders on the balcony. The bodyguards can also be seen at various times sitting in the outer office hooking rugs for the director's secretary. This has created some embarrassing moments, when the director will suddenly and unexpectedly charge out of his office to go to the State Department or elsewhere for a meeting, while the bodyguards try to untangle themselves from their rug-hooking to catch up with him.

There are very few leaks of information from the executive suite. Those closest to Helms, as said before, are men who know which side their bread is buttered on. The only inside stories that manage to leak out are those that Helms desires get out. These normally deal with the political infighting that goes on at the second and third levels of the agency. The one exception to this general rule occurred when Helms was Deputy Director of CIA under Admiral Rayburn, the director in 1965–66. Some rather juicy gossip about Rayburn's performance would work its way down to the lowest levels of the agency. One piece of gossip alleged that the admiral, who had headed up the Polaris submarine program as his last act in the Navy, admitted shortly after taking over CIA that he was not "up to speed" on world politics. The story had it that he was given a daily fifteen-minute briefing on a particular country by the staff, so that he could catch up on the political and diplomatic scene. The day that the Libya briefing was given, the story has it that Rayburn was provided with a complete rundown of the country, including basic social, economic, and political facts. He was told, for example, that the country was run by an oligarchy. At the end of the briefing, when asked if he had any questions, Rayburn allegedly asked to see the biographic file "on this fellow Ali Garky."

During one brief period of CIA's history there was a director who came to the agency without any particular background in intelligence. John McCone had proved himself as an administrator, and he instituted a number of changes while he ran CIA. For those of us on the analytical side of intelligence, his tenure was known as the "Let a hundred blossoms flourish" period. The intellectual level of meetings among intelligence officials at CIA and other agencies improved greatly under McCone. He was in the habit of putting difficult and precise questions to those performing formal analyses and plans, challenging them and forcing them to defend their judgments.

Breaking cleanly with tradition, McCone brought specialists and analysts into conferences and decision making at a much higher level of policy than ever before. Often he took such men with him to meetings at the cabinet level and to the White House. This exposed the CIA men to policy considerations as never before and put policy makers more closely in touch with the experts on whose facts they were acting.

As chairman of the United States Intelligence Board, McCone again broke with tradition and won himself a reputation for objectivity by frequently overruling the proposals of his own agency. McCone also tried but failed to end the interagency rivalry. He spent a great deal of time in bitter dispute with Secretary of Defense McNamara about the division of labor and the cost of technology.

The high-water mark of McCone's objectivity occurred in

1963, when the limited nuclear test-ban treaty was under consideration. McCone, as the former director of the Atomic Energy Commission, was personally in favor of the treaty. He had backed such an idea since his years at the AEC. He wanted the facts of the case to be known clearly, and he surprised the entire intelligence community and enraged the White House by supplying the opposition in Congress with a CIA staff expert. The man assisted the powerful and influential Senator John Stennis of Mississippi, the chairman of the Armed Services Committee, in preparing his opposition case against the treaty. McCone viewed such a move as consistent with his view of CIA's role to inform government as fully as possible; such a move has never again occurred.

McCone also took steps to reorganize CIA from within. He noted that his three deputies—for intelligence production, clandestine operations, and support—were all vying for his time and attention. He set up the number-three slot in the agency, named an executive director to fill it, and made the three deputies go through this man. This provided a mechanism for badly needed centralized planning and policy formulation within the agency. It reduced the three deputies to equals and ended, for a time, the bitter rivalry for the director's attention. In the past the clandestine services chief had reigned supreme in the informal organization of the agency. He always had Allen Dulles's ear, and his two colleagues went begging.

McCone, with his scientific background at the Atomic Energy Commission, was not pleased with the agency's scientific efforts. After studying the problem, he pulled together all the scientific elements of the agency from their scattered enclaves and formed a fourth deputy directorship for science. It took more than two years to accomplish this because of the tremendous resistance within the bureaucracy.

The contrast between Allen Dulles and John McCone, who replaced him, is sharp. To Dulles, a gambling man, the possibilities of losses were real but the chances of success were more important. A 20 percent chance to overthrow a leftist regime in Guatemala with a CIA-sponsored invasion was all he wanted to give it a try. He charmed President Eisenhower with tales of extraordinary snooping and romantic derring-do. As long as his brother John was Secretary of State he had no need to chafe under political control. Neither of the Dulles brothers earned their reputations by taut and businesslike administration. Both placed supreme confidence in their own personal judgment.

Admiral Rayburn, who was appointed director of CIA in 1965, earned his reputation as the developer of the Navy's Polaris submarine, but he had no previous experience in intelligence. He was not particularly close to President Johnson or other high administration officials. He got off to a bad start by taking over on the day President Johnson dispatched United States troops to Santo Domingo, and he was blamed by many for coming up with the mishmash of evidence on which State rested its case for invasion. Rayburn was chosen, after a six-month search, primarily to serve as a front man with Congress. He had earned high marks in his dealings with Congress while heading up the Polaris program, but as director of CIA he failed to maintain his high standing, for Congress soon came to have little confidence in his grasp of intelligence matters. This was partly due to his lack of experience but it was also partly due to Richard Helms's influence. In a conversation with me some years after he retired, Rayburn confided jokingly, "I thought for a time when I was director of CIA that I might be assassinated by my deputy." His deputy, of course, was Helms. When I pressed him on this point he refused to say more. One of the ways in which Helms set out to take over Rayburn's job has already been discussed. Another involved an arrangement Helms set up with the overnight Watch Office. Whenever the White House called CIA, Helms was informed first of the request. He, in turn, passed the information along to Rayburn. This way Helms got the entirety of the request and supplied Rayburn with whatever he thought prudent before he went off to the White House with the answer. As subtle as this is, Helms had to be extremely careful in what he gave the director and what he did not. In many cases Rayburn had to call Helms to the White House after his own arrival to supply them with a more complete answer. Of course Helms came off looking like the White Knight in such a situation. Rayburn also tried to make some needed changes within the agency but failed disastrously. He told me, "The wall of entrenched bureaucrats below me was fantastic. Whenever I suggested any changes they spent the next several days coming up with reasons why not. There was no communication; it was open warfare."

There have been more than a dozen attempts at reforming the intelligence community since it was formed in 1947. In many cases these attempts were prompted by some intelligence crisis. They are all notable for their lack of success in coming to grips with the problem. If any one reason can be attributed to this lack of success, it is the personal involvement of CIA in investigating itself—a most questionable arrangement, which springs from the myth that intelligence is such a specialized art that intelligence officials must take investigators by the hand and lead them through the community so they can understand it. Of course they always manage to divert the investigators, and they never reveal where any of the bodies are buried.

President Truman called three men together with intelligence experience and had them investigate the structure of federal intelligence in 1948. Allen Dulles, William Jackson, and Matthew Correa came up with recommendations that pointed out several flaws in the structure. Primary among these was the fact that most of the top-management slots in intelligence were filled with military officers, many of whom knew little of intelligence. In true government fashion, however, their report was sent to CIA for comments when it was finished. The very officials whom the report lambasted now had to sit down and review it. Their reply was not at all responsive to the report, and it finally took a National Security Council directive to have some of the recommendations implemented. Despite the NSC directive, the CIA staff still resisted and whittled away another year before implementing those that were absolutely necessary.

In 1948 the Hoover commission on government organization took a look at the intelligence system and concluded that intelligence people were not paying sufficient attention to scientific developments. The community resisted the commission's recommendations that they get involved in this field until the Soviets detonated their first atomic device. Then it moved to set up scientific shops throughout the community.

In 1954 another task force was set up to look at intelligence. Headed by General James Doolittle, this group took a long look at the agency's overseas clandestine activities and made several fundamental recommendations concerning their control. Allen Dulles strongly influenced the recommendation that an interagency group be set up to monitor and actually control all CIA's overseas actions. The group was set up with the President's special assistant for NSC matters at the head. The director of the CIA, the Deputy Secretary of Defense, and the Undersecretary of State for Political Affairs also sat on the group. Because of the fraternal relationship of John and Allen Dulles and their closeness to Eisenhower, the group exercised little control that Allen Dulles did not personally endorse. In effect no control over the community resulted.

In 1955 another Hoover task force on government organization took a look at intelligence and recommended that a congressional joint committee and a presidentially appointed board of outside consultants be established to oversee and control intelligence activities. Allen Dulles had no desire to share his secrets with Congress, so his efforts were aimed at killing that portion of the report. He was successful, and, in victory, he acquiesced to the establishment in 1956 of the President's Foreign Intelligence Advisory Board. This group was to be a permanent body that would report directly to the President. It was headed by the distinguished Dr. James Killian, president of MIT. The only useful function this first board performed was to give impetus and support to the U-2 program, a pet of Dr. Killian's. It did not look into covert overseas operations except on a post-mortem basis.

Allen Dulles saw to it that the group was nothing more than a front. Lyman Kirkpatrick, in *The Real CIA,* described the first briefing the group was given. "The opening briefing that CIA gave this distinguished board was brutal. It lasted about eight hours and was in truth a saturation effort on the work of the CIA. The board happily recovered from their baptism of fire and settled down into their established procedure of meeting about every month for a day or two and studying the most important problems affecting the CIA and other intelligence agencies."

The staff of the President's board was drawn from the upper staff echelons of CIA. These men did the homework for the board and dutifully reported back to the director what areas the board wanted to investigate. Their impartiality can be seriously questioned.

In 1959 Soviet Foreign Minister Gromyko attacked United States intelligence and claimed it was creating a dangerous situation in Berlin. Eisenhower personally took direction of a look into intelligence. As a result, the Bureau of the Budget increased its review of the size and scope of the United States intelligence effort. Maurice Stans, then the director of the Bureau of the Budget, proposed to Eisenhower that the bureau be allowed to study two major areas of intelligence. Eisenhower agreed that these studies should be completed before his administration left office. The next step, of course, was to call the agency and other members of the board to a meeting with Stans to set up the necessary procedures. The proposals of Stans never got beyond the talking stage. The discussions resulted in such complete disagreement that nothing happened.

After the shootdown of the U-2 the following year, the Bureau of the Budget again tried to pry open the lid on intelligence and presented a proposal to the President's Foreign Intelligence Advisory Board. The board, respecting the wishes of

Allen Dulles, decided that such a study was too broad a subject for the Bureau of the Budget. Instead, it directed that the study be made by a special task force made up of representatives of the State Department, the Defense Department, the White House, the Bureau of the Budget, and the CIA. Who did the board pick to head up the group? Why, the director of the CIA, naturally. The group met several times and finally issued a watered-down report that recommended several cosmetic changes to the incoming administration.

When John Kennedy came into office he decided to do away with a goodly amount of the formal bureaucratic empires that had sprung up under Eisenhower, among them the President's Foreign Intelligence Advisory Board. After the Bay of Pigs fiasco, however, he decided that perhaps such an instrument would be useful. It was reconstituted under the direction of Dr. Killian. The President directed the board to investigate the whole intelligence community and recommend changes. After a decent interval Kennedy relieved Dulles and selected McCone to head the agency. Dulles managed, however, to leave his imprint—the board soon learned the fact of life that abroad CIA answered to no one but the director. Kennedy issued a letter reinstating the ambassadors to their position of primacy overseas. He followed this letter with a secret cable to all posts abroad saying that he specifically meant that CIA would come under the ambassadors' control. The board wrestled with the idea of splitting up CIA and scattering it to the winds of government. They wanted to take the clandestine operations function and plant it either at the Pentagon or in a special agency. Moreover, they considered divesting CIA of some of its collection assignments. Dulles convinced the board that neither of these steps was advisable. The report to the President finally recommended that things should pretty much stay as they were. And so the tale goes. In 1963, after the Diem coup, another investigation ended up reducing CIA's covert political action in South Vietnam.

Clearly lacking since 1955 has been a thorough public investigation of the intelligence community in the style of the Hoover commission study. The internal attempts at reform have simply failed to come to grips with the fundamental organizational ills of the community. They have not been impartial and they have all resulted in glib, well-written reports which acquit many, condemn few, and generally result in a few minor cosmetic changes that, in reality, avoid or hide the basic problems.

The President's Foreign Intelligence Advisory Board still exists, but it is a joke within the community. I have witnessed this august body in operation when it meets every month for a day or two. The members are treated to a morning of world situation briefings that leaves most of them nodding in their chairs. They spend the afternoon reviewing the minutes of their last meeting and being told what the staff has done since. The next morning, fresh from a round of drinks and dinner in town, they usually tell the staff what they want looked into. "Perhaps we ought to be doing a little more of this and a little less of that" is the kind of statement that usually springs from the mouths of the members. When they meet next month, the staff tells them the director of CIA has been told that he should be doing a little more of this and a little less of that. The board is usually happy with this arrangement, for to really follow up they would have to spend considerably more than two days a month in Washington. The board is treated very lightly in the executive suite at CIA. The director refers to the executive secretary of the board as "that little gnat" that keeps coming around every so often to bother him. He usually asks one of his staffers to swat the gnat for him.

Aside from these formal governmental attempts to reform CIA there are always numerous attempts underway at a lower level within the community to bring about change. Two instances come to mind that serve to underscore the attitude that prevails at the top. Many more could be told by every man in intelligence. In 1967 it became obvious to a man named Hamilton in the director's executive suite that things were getting out of hand in the field of intelligence collecting. He convinced his boss, the deputy director, that the agency should take a look at this to see what could be done. His boss brought the subject up at a morning staff meeting with the director and he said it was a good idea. Moreover, he added that perhaps the study should be done by the Inspector General's office—which would give it more impact when finally released. Hamilton was put in charge of the study team, and off they went for several months of documenting what is collected and to what uses it is put. Hamilton was a straightforward intelligence officer with considerable espionage experience in Eastern Europe and command positions throughout the agency. He didn't mince his words. When all the evidence was in, Hamilton sat down and wrote a frank report of conditions. The first sentence of his report is a legend within the halls of CIA today. It said, "The United States intelligence community is collecting entirely too much information." He went on to say that much of what is collected is merely stored away without being used. The report pinpointed the areas of useless collection, the duplication of collection efforts, and closed with recommendations concerning what should be eliminated and what should be cut back.

The very fact that his first sentence achieved legendary status within the agency stands as moot testimony to the kind of finished reports that come out of the top of the intelligence structure. No one likes to state a position clearly and forthrightly. Rather they prefer to "balance" whatever they say with "both sides of the story." Had some of the more skilled bureaucrats done the report it certainly would not have started out like Hamilton's version. More likely they would have said something like: "A detailed examination of United States intelligence collection indicates that, despite some duplication and extraneous collection, the overall thrust of efforts contributes solidly to national goals."

Hamilton closed his report by recommending that the director convene a meeting with other heads of the community and begin a program to scale down all United States collection efforts. He provided him with chapter-and-verse statements of where the group could begin their reforms.

The report was finally passed to the director at his morning staff meeting. Printed copies were handed out to all the deputies, and Hamilton gave a short fifteen-minute briefing on the subject. While he was talking, the various deputies were reading the printed version. Their reactions were similar. Whenever they saw the other guy's ox getting gored, they smiled and nodded affirmatively. Whenever their own ox got it, they screamed. After the briefing a regular shouting match broke out. All the deputies wanted Hamilton's hide. The meeting broke up with the director asking that they all take a look at the report and come back with their comments. A week later the report was the subject of a special staff meeting. This time the deputies came armed for war. Each defended his own collection programs. They all took a similar tack in their assault on Hamilton. They let it slip in their formal briefings that Hamilton was "slipshod" in his investigation. He spoke to "the wrong people," those who didn't have a "full understanding of the problem." He failed, they said, to come to the boss in his investigations.

To make a long story short, Hamilton's report was filed away in the director's office and nothing was done about it. The director merely told his deputies to set up a working group to go into all aspects of the report. This, in effect, was the kiss of death. The director knew that they would whittle it to shreds if they were given enough time. They did. As for Hamilton, who had been a comer in the front office, he was transferred within a month to become the deputy director of training.

In 1969 the National Security Agency came under the gun at budget time. There was one particular collection program that had stood out like a sore thumb for its inability to produce any worthwhile intelligence. For years NSA had been collecting tape recordings of Soviet "scrambler" communications. This is a form of radio communication in which the signal is scrambled on the airwaves. It is refiltered by the receiving station according to a random mathematical formula, and it comes out in the clear. The statistical odds against breaking this form of communication, if one does not have the exact type of receiving and sending gear as the Soviets, is conservatively estimated at around one million to one. The trend in this type of communications system is toward even better gear. NSA was spending approximately one hundred million dollars per year to collect this information. Once collected, however, it was merely stored away in vaults at NSA headquarters, as NSA's mathematicians had not yet devised a formula for breaking it out. The deputy director of CIA called a meeting with NSA and all the other members of the community. He told them the program was slated to be canceled. NSA protested and demanded a reexamination of the evidence. When they came back for the next meeting one week later, the NSA staff had come up with figures showing that only fifty million dollars was being spent on the project. The other fifty was tucked away in other parts of the NSA budget. Nothing was solved at this meeting. At the next three or four meetings the cost of the scrambler project suddenly diminished to less than ten million dollars. Bits and pieces of the original program began showing up under other approved collection projects. No one protested this NSA action. As a matter of fact, most members of the group quietly applauded and made notes on how it was done, for their own future reference. The final result was a slick briefing given to the United States Intelligence Board in which NSA demonstrated that for a relatively minor investment of eight million dollars they were storing up information that could rewrite world history at some future date—if their mathematicians ever devised systems to read the stuff. The leaders of the community felt that the program was worth continued investment.

The idea that the intelligence activities of the United States are under continual and close congressional scrutiny is, perhaps, the politest fiction in Washington. The overall effect of the fragmented, disjointed, and highly partisan congressional role in intelligence is near zero.

More important than what role Congress plays in overseeing CIA is the little known, but potentially dangerous, fact that CIA actually has a direct hand in picking what members of Congress will serve on the committees charged with supervising intelligence activities. The excuse for giving the agency a voice in the selection of congressmen is to make sure that only "secure and responsible" members are chosen. The net effect of this privilege over the past ten years has been that the agency usually manages to have itself checked by its best friends in Congress, those who can best shield it from more critical members.

There are four committees of Congress with some responsibility for looking into intelligence. In both the Senate and the House, the Appropriations and Armed Services Committees have CIA intelligence subcommittees. Their members take a piecemeal look at the impact of intelligence on either the annual budget or the military. None of the four committees takes an overall look at the entire structure of intelligence. None considers the entirety of the intelligence budget. Left out of the picture altogether are the important House and Senate Foreign Relations committees. The only part of the intelligence community which comes within the jurisdiction of the Foreign Relations Committee is the Bureau of Intelligence at the State Department. The committee has done little in the way of formal overseeing of that bureau, its staff counsel told me, although there are a variety of informal contacts maintained. There are no formal arrangements whereby the Foreign Relations Committee is brought into the CIA subcommittees of Appropriations and Armed Services. Informally, three members of the Foreign Relations Committee are invited to meetings of these subcommittees. The Foreign Relations Committee can and does call members of the intelligence community before it for questioning. In 1970 this was done on eight occasions.

Efforts to regain a greater measure of congressional supervision of the intelligence community have met with surprisingly little success in the last twenty-four years. Since 1947, for example, over two hundred resolutions have been introduced in the Senate calling for stricter and more systematic congressional surveillance of the entire community. An even greater number of such proposals was made in the House of Representatives. None of these proposals has had any impact on the original congressional system for overseeing set up in 1947. Congress forfeited its traditional controls over elements of the executive branch in the case of the CIA. In principle, however, congressional control over intelligence remains.

The question of congressional control of CIA first became an issue in early 1956. Senator Mike Mansfield, with thirty-four co-sponsors, introduced a bill to form a Joint Committee on Intelligence in Congress. It would be patterned after the Joint Atomic Energy Committee with its own staff of experts and permanent status. The idea was to share the responsibility for overseeing intelligence among the three committees of Congress with direct interest in the subject—Appropriations, Armed Services, and Foreign Relations. Mansfield wanted to probe deeply into the intelligence structure to find out what was going on within the community. His bill would have given the joint committee power to study all of the activities of the CIA, to study the problems related to gathering intelligence which affects national security, and to study the coordination and use of intelligence by the various departments and agencies of government. Mansfield was supported in his plan by the 1955 Hoover commission study of government organization, which recommended that a joint committee be established. After debate the bill was defeated in the Senate, where fully another ten years was to pass before it arose again as a major issue.

In 1966 Senators Fulbright and McCarthy drafted a resolution in the Foreign Relations Committee and brought it to the Senate floor for a vote. It called for the creation of a committee on intelligence operations made up of nine members drawn from the three committees with interests in intelligence activities. Before this resolution even saw the light of day, however, major compromises had been made. McCarthy originally intended to present a resolution which would have granted the same investigative powers that were proposed in 1956. The bitter infighting that went on behind the scenes resulted in his original aim being reduced to a request to merely· expand the existing subcommittee system to include three members of the Foreign Relations Committee in the picture. Even in this emasculated form the resolution was effectively killed when the Senate voted to send the resolution to the Armed Services Committee for action. It never came out of committee.. President Johnson, who could have settled the dispute by ordering CIA to give full information to the Foreign Relations Committee, stayed out of the fracas. Apparently he couldn't separate Fulbright's and McCarthy's criticism of his Vietnam policy from the CIA issue.

It is very difficult to ferret out all of the reasons why congressional reluctance to change is so great. Perhaps the most pertinent reason is that a change in the status quo would call for the sharing of some power by the senior members of Congress.

As far as the formation of a joint committee is concerned, there is ample precedent for such a setup. Congressional surveillance of atomic energy has existed since 1946. This area is as sensitive as foreign intelligence. An identifiable committee of Congress dealing with all of intelligence would promote new confidence between Congress and CIA. The need for such a committee is buttressed by the well-known fact that studies of CIA by ad hoc or temporary groups have not been effective. Moreover, the present system allows for the continued heavy use of the secrecy excuse. This policy of secrecy for secrecy's sake invites abuse and prevents Congress and the nation from knowing what kind of intelligence apparatus we have.

Opponents of change argue that the present setup is more than adequate. They also claim that the functions of the CIA are essentially executive in character and immune from deep probing by Congress. They state that CIA has been adequately investigated by the present committee structure and that the proposal to create a joint committee raises a constitutional issue of separation of powers between the executive and legislative branches. Intelligence, they say, is exclusively the prerogative of the President and closely associated with the conduct of foreign affairs. As far as the Atomic Energy Committee precedent is concerned, opponents of change simply state that it is not valid to compare the two subjects. Intelligence, in their view, is not comparable.

Behind these publicly stated reasons lurks another—that granting Congress wider surveillance over CIA would upset the principal allies of the United States. Intelligence units in many allied countries enjoy immunity from detailed legislative supervision. Wider congressional surveillance would raise fears among allies that sources might be blown by indiscreet leaks from the American Congress.

As a result of the 1966 Fulbright-McCarthy attempt to broaden congressional oversight of CIA, the chairman of the Senate Armed Services Committee invited the three senior members of the Foreign Relations Committee to sit in on the CIA subcommittee meetings. Senator Fulbright described to me what goes on in those meetings. "They get very little done. They do not keep any minutes of the meetings; it is all very hush-hush. The ten-minute rule is in effect, so the members have little if any chance to dig deep into a subject. The director of CIA spends most of the time talking about the Soviet missile threat and so on. The kind of information he provides is interesting, but it really is of little help in trying to find out what is going on in intelligence. He actually tells them only what he wants them to know. It seems to me that the men on the committee are more interested in shielding CIA from its critics than in anything else."

Obviously there are conflicting arguments on the value of these meetings. Some say they are comprehensive and that the director holds back nothing. Others, such as Senator Fulbright, say nothing of value transpires. Several things are clear. The subcommittees exercise no real control because they are not advised before or after covert operations are launched. The senior members of all four committees in the House and Senate are clearly men whose prime interest seems to be protecting the CIA from its critics. The director of CIA controls what information is provided to the committees. Some members of Congress do not want to know any classified information for fear they might leak it in a speech or press conference. For all these reasons there is a large body of substantial evidence and opinion in and out of Congress that favors more specific monitoring of intelligence activities.

X

The Boom of <u>Your</u> Voice

What is to be done about CIA? I hope that many of the myths surrounding CIA have been dispelled. CIA is not a ten-foot ogre. It is merely a human institution badly in need of change. CIA is not the invisible government. Rather, it is a tired old whore that no one has the heart to take in off the street. She needs a hot bath, a clean set of clothes, and a good rest, not to mention a few good meals, before she can again assume an air of respectability. As I stated at the outset I am a believer in the necessity for having the CIA. It is a vital part of the American government and must continue to be so. My concern stems from the realization that United States intelligence is in very bad condition, and no one within government seems to give a damn. Or, those who have tried to render changes have met with such overwhelming obstacles that they have thrown in the towel.

A summary of the major problems facing intelligence is discouraging. The most crucial aspect is at the working level. There is a great deal of frustration among the men and women at this level because there is a seeming lack of concern for them at the top. Technology is king, and the analysts and operators alike are subordinated to it. A "could-not-care-less" attitude is prevalent; too many people are doing just what they have to do and little more. After a year or so in intelligence, they learn that initiative gets one in more trouble than it's worth. Any new idea, unusual approach to a problem, or questioning of the established order of things is treated as a form of heresy. Most people learn quickly.

The confusing welter of committees, study groups, and overlapping lines of authority and responsibility leaves most men and women wondering just whom they work for, what it is they actually do, and why. It is difficult for most to perceive just how they fit into the overall scheme of things. These are not uncommon criticisms in today's world, given the highly organized society we have created for ourselves. It cannot be allowed to persist in intelligence, however, because this is not a common pursuit. Its goals and influence are broader than mere corporate profit.

The entire intelligence community is a child of compromise. It merely represents an arena in which conflicting budgetary interests at the Pentagon and policy goals of the State Department are horse-traded. It has no individuality, as its membership is largely composed of men and organizations whose interests lie in protecting their bailiwick and managing intelligence to suit their needs. The departmental approach really works only in theory. The shibboleth of "coordination" is a farce, representing in large part the watering down and soft-peddling of tough issues. Each of the separate agencies is an institution in itself. Because of the enormous complexity of trying to blend all these activities together, the major problem is averted. No one has had the courage to face up to the fact that the departmental approach to intelligence is now obsolete. It simply won't work anymore. The community and its leaders all realize this, but no one wants to rock the boat and admit it openly. Why? Because it is simply easier to muddle along with what you have than to make the radical changes that are necessary. It is this attitude that creates hundreds of committees, that spawns a ridiculous degree of duplication of effort, that generates enormous and backbreaking loads of paperwork, that allows major inequities in personnel policies, and finally, that forces the entire community to assume the most defensive posture it can to keep the wolves away from its door. The sages of intelligence today, those old duffers who fought the valiant fight required to form CIA, will brand me as naive. "It can't be done. We tried once back in the forties and it was a bloody fight." What they are really saying is several things. First they mean they are happy with what they devised. They don't want to do something at the end of their careers that says their original decisions were perhaps wrong. They are admitting that they haven't tried to improve on the system they originally established. These men are very clever, too. They won't come out and address the problem directly. Rather, they will pose an intellectually appealing line of reasoning that goes like this: "Dear boy, don't you realize that intelligence is an imprecise art form? It has been this way since the dawn of time. We can't simply bridle the imaginative creativity of intelligence officers and make them conform to a mold. We have to shift with the ebb and flow of events. We can't allow ourselves to be precisely and functionally organized like other parts of government." Not given to fully appreciating such profundities, particularly since I spent a good many years where this supposed art form is played out, I don't accept this cocktail party baloney. There is an old school notion afoot among the well-bred leaders of intelligence that these problems will somehow go away and that they, as generalists, can maintain adequate control through the boom of their voices and the fact that they "know" old George over there at the Pentagon or at State.

This chummy feeling that everything is under control has

also prevented today's intelligence leadership from realizing the full impact of technology on intelligence. Only a few at or near the top will admit that technology is a runaway horse, not responsive to the boom of anyone's voice. In my opinion, the unbridled reliance on technology contains the seeds of intelligence's own destruction. It must be channeled and controlled day by day. Searching, fundamental questions must be asked about the precise role technology is to play in intelligence. It can provide enormous support to the intelligence community, but it can also quite easily make the production of intelligence subordinate to itself. I submit that the community is quite close to that point today.

Lastly, I submit that the events of the past six years point rather clearly to the distasteful conclusion that Richard Helms, or any other professional spy, should not be allowed to head up the intelligence community. The job does not require a man versed in intelligence, so much as it requires a highly skilled manager and administrator. The community today is not the tiny enclave of independently wealthy public servants who performed so admirably during World War II. It is a conglomerate industry with diverse functions and a worldwide responsibility to collect, process, and pass along information. Given the competitive nature of the present intelligence establishment, it would almost seem doubly necessary to bring in leadership with no internal fiefdoms to protect, with an objective and impartial outlook, and with a mind clear enough to ask the searching basic questions and challenge the existing order of things within the community.

The broader implications of allowing intelligence to continue along its present path are worrisome. Most fearful is the fact that the entire structure is today so unwieldy that it could inadvertently stumble into a continuing series of international incidents, any one of which could lead us to war. The USS *Liberty,* the *Pueblo,* and the *EC-121* incidents are three classic examples of bureaucracy gone awry.

Added to this substantial worry is the fact that a worldwide intelligence net, active as the American one is today, can do very little to serve the basic policy thrust of reducing American presence abroad such as proposed in the Nixon doctrine. The mere presence of intelligence operatives in a country automatically assures that a continued and pervasive interest in that country will be fostered by the Washington intelligence agencies. In July, 1969, when the Honduras–El Salvador war was going on, it was jokingly remarked that there were more intelligence people in Washington and the two countries working on the war than there were citizens of the two countries fighting it.

As the "daily take" of intelligence increases around the world it seems to almost guarantee that significant developments will be lost in the ever-increasing swirl of paper. With no rational ceiling or limitations on intelligence collection the volume of material is bound to increase. In such a situation it becomes more and more difficult for intelligence to perform its primary mission of keeping the President informed.

Perhaps the most important facet of today's intelligence problems is the lack of confidence among the American public in regard to its government. The idea is afoot, based on good evidence, that United States intelligence is now turning inward on the citizens of this country. Newsmen, students, dissenters, militants, and college professors have a distinct distaste for intelligence. If this persists much longer the ordinary citizens of this country will come to suspect that they, too, are being watched by intelligence. The next logical step then would be for an administration to do exactly what its people suspect it of doing—start mounting intelligence operations against citizen groups and assemblies.

The problems of intelligence, then, seem to cut across many lines. There is the organizational mechanics of intelligence, but this dims in comparison to the far broader difficulties of secrecy in government and the role of intelligence in our society. It is the aspect of secrecy that causes many of the other ills. Left to its own devices, intelligence is incapable of policing itself. The result has been the ever-swelling expansion of the intelligence structure. It is time, perhaps, to back away from this enormous structure of intelligence and ask again some basic questions.

A total reorganization of the effort is sorely needed. Perhaps the community should be formed around the basic processes involved in intelligence—collection, processing, reporting, and operations. Today each one of these four processes is engaged in by each of the nine federal agencies in intelligence. That they duplicate each other's efforts is well documented. That they waste considerable amounts of time, money, and human resources is implicit. Within the federal structure the Director of Central Intelligence could remain where he sits today, answerable to the National Security Council and the President. Beneath him, however, it seems time to seriously consider creating a department of intelligence collection which would gather under one roof all of the intelligence-gathering tasks, from the traditional human contacts maintained around the world to the most sophisticated of space satellites. With one man in charge, the director would at least have a specific place to go when he had a collection problem. Moreover, the entire effort could more rationally be controlled. Duplicate collection efforts would be immediately visible, and extraneous efforts could be eliminated. Budgets could more sensibly be controlled without the ability, as now exists, of hiding collection under various other portions of an agency's budget.

The greatest strides toward economy and efficiency could be realized with a department responsible for processing the vast amounts of information collected today. Here, where the computer is just now coming into its own, a consolidation of efforts would save untold millions. Today each of the nine departments in intelligence is building up its computer systems with little or no attempt to understand where the other agencies are going in this expensive field. A department for processing would also serve as an independent check on the collection effort. They could more readily identify duplicate and useless areas of collection. Today no one in the intelligence computer business would raise a voice about the volumes of useless material being collected because he would be damning his own organization.

A department of analysis would, perhaps, be the most vital element in the community. Staffed with personnel from the present nine agencies, the old argument about vested interest and only one person looking at the problem would be largely discredited. The diverse analytical functions could be divided up considerably more efficiently than they are now. Sufficient leeway would exist organizationally to allow for the diversity of opinion that everyone today screams about as being the one reason we can't get rid of the departmental approach to intelligence. Glib spokesmen also say they'd like a little bit of duplication to keep everyone honest. That is similar to wanting to be a little bit pregnant. It would also be possible to establish a net evaluations group in such a new department to look at the strategic areas of intelligence that today are burdened with budgetary considerations. This group could assess the thrust of United States military spending and research at the same time that they are assessing the thrust of Soviet and Chinese efforts in the field. Then, perhaps, the chances for less vested interests coming to play in intelligence would appear. Such a unit could have considerable impact on congressional appropriations. Instead of today's system, with the Pentagon marching to Capitol Hill each spring to sell fear, we might be able to evolve a less emotional approach to military spending.

A department for operations would again collate all of the diverse intelligence operations going on abroad. It would give the President and the rest of government one responsible official to check with when operations were being considered. They would be able to better control these worldwide efforts more reasonably.

Obviously with such a complex subject there would be some need for coordination among the four major elements of the community. But this could take place at a higher level, and, hopefully, be kept to a minimum. With the situation as it is today, committees gather to decide on installing a gasoline pump at an overseas location and then producing a feasibility study on the subject.

The benefits of a clear-cut functional approach to intelligence speak for themselves. It would solve many of the now existing problems that characterize a career in intelligence. It would create others also, but it is doubtful if these new problems would be as serious as the current ones.

In the established order of things the only person who can effect the needed changes in intelligence is the President. It works for him, and he has the clout to order changes. Presidential displeasure with intelligence is no secret. President Nixon has taken steps to bring about change—he had a detailed study of intelligence made and several changes were considered. But he made one tragic mistake in his approach to solving the intelligence dilemma: he let the intelligence community take a major part in the study. History has shown what happens in such cases, and today it is happening all over again. This study has followed the path of all the others. Nothing more than cosmetic changes were rendered. The government has once again avoided coming to grips with the basic organizational obsolescence of the community. What has resulted is some minor reshuffling of duties at the top. This, of course, has necessitated the creation of more committees to service the needs of this realigned superstructure. They will not render any changes that affect the workings of intelligence.

Nixon invested Helms with new authority to oversee all the intelligence agencies, paring away budgetary fat and professional overlap wherever possible. With Helms elevated to superstar status, the day-to-day running of CIA fell to his deputy, Marine Corps Lieutenant General Robert Cushman. In the White House, Nixon solidified Henry Kissinger's powers to evaluate intelligence reports and, in particular, to make them more responsive to the needs of the policy makers.

Outwardly these maneuvers might appear to be a mild bureaucratic rebuke to the intelligence community; their real punch was delivered in a top secret presidential "decision memorandum" spelling out Nixon's dissatisfactions and desires in meticulous detail. His major complaints are faulty intelligence, runaway budgets, and a disparity between a glut of facts and a poverty of analysis.

Though the President holds Helms and CIA in high personal regard, he has been irritated by a series of intelligence community failures. The SALT talks had to be delayed for months while the White House tried to sort out discrepancies between the various agencies on how well the United States could detect possible Soviet violations of any arms control agreement. Estimates of the Vietcong supplies that used to flow through the Cambodian port of Sihanoukville were off by several orders of magnitude, and there was a complete failure to predict the ferocity of North Vietnamese resistance to the ill-starred campaign in Laos in 1970. The elaborate commando raid on an empty prison camp in North Vietnam still rankles, and the White House blames the intelligence community for not catching sooner the Russian-built surface-to-air missiles that suddenly sprouted in the Middle East cease-fire zone in 1970.

Political analyst Joseph Kraft summarized his feelings about the most recent changes in intelligence in November, 1971. He wrote:

> The reorganization of the intelligence community announced last week looks at first glance like a mere administrative tightening. The producers of raw intelligence are simply being made more responsive to the needs of the consumers in the White House.
>
> But the Nixon administration is no more free than most others of the itch to enforce conformity. Unless very carefully watched, the new setup could be one more device for destroying independent centers of analysis and information inside government.
>
> The reorganization has two main components. For one thing Richard Helms, the director of Central Intelligence,

has been given authority to coordinate his own budget with those of the intelligence units within the Defense and State Departments.

Since Mister Helms, as CIA director, is a member of most of the high-level policy committees in government, he is alert to the intelligence needs of the President and his closest advisers. Presumably he will be able—perhaps with a considerable saving of money—to make the work of such intelligence outfits as the National Security Agency and the Defense Intelligence Agency more relevant to White House needs. His part of the reorganization seems relatively straightforward.

The second part of the reorganization involves what is called net assessments. That is a fancy term to answer the question, How does the strategic balance stand between Russia and the United States? That question with deep ramifications in politics and economics as well as foreign policy is to the various private and public interests that come to a head in government what a piece of red meat is to a pack of starving dogs.

Under the Eisenhower administration the net assessment was handled by a secret subcommittee of the National Security Council headed by a general officer and working out of the Pentagon. In the Kennedy and Johnson administrations, the net assessments were essentially made under the direction of the Secretary of Defense, Robert S. McNamara, in the Systems Analysis Division of the Department of Defense.

Under the Nixon administration there has been no central responsibility for net assessment. The result has been a chaotic battle featuring many protagonists. In general, the Secretary of Defense, Melvin R. Laird, with the backing of his director of research, John Foster, and to the delight of congressional hawks, has tended to rate the Soviet threat very highly. The CIA, to the delight of the congressional doves, has been more skeptical about the Communist menace.

Under the new reorganization, responsibility for making the net assessment will be vested in a group working under the head of the National Security Council staff, Henry Kissinger. The official immediately responsible for the net assessments will be Andrew Marshall, who now leaves the RAND Corporation, where he has been serving as an analyst, to take the place on the security council staff.

Mr. Marshall is by all accounts an extremely good man—experienced, reliable, and discriminating in judgment. Presumably he can do a serious job of pulling together the vast range of complicated data required for making the net assessment.

But it is a serious question whether that office should be performed in such close range to the White House. For the atmosphere in the White House is heavily political. There is no great disposition toward detached analysis, still less to hear news out of keeping with prejudices and commitments.

A nice case in point is the Defense Program Review Committee set up under Dr. Kissinger back in 1969. The purpose of that group was to cast a cold analytic eye on the defense budget, and some of the best analysts in and out of government signed on to do the staff work.

But the President has backed the big spending program of Mr. Laird. The review committee has been allowed to wither on the vine. Half a dozen of the analysts connected with it have resigned, and the senior official presently concerned, Dr. K. Wayne Smith, is rumored to be leaving soon.

No serious high-level critique of the defense budget is now being made anywhere in government. That is one of the reasons the Congress and those of us in the press are floundering so when it comes to defense expenditures.

What all this means is that the new intelligence setup should be watched with great care. It looks like a sensible arrangement. But it could easily become one more instrument for restricting information and criticism to the disadvantage of all of those on the outside of government.

Senators Stuart Symington and J. W. Fulbright reacted to the announced changes by saying that President Nixon had reshaped the nation's intelligence network to vest more control in the hands of Henry Kissinger without obtaining congressional advice.

Senator Symington called in a Senate speech for a full review of the changes by the Senate Armed Services Committee. He charged that critical aspects of intelligence analysis had been taken out of the hands of career professionals and turned over to the military and White House staff.

Senator Fulbright, asked by a reporter for comment, said the reorganization was a further erosion of congressional control over the intelligence community. The Arkansas Democrat noted that Kissinger, in his position as White House adviser, was insulated from congressional scrutiny.

Senator Symington said the reorganization might turn out to be a constructive move. But he said it was impossible for the Congress or the public to know, since the White House announcement had not given an explanation of what had caused the shakeup or of the remedies which have now been unilaterally decreed.

He said the White House apparently does not consider either the organization or the operation of the intelligence community to be matters of concern to Congress. "To my knowledge there was no advance consultation whatsoever with the Congress regarding this reorganization, or even any advance notice of what had been decided," he declared.

Senator Symington asked how Helms's leadership role would

be enhanced, as the White House said it would be, by the creation of a new and obviously more powerful supervisory committee chaired by the adviser to the President for national security affairs, on which new board sits not only the Attorney General but also the chairman of the Joint Chiefs of Staff.

"Has this new White House committee been given authority or responsibility which heretofore was the responsibility of the CIA and which the Congress under the National Security Act vested in the agency?" Mr. Symington asked. "How can the integrity of the intelligence product be assured when responsibility for the most critical aspects of intelligence analysis is taken out of the hands of career professionals and vested in a combination of military professionals and the White House staff? This arrangement can bring the most important aspects of intelligence production and coordination directly under the White House and thus within the scope of what the President believes he can deny to the Congress through the exercise of executive privilege."

Symington said that he wrote Senator John C. Stennis, chairman of the Armed Services Committee, urging that hearings on the intelligence shift be held before either that committee or its subcommittee on the CIA. As a senior member of both groups, Symington disclosed that, despite claims that there is constant congressional supervision of the CIA, the Senate CIA subcommittee did not meet once in 1971.

It is important for the President to be aware of the depths of the problems facing him within the intelligence community. He must not be sold a bill of goods that all is well at the lower levels, and that all that is needed are some minor changes at the top. The President has the power to effect the most needed change in intelligence, the dropping of the secrecy veil. Fully 85 percent of the material in intelligence that I have dealt with deserves not to be classified, yet it is. The Pentagon papers showed that much of what is marked top secret concerns itself with hiding the official thinking within an administration. An executive order redefining the use of classified material would go a long way toward reducing the volume of material that must be classified.

Secrecy wreaks its worst havoc in the area of the intelligence budget. For years now, the tradition has been to be as stealthy with the intelligence budget as one would be were he running a clandestine operation abroad. The only losers in this proposition are the people of the United States, for it is they who are paying the five billion dollars a year with no way of knowing why or how it is being spent. The argument offered in defense of this practice is that we cannot allow the Soviet Union to know how much we are spending on intelligence. This argument sounds interesting, but I submit that the Soviet analysts working the American desk in Moscow have our intelligence budget figured out a lot closer than the most informed American citizen. Moreover, when you stop and think about it, what difference does it make if the Soviets know how much we are spending on intelligence? Can they change it? No. The only development I can see coming out of a yearly publication of the intelligence budget is, perhaps, the winning of a few defectors from the Soviet intelligence service who might be enticed to come over to the other side in the hope of getting a pay raise themselves. Seriously, though, we make no attempt to hide our more important defense budget. Each year the congressional hearings on defense appropriations are made public with each and every program justification fully provided for the public. This is of far more crucial value to the Soviet Union than the intelligence budget. The time has come to stop playing schoolboy games.

Because of the current reputation enjoyed by intelligence it would seem advisable for the President to convene a public and governmental board to redefine for the American people the exact role of intelligence within the American system. Many reasonable men would go along with the necessity for having a certain minimal amount of secrecy in government operations if they understood the prevailing philosophy for such a venture and knew of the limitations on such reliance on secrecy. Today, suspicions abound among the general public as to what the government is up to in the murky area of intelligence. The difference must be reconciled between a free and open government and society and the need for keeping government secrets.

To ensure the continuing confidence of the people and its elected representatives the President might seriously consider rewriting the character of the President's Foreign Intelligence Advisory Board. This board could serve as an ombudsman for the people and prepare a yearly unclassified report on intelligence for Congress. Such a report would describe the extent of intelligence activities underway during the year. Problem areas and the solutions applied could be explained. Moreover, this annual report would provide the President a yearly opportunity to update his thinking on intelligence matters, and, in effect, serve as a vehicle to keep him not only honest, but constantly thinking about the role of intelligence. If the President was required to divulge the sketchy nature of the intelligence on which he based his Son Tay prisoner-of-war-camp raid into North Vietnam, odds are he would have given serious second thoughts to approving the fiasco.

The existence of a veil of secrecy poses a continuing problem. It affords bureaucrats a device to hide from public scrutiny, and thus emboldens them to carry on with a sort of messianic zeal, as if they are the only ones privy to the real truth. What has been lacking in the intelligence community is a continuing responsibility for public accountability. The President should seriously consider some minor changes in the National Security Act to allow a full and impartial investigation of intelligence by a public body every five years. Their report should be the basis for thorough congressional debate on the subject of intelligence.

Senator J. W. Fulbright traces the current attitude of Congress toward CIA to the anti-Communist fervor of many of its members. To a great degree this is the truth. In no other area of government will you find Congress as lackadaisical as in intelligence. The one jealously guarded prerogative of Congress over the years has been its investigative authority. Yet, since

1947 it has consistently forfeited its responsibility as far as intelligence is concerned. Above all else, this is the only effective device Congress has for getting to the source of the problems within intelligence today. No amount of carping and rhetorical splendor will suffice. It must dig in deeply if it is going to effect change in this vital area of government.

A congressional investigation and public debate on intelligence is long overdue. The members of both houses of Congress that I interviewed were all reluctant to have Congress investigate CIA. They offered excuses ranging from the fact that they don't want to know what's going on for fear they might let classified information slip to stating they are fully confident the President has it all under control.

The facts speak otherwise. Congress, by default, has lost any reasonable semblance of control over intelligence. A rebirth of interest in the subject is sorely needed. If such an investigation is conducted, the committees conducting it should by no means content themselves with merely calling the leaders of the intelligence community before them. If they do, they will simply be treated to a series of "all-is-well-on-the-western-front" briefings, replete with slides and color charts "proving" why all is well. Congress needs to get off its collective duff and visit each of the agencies involved in intelligence. Congressmen should hold private, confidential discussions with men and women throughout each of these agencies at all levels to find out what is on their minds. They should ask them in confidence what they think is wrong with intelligence. They might be surprised at the considerable amount of frustration and even disgust that exist at the various levels. They might also hear some well-thought-out solutions to many of the current problems in the community.

Congress should also be concerned that CIA and the entire intelligence structure be made truly accountable to it. The first step in this direction is an admission that Congress is not presently organized to deal rationally with the intelligence community. The four committees that now look into the subject are limited to rather narrow perspectives. The two appropriations committees are simply interested in the CIA budget—which is hidden in various other departmental budgets such as Defense, State, Agriculture, and Commerce. Congressmen, in effect, never see the entirety of CIA's budget, so how can they hope to control it?

The Armed Services committees are only interested in the impact of intelligence operations on military effectiveness. They do not concern themselves with the larger questions of what intelligence is collecting, how the community is managed, or the other kinds of problems that committees like the Government Operations subcommittees investigate.

In my view a joint committee of both houses of Congress is very much needed to keep continuing tabs on intelligence. It should be composed of men from committees with interests broad enough to take a full look at intelligence. The entire structure should concern them.

Thanks to Mr. Agnew, the normally bold press and TV in this country has pulled in its horns in many areas. Intelligence is one of these areas. The media have a continuing responsibility to themselves and the people of this country to report on intelligence. They should mount a relentless campaign on the subject, digging under every rock they find to see what is going on today. They should demand to know how CIA can get away with a simple "no comment" whenever intelligence problems arise. They should probe into the origins of the secrecy that surrounds intelligence. They should seek comments from former governmental officials on the subject and fully explore how intelligence contributes to national policy. In a word, they should turn loose some of their talent onto this subject in an effort to inform their readers and viewers what is up in intelligence. There are so many teasing tidbits that have leaked out in the past several years that it causes one to wonder what has happened to the supposedly native curiosity of the American media.

The key to getting anything meaningful done about the current state of United States intelligence is citizen interest. This nation did not become alarmed about drugs while they were ruining the lives of hundreds and thousands of blacks in our urban ghettos. But as soon as the problem began to creep into suburbia the uproar started. Why? Because citizens who still had some faith in the system were involved. They took action on their own to get something done. They contacted the press, the Congress, and the President. The same could hold true with the problems of intelligence. As long as it remains an arcane field with only limited professional interest, nothing meaningful will be done to resolve the major problems. Our leadership elements do not tackle a problem until the noise of constituent complaints reaches a level where it can no longer be ignored.

The problems of intelligence have a direct influence on your own life also. To start off, you and your neighbors are footing the five-billion-dollar annual bill. You deserve to know how and why your hard-earned money is being spent the way it is. More important than the money angle is the fact that intelligence has a sizable influence on the foreign policy of the United States. Three times during the sixties, intelligence brought this nation to the brink of war. The nature of the beast is such that unless radical changes are made it is almost certain that other equally volatile intelligence fiascoes will occur. This is particularly true with the increased need to maintain surveillance on the Soviet Union if we ever sign a strategic arms agreement with Moscow. Moreover, since Nixon has rediscovered the existence of China we may ultimately find ourselves with diplomatic representation there—an automatic guarantee that CIA will unleash its phalanx of "old China hands" who have been sitting on the sidelines waiting these past two decades for just such a break.

Finally, some mention should be made about the potential for intelligence turning inward on the citizens of this country. The seeds for this type of action on the part of an overzealous intelligence staff have already been planted with the Army's stumbling into domestic intelligence during the 1968 elections. You can bet that the next attempt in this field will not be as amateurish as the last. You can also bet that after the Army attempt was exposed, the staffers at CIA responsible for covert political action studied just what the Army did—not to assist the government to stop this sort of thing, but rather to see where the Army screwed up and to devise a better way of doing it, just in case they were ever called upon to mount a similar operation. If it is deemed necessary, the President will not rely on those clods in uniform. He'll turn to the professionals at CIA and the FBI. I'm not saying that this kind of activity is presently going on. As a matter of fact I believe otherwise. What I am saying, however, is that the potential definitely exists for the mounting of such operations. Their initiation would depend on the mood of the country.

In the final analysis it is up to you. It is the boom of your voice that will bring about the necessary changes. As an individual you no doubt have a feeling of impotence when it comes to influencing your government. Collectively, however, you have a tremendous impact. It requires only that you get a slight ground swell started, and the American system will take over from there. And it is relatively simple to get that ground swell started. By writing to your local newspaper and TV stations you can get the ball rolling. Ask the program manager and managing editor why they never provide any coverage on intelligence. Ask what they think of the contradictory nature of CIA's policy of secrecy. Suggest that they invite government officials and academic experts to discuss the subject. Suggest that the editors seek out the opinion of your local congressmen and senators on this vital subject for publication or airing. You'd be surprised at how quickly your elected representatives respond to a press inquiry from their home area.

To further fuel the fire, write directly to your congressmen and senators. Ask their views on the situation. Ask why they allow the present situation to persist. Ask if they plan to do anything about it in the future. Finally, ask that they provide detailed reasons for their positions. Don't be satisfied with canned handouts. If the replies strike you as bland statements with no heart in them, write more letters demanding fuller explanations. It wouldn't take too many letters to start your senators and representatives thinking about the subject.

The President should also be written. He is the one man who can bring about the necessary change by simply ordering it. Ask him why he hasn't done something about it. Ask him if he is satisfied with the intelligence that he receives. You might also remind him that since you are footing part of the five-billion-dollar annual intelligence budget you'd like to know just how that money is being spent.

If you have doubts about the boom of your voice just recall the ground swell that developed in favor of Lieutenant Calley after he was convicted. That caught on like wildfire, and the President intervened almost immediately. Ask yourself why he did that. The answer is simple. He moved because thousands of people wrote and wired about the issue. I, for one, have not lost faith in our system. It takes a little prodding, pushing, and shoving, but it works. Try it out; you'll be surprised.

*Some other books published by Penguin
are described on the following pages.*

Richard J. Walton

COLD WAR AND COUNTERREVOLUTION
The Foreign Policy of John F. Kennedy

This radical reevaluation, based squarely on the available evidence, reveals that Kennedy was a hawkish counterrevolutionary whose vigorous anti-communism prevailed over his sympathy for the oppressed peoples of the world. Although he had political skill and several great achievements to his credit, Kennedy's chief legacy was the miscalculations of Cuba, Berlin, and Vietnam. As this courageous book makes clear, it is not too early to subject that legacy to strict historical scrutiny. Between 1962 and 1967 Richard J. Walton was the Voice of America's principal United Nations correspondent.

Richard J Barnet

ROOTS OF WAR

This is the first comprehensive survey of the forces
in American life that have kept this country in a
succession of wars for more than a generation.
Why has killing in the national interest become
routine? How much does personal ambition affect
foreign-policy decisions? What is the role of business in determining foreign policy? How important
is public opinion? These are only a few of the
questions this book considers as it argues that the
United States can never change its foreign policy
until it comes to grips with the forces now shap-
ing that policy. Richard J. Barnet is co-founder
and co-director of The Institute for Policy Studies.

Walter and Miriam Schneir

INVITATION TO AN INQUEST
Reopening the Rosenberg "Atom Spy" Case

This carefully documented review of the twentieth century's most controversial espionage case is the result of Walter and Miriam Schneir's years of research on the events leading up to the 1953 execution of Julius and Ethel Rosenberg—convicted of spying for the Soviet Union. Re-creating both the trial and the atmosphere that surrounded it, the Schneirs ask—and answer—some eye-opening questions: Were the Rosenbergs tried in the press rather than in the courts? Were their accusers untrustworthy? Were the Rosenbergs guilty? "A vital social document . . ."—*The Nation*.

John A. Parrish, M.D.

12, 20 & 5
A Doctor's Year in Vietnam

A young doctor who spent a year behind the front
lines in Vietnam wrote this extraordinary memoir.
12, 20 & 5 is not a political or a military book;
rather, it is a haunting journal of one man's ago-
nized confrontation with war. In blistering prose
Parrish evokes a nightmarish scene of fear, sex,
alcohol, and blood. The people he portrays are
unforgettable—from Bill, the tough chief surgeon,
and Myron, the shy internist, to Suzy, the prosti-
tute, and Maria, the nun. Running through all
that he writes is the knowledge that every moment might be his last. The title recalls the three
numbers announced as each helicopter arrived
bearing more men: litter-borne wounded, ambu-
latory wounded, dead.

Clive Limpkin

THE BATTLE OF BOGSIDE

This is a photographic report from one of the centers of strife in Northern Ireland. Bogside is a Catholic section of Londonderry where in 1969 a police rampage resulted in several deaths. Since then neither the police nor the English army has entered Bogside, making it a self-governing district probably unique in the Western world. Taken from both sides of the barricades, the exciting photographs in this volume are a record of the battle and of life in Bogside from 1969 to 1972. There is almost no text, but the two hundred photographs tell more than any words could. Clive Limpkin is a newspaper photographer who has spent most of the last three years in Londonderry.